LITERATURE AND COMPLAINT IN ENGLAND, 1272–1553

Literature and Complaint in England, 1272–1553

Wendy Scase

OXFORD
UNIVERSITY PRESS

OXFORD
UNIVERSITY PRESS

Great Clarendon Street, Oxford OX2 6DP
United Kingdom

Oxford University Press is a department of the University of Oxford.
It furthers the University's objective of excellence in research, scholarship,
and education by publishing worldwide. Oxford is a registered trade mark of
Oxford University Press in the UK and in certain other countries

First published 2007
Reprinted 2013

Published in the United States of America by Oxford University Press
198 Madison Avenue, New York, NY 10016, United States of America

British Library Cataloguing in Publication Data
Data available

Library of Congress Cataloging in Publication Data
Data available

ISBN 978-0-19-927085-9

For Lizzy

Acknowledgements

I acknowledge with great gratitude the generosity of the Leverhulme Trustees in supporting the research and writing of this book. The award of a Leverhulme Research Fellowship for 2004–5 meant that instead of trying to complete the project in snatched intervals, I had extended time for access to research archives and libraries, and for reading, writing, and thinking. I am grateful to the anonymous readers commissioned by Oxford University Press for their insightful reports and comments. Several historians of medieval law and politics have generously shared their expertise with me and tolerated a literary colleague's questions about medieval judicial processes and sources, in particular Gwilym Dodd, Anthony Musson, and Mark Ormrod. Of course, responsibility for the arguments in this book, and for any errors, is my own. I am very thankful to the Bodleian Library, University of Oxford, to the British Library, to the President and Fellows of Magdalen College, Oxford, and to the Keeper of the National Archives (Public Record Office) for permission to reproduce photographs of materials in their care, and to the curatorial staff of these institutions for their help. I am most thankful to my colleagues and students in the Department of English at the University of Birmingham for patiently tolerating my preoccupation with this project, especially as the deadline loomed. I thank audiences and readers who have discussed aspects of the material with me when I have presented them in papers and essays. My greatest debt, as always, is to my family, who have supported me in countless ways. My husband, Roger Scase, has been stoic and generously supportive through all of the phases of my work, and our daughter, Elizabeth, the dedicatee of this book, has cheerfully humoured her mother's odd enthusiasm for bills without complaint.

A Note on Conventions

In quotations, words interpolated by the author are enclosed in square brackets. Angle brackets enclose matter interpolated by the editor or author of the text cited.

Contents

Acknowledgements   vii
List of Illustrations   xi

Preface   1

1. Judicial Plaint and Peasant Plaint   5

Peasant Plaint and Judicial Reform   5
Peasant Plaint in the Royal Courts   11
Peasant Plaint and New 'Villeins'   17
Peasant Plaint and Vernacular Poetry   33

2. Complaint, Clamour, and Libels   42

Criminal Justice and Satirical Complaint   42
Complaint and Clamour of the People   54
Clamour of the People in the Later Fourteenth Century   62
Clamour and the Appellants   65

3. The Literature of Clamour   83

The Beginnings of Clamour Literature   83
Lollard Petitions and Libels   87
Lollard Bills and the Literature of Clamour   101
The Clamour Literature of the 1450s   110

4. Transmission, Response, and Development: Clamour Writing 1460–1553   137

Clamour in Yorkist and Early Tudor England   137
Developments in the Transmission of Clamour   143
Reformation Responses to Clamour Writing   149
Complaint from the Dissolution to the Fall of Somerset   157

5. Literature, Complaint, and the *Ars Dictaminis*   170

List of Abbreviations   187
List of Works Cited   188
Index   205

List of Illustrations

1. TNA (PRO), SC 8/20/997. The Mercers' Petition against Nicholas Brembre. Reproduced by kind permission of the Keeper of the National Archives.   73

2. TNA (PRO), SC 8/20/997. (Detail). The Mercers' Petition against Nicholas Brembre. Reproduced by kind permission of the Keeper of the National Archives.   74

3. TNA (PRO), SC 8/20/1004. The Painters' Petition against Nicholas Brembre. Reproduced by kind permission of the Keeper of the National Archives.   75

4. TNA (PRO), C 49/9/22. Libel against Alexander Neville. Reproduced by kind permission of the Keeper of the National Archives.   78

5. Oxford, Bodleian Library, MS Digby 98, f. 195^r. Pro-Wycliffite poem 'Heu! Quanta desolatio' on single sheet (now bound with codex). Reproduced by kind permission of the Bodleian Library, University of Oxford.   96

6. TNA (PRO), KB 9/203/1. John Whitelock's Petition. Reproduced by kind permission of the Keeper of the National Archives.   107

7. London, British Library, Cotton Roll IV. 50. Petition of the Cade rebels at Blackheath. Permission British Library, Cotton Roll IV. 50.   116

8. London, British Library, Cotton Roll IV. 50, dorse. Petition of the Cade rebels at Blackheath. Permission British Library, Cotton Roll IV. 50.   117

9. Oxford, Magdalen College, Magdalen Misc. 306, pp. 2–3. Petition of the Cade rebels; possibly the copy obtained by John Payn for Sir John Fastolf. Reproduced by kind permission of the President and Fellows, Magdalen College, Oxford.   119

10. Oxford, Magdalen College, Magdalen Misc. 306, p. 4. Petition of the Cade rebels, outer leaf showing folds; possibly the copy obtained by John Payn for Sir John Fastolf. Reproduced by kind permission of the President and Fellows, Magdalen College, Oxford.   120

11. London, British Library, Additional MS 34888, ff. 36^v–37^r. Commons' petition against William de la Pole, Duke of Suffolk, top sheet of roll of two sheets, now bound as bifolium with the Paston Letters. Permission British Library, Additional MS 34888.   123

12. London, British Library, Additional MS 34888, ff. 38^v–39^r. Commons' petition against William de la Pole, Duke of Suffolk, bottom sheet of roll of two sheets, now bound as bifolium with the Paston Letters. Permission British Library, Additional MS 34888.   124

13. Oxford, Bodleian Library, MS Eng. hist. b. 119, f. 3^r. Bill against William de la Pole, Duke of Suffolk, replying to points in his defence. Middle sheet of a roll of three sheets, now bound as leaves. Reproduced by kind permission of the Bodleian Library, University of Oxford.   126

14. Oxford, Bodleian Library, MS Eng. hist. b. 119, f. 4^r. Bill against William de la Pole, Duke of Suffolk, replying to points in his defence. Bottom sheet of a roll of three sheets, now bound as leaves. Reproduced by kind permission of the Bodleian Library, University of Oxford.   127

15. London, British Library, Cotton Roll II. 23, showing the end of a petition of Cade's rebels and the beginning of 'Boothe, be ware, bissoppe thoughe thou be', a verse libel against William Booth. Permission British Library, Cotton Roll II. 23.   132

16. TNA (PRO), SP 10/9/12. Libel against the enemies of Protector Somerset. Reproduced by kind permission of the Keeper of the National Archives.   163

17. TNA (PRO), SP 10/9/12, dorse. Reverse of libel against the enemies of Protector Somerset, showing instruction 'Rede it and gyue it ffurth'. Reproduced by kind permission of the Keeper of the National Archives.   164

18. *Pyers plowmans exhortation vnto the lordes knightes and burgoysses of the Parlyamenthouse*, title-page. Permission British Library, 238.a.11.   166

Preface

This book is an account of complaint and the shaping of literature in England. When I speak of 'complaint', I refer, first and foremost, to the expression of a grievance as a means of obtaining a judicial remedy. The thesis of the book is that the judicial institutions of written complaint which emerged dramatically in the reign of Edward I came into dialogue with literary production, becoming part of, and centrally informing, a wider literature of complaint. Although, as I shall show, this literature comprises texts and practices of widely differing kinds, its components share common material characteristics, production practices and infrastructure, themes, and, above all, theories of complaint.

Complaint is of course a medieval word with uses both in law and in literature. In the writings of our period it is a motile, slippery term, moving between legal, rhetorical, formal, and generic applications, and never quite settling in use in any of these areas. In law, a *pleinte* is the expression of a grievance as a means of initiating litigation.[1] *Pleinte* is related procedurally and conceptually to the *querela*, the *libellus*, the *bill*, and *clamour*. The precise legal status and the proper forms of expression of *pleinte* were under development during our period. In literature, *compleinte* is sometimes associated with the names of the French lyric *formes fixes* poems, such as the *ballade* and *virelay*, but it never designates a fixed form itself.[2] Middle English terms derived from *planctus*, *compleinte*, and the verbs *pleinen* and *compleinen*, sometimes seem to describe a manner of expression, for example *pleinte wise*, and *complayning wyse*, but these expressions do not have a precise rhetorical meaning.[3]

Reflecting its motility in medieval usage, *complaint* has been a problematic category in modern critical vocabulary, proving to be a term difficult to apply with much analytical purchase. For the *Manual of the Writings in Middle English*, *complaint* covers a multitude of genres and texts of broadly reformist outlook and purposes.[4] There have been some attempts to press the term into more thoroughgoing analytical service. In *Complaint and Satire in Early English*

---

[1] Harding, 'Plaints and Bills', is still the classic study of the procedure, and includes much useful comment on the terminology. Harding, *Medieval Law*, 147–90, offers an updated survey and much comparative continental (mainly French) material.

[2] Wimsatt, *Chaucer and his French Contemporaries*, 29; Champion (ed.), *Charles d'Orléans: Poésies*, i. p. xxxiv, points out that the 'complaints' of Charles d'Orléans have very varied forms.

[3] *MED pleint(e* (n.) 1 (a) (*Ancrene Wisse*); *compleinen* (v.) 1 (a) (Usk, *Testament of Love*). Kerrigan points out the significance of the word's etymological relationship with Latin *plangere*, literally, 'to beat the breast' (Kerrigan (ed.), *Motives of Woe: Shakespeare and Female Complaint*, 7).

[4] Robbins, 'Poems Dealing with Contemporary Conditions', includes section eight 'The Wicked Age: Satires and Complaints', a classification which has five sub-divisions organized on thematic lines.

Literature, John Peter proposes that complaint should become a 'technical term' to characterize a variety of distinctively medieval writing, distinguished from satire by its hectoring, generalization, and lack of wit. Langland typifies complaint; Chaucer typifies satire.[5] Elliott suggests refinements to Peter's analysis, proposing that complaint is 'a distinct literary type' that comprises texts of two kinds: 'those that contemn the world and those that want to reform it'.[6] Davenport contrasts *complaint* with *narrative,* arguing that these are two modes of writing which most engaged Chaucer. Complaint comprises several varieties, but for Chaucer it is 'a type of expression, or a rhetorical device … not … a poetic form'.[7] Kerrigan relates Shakespeare's *A Louers Complaint* to 'female complaint', a 'subgenre' of 'complaint' or 'lament', which, encompassing classical laments, ballads, courtly lyrics, and other genres is an 'ample, generically complicated literature'.[8]

In this study I propose that English law imposes structure on complaint, that a force-field is created in which complaint textuality is theorized and a literature of complaint emerges. This process begins with the emergence of written complaint in particular circumstances in the later thirteenth century. I trace the development of the forms and phrases of complaint, the emergence of the infrastructure for the production of plaint texts (the persons, the training, the textual resources), and the formation of the judicial institutions and processes built around complaint. This book offers an account of how the culture of judicial plaint interfaces with, and helps to shape, literature.

When choosing which literary texts to focus on, I have been required by constraints of space to be very selective. I have focused on those texts that most powerfully demonstrate the impact of judicial complaint on the formation of literary practice. These are very often, indeed are mostly, rather neglected, despised, marginal texts. I originally hoped to include more analysis of mainstream literary works, particularly an extended discussion of love plaints, but I have reluctantly had to exclude much of this material because of space constraints, and confine myself to a few selected examples of how complaint culture provides a framework in which to read the more canonical texts. I have also been extremely selective when treating the vast mass of sixteenth-century material, choosing examples which best illustrate responses to earlier texts and traditions. I hope to expand on my study of both categories of material in greater detail elsewhere.

The first four chapters follow in a sequence that is broadly chronological, though there are overlaps between chapters, and broad themes are followed throughout the whole sequence. The book begins with materials from the reign

---

[5] Peter, *Complaint and Satire,* citation from 13.

[6] Elliott, 'Middle English Complaints', citations from 26, 34.

[7] Davenport, *Chaucer: Complaint and Narrative,* 6; and cf. Davenport, 'Fifteenth-century Complaints and Duke Humphrey's Wives'.

[8] Kerrigan (ed.), *Motives of Woe: Shakespeare and Female Complaint,* pp. v, 1–2. Kerrigan's introductory essay in this anthology of female complaint texts is the best available discussion of the various literary traditions of complaint.

of Edward I, when written plaint first seems to have gained importance in the judicial process, and when the first related literary texts appear. The first chapter focuses on the formation of a definition of legally admissible plaint, and on what is excluded by this definition, telling this story through analysis of 'peasant plaint'—the tradition of plaint most subject to pressure and innovation because at once included and excluded by the new judicial process. Chronologically, the story finishes with the close of the reign of Edward VI, with an account in Chapter 4 of the complaints of Pyers Plowman and similar peasant plaintiffs who echo their forebears from the reign of the first king Edward. The echo offers a rational place to finish the book, though the story itself goes on with the libels and pamphlets of the seventeenth century and beyond—into a mass of material which simply could not be considered in the space of this book. In Chapters 1–4 I describe the gradual emergence and development of what I call a 'literature of clamour'. The literature of clamour relies on judicial plaint for its claims to legitimacy, its topics, its forms and language; for analytical terms such as *bill*, *libel*, *petition*, and *plaint* (my own usage of these terms in this book invoking their complex, motile legal connotations in the period); and sometimes even for the means of its material production and transmission. In the final chapter I consider the implications of this story for literary history. I propose that, though it concerns largely neglected and despised, subliterary materials for the most part, the story of clamour literature entails some profound revisions of our narratives of how English writing emerged as a legitimate mode of literary and judicial communication, and of how literature was structured and theorized.

In Chapter 1 I describe the emergence and development of judicial complaint in the context of judicial reforms associated with the reign of Edward I. I show that the new plaint arises with the definition of both the procedures and the agents of complaint. I explore the ways in which this definition of plaints and plaintiffs gives shape and definition to plaint which is inadmissible because it is the plaint of those who are not legal subjects, the grievances of villeins. But while peasant plaint could be excluded from a hearing in the courts, it was also, in some contexts, admitted as legal plaint. I explore the ways in which peasant plaint is positioned in relation to judicial plaint in a range of judicial and literary texts. In the last section of the chapter I suggest that the new institutions of plaint gave vernacular poets opportunities to position English poetry in relation to judicial writing, and thus gave them opportunities to imagine how English composition could become a legitimized literature. The chapter focuses on the period in which this discourse was emerging. In later chapters we encounter again the topics and strategies of peasant plaint, following them through to the ploughman texts of the sixteenth century.

In Chapter 2 I outline the far-reaching changes in criminal justice associated with plaint procedure, and trace the ways in which the implications of the procedure were worked out, explored, developed, and contested. I show that the new plaint procedure created a flexible variety of ways of initiating criminal judicial process which are encompassed by the term *clamour*. I trace the ways in which satirists explored the limitations and dangers of this procedure and negotiated the position of their satirical plaints in relation to legal plaints. I trace the gradual expansion of the category of valid plaint and explore how *clamour* encompassed, potentially, a wide variety of texts. I analyse the first vernacular libels and legal complaints, relating their production to the creation of this flexible category of clamour. These texts build on the exploitation of peasant plaint, and look forward to the spread of the vernacular as a medium for complaint and to the further refinement of petitions and linked literary modes in the fifteenth and sixteenth centuries.

In Chapter 3 I argue that the literary ideas and forms associated with plaint procedure inform a body of writing which I term the 'literature of clamour'. The literature of clamour is first recognized when we detect widespread dissemination of petitions associated with the rising of 1381. The first *surviving* texts from the literature of clamour are lollard petitions and associated writings. I show that these texts interface with other clamour campaigns to form a corpus of literature. The first full corpus of clamour literature to survive dates from the 1450s. With this material we can trace the production and reception of clamour literature across a wide social spectrum and field of political activity. We can see clamour writing maturing as a literature with a sense of tradition detectable in the recycling of material, in the appearance of collections and collectors, and in the emergence of a sense of precedent.

In Chapter 4 I examine the continuation of clamour traditions after the 1450s. I explore the transmission of medieval clamour texts in later medieval and early modern England, and describe how clamour tradition is appropriated and developed by early modern writers. I analyse representative examples of printed texts, and follow the continued use of the manuscript libel. I suggest that there is clear evidence for continuity from the earliest examples through to the libels of the seventeenth century.

In Chapter 5 I draw together and extend discussion in the foregoing chapters of complaint writing as a mode of literary analysis, theorization, and composition. I conclude that legal definitions of plaint create a force-field in which complaint texts may be composed, analysed, and theorized, and a structure of literary relationships created and exploited. I argue that, as a response to these stimuli, complaint writing is a vigorous, experimental practice of the *ars dictaminis*. The interest in producing clamour texts stimulates experimentation with the arts of the *dictamen*, including the vernacularization of letter and document composition. I propose that this project is closely associated with, and stimulates, vernacular literary production. I offer some key examples of the impact of the clamour project on poets of the later fourteenth and fifteenth centuries, and conclude with a review of the evidence for this textual practice across the period 1272–1553.

1

Judicial Plaint and Peasant Plaint

PEASANT PLAINT AND JUDICIAL REFORM

'Ad regem vadam', dixit miserabilis Adam;
'Coram rege cadam, causam scriptam sibi tradam'.
Ibant psallentes, magnum risum facientes,
Sed redeunt flentes, fiunt sine fine dolentes.

Poem on Disputed Villein Services[1]

['To the king I shall go', said Adam the wretch;
'Before the king I shall fall, I'll deliver him a bill'.
They went off singing, making much mirth,
But they come back weeping, lamenting without end.]

From near the beginning of the reign of Edward I comes one of the earliest, fullest, and most intriguing descriptions of complaint in the medieval English courts. The passage quoted above is from the *Poem on Disputed Villein Services,* an eighty-three-line macaronic poem which recounts how some tenants of Leicester Abbey brought, and lost, a case against their lord in the king's court. Motivated by 'a thousand oppressions', the villagers of Stoughton confidently take their plaint to the king's court. Once they are at the court, the sergeant warns them that a jury will dispute their claim, while the cost of paying a pleader proves prohibitive. Fearful of worse penury, the peasants decide not to pursue their case, and return to the abbey lamenting that they will be villeins for ever.

We can, of course, relate the poem to a long literary tradition of complaint against servitude.[2] John Ball's famous sermon, which, Walsingham alleges, rallied

---

[1] Ed. Hilton, 'Poem on Disputed Villein Services', 95–7, 95.

[2] In its scant critical notices it has been seen in this way. Hilton sees the case to which the poem alludes as one example of many instances of peasant resistance to lords in the courts before the 1381 rising, and views the poem as typifying the 'emotional reaction' of lords to such resistance (Hilton, 'Peasant Movements', 81; Hilton, 'Poem on Disputed Villein Services', 94). Richard Firth Green sees the case as an example of a conflict between folklaw and the king's law, and the poem as monastic 'memorialization' of this conflict in verse (Green, *Crisis of Truth*, 168).

the commons to rebel against their lords in 1381, draws on this long tradition of medieval complaint against the injustices suffered by the peasant:

> Whan Adam dalf, and Eve span,
> Wo was thanne a gentilman?

Continuansque sermonem inceptum, nitebatur, per verba proverbii quod pro themate sumpserat, introducere et probare, ab initio omnes pares creatos a natura, servitutem per injustam oppressionem nequam hominum introductam, contra Dei voluntatem; quia, si Deo placuisset servos creasse, utique in principio mundi constituisset quis servus, quisve dominus, futurus fuisset.[3]

[Continuing the sermon, he attempted, using the words of the proverb that was his theme, to introduce and to prove that all were created equal by nature from the beginning, servitude being a wicked introduction through the unjust oppression of men against the will of God: because, if God had wished to create serfs, undoubtedly at the beginning he would have decreed who was to be a serf and who a lord.]

As the chronicler himself acknowledges, the text of Ball's sermon was proverbial. Paul Freedman has traced examples of this kind of complaint against servitude as early as the ninth and tenth centuries.[4] The *Colloquy* by Ælfric (*c*.955–*c*.1010) famously has the ploughman describe his heavy labour for a hard master: 'magnus labor est, quia non sum liber' ('the labour is great because I am not free').[5] The *Carmen ad Rotbertum regem* (*c*.1025) by Adalbero of Laon describes 'servi' as those who receive only sorrow in return for their labour.[6] The story of Adam and Eve was one of several biblical narratives available as a framework for understanding the hardships experienced by those who labour. Biblical history provided other important models: Noah's son Ham was a type of the lord; the Jews enslaved by the Egyptians typified the dominated.[7] Chronicle histories of conquest and enslavement in England before and after the Norman conquest provided fulfilments of the type, as well as antecedents of later medieval English peasants.[8]

But *Poem on Disputed Villein Services* also does something new. It raises the question of how peasant plaint relates not only to literary tradition but also to plaints in law. The poem can be related to an actual lawsuit. In 1276–7 the abbot of Leicester, William Schepished, sought to prove that the tenants of Stoughton held their land as his villeins and could therefore not dispute the services asked of them.[9] The court roll records that the villagers acknowledged their villein

---

³ Riley (ed.) *Walsingham … Historia Anglicana*, ii. 32–3.   ⁴ Freedman, *Images*, 40–55.
⁵ Garmonsworthy (ed), *Ælfric's Colloquy*, l. 35.   ⁶ Freedman, *Images*, 17–18.
⁷ Ibid., 91–8.   ⁸ Ibid., 126–30.
⁹ TNA (PRO), KB 27/26/9d; cf. Farnham, *Leicestershire*, 152–4. Hilton was almost certainly right to describe the case as one about disputed villein services, however, the cause at issue in court was and had to be that of villein *status*. Proving villein status was by no means straightforward. The main method was by 'suit of kin'; the production in court of relatives who acknowledged themselves to be villeins provided proof, since status was hereditary, but 'mixed' marriages, bastardy and so on

status. The record uses the precise and distinguishing language of villeinage, recording that they hold land of the abbot making redemption of flesh and blood and other customs 'per voluntate ipsius Abbatis', at the will of the abbot.[10] The peasants' legal status is indicated in precise legal terms in the poem too. The court roll records that the abbot stated that he was not bound to answer the villagers' claim, and only did so to show their malice. By making this 'without prejudice' statement, the abbot takes care not to recognize their legitimacy. The implications are that, as villeins, the villagers have no right to complain against the abbot in the royal court. The poet underlines this point about the villagers' status in various ways. As soon as the villagers arrive at court, the 'narrator' (pleader) Allan questions their assumptions that they are plaintiffs in the case, and the abbot the defendant:

> ... dixit narrator Allanus
> 'Rustice Willelme, causam, tibi supplico, tel me:
> Ad quod venisti sensu sine credo fuisti.
> Tu male discernis, reus es quia dominum spernis ... '[11]

> [... said Allan the pleader
> 'Rustic William, your case, I pray you, tell me:
> For what you have come, senseless I dare say you have been.
> You misunderstand, the defendant is you because you scorn the lord ... ']

On the contrary, Allan asserts, the peasant is the defendant—the one liable to a penalty ('reus')—because he has scorned his lord. Sardonically, the poet concludes with a French tag, 'Uncore a la curt le rey, usum menie la ley' ('in the king's court, usage still leads the law'); the law in the king's courts has been soundly built up by means of many precedents.[12] The poet concludes that the serf must hold the status of 'purus servus' for ever, echoing Bracton's differentiation of 'pure' villeins from those with privileged status.[13]

This denial of the peasants' status as legitimate plaintiffs is shown to have implications for the standing of their plaint. The poet, like the abbot, seeks to show that the peasants' plaints were not to be heard in a royal court of law. The name Adam (the name of the villager who carries the written plaint) is the only one given in the poem that is not corroborated by the court record. Arguably, 'miserabilis Adam' identifies the villager—and his fellows—with the first labourer, condemned by God to toil on account of his sin. Miserable Adam's peasant plaint is defined in relation to written bills of complaint.

---

made the tasks facing courts very difficult, and exercised legal theorists such as Bracton (Hyams, 'Proof of Villein Status'). For the legal procedures see Hyams, 'Action of Naifty'; cf. Hyams, *Kings, Lords and Peasants*, 162–71.

[10] TNA (PRO), KB 27/26/9d.   [11] Hilton, 'Poem on Disputed Villein Services', 95.

[12] Ibid., 97. I follow the interpretation and translation of Hilton, 'Freedom and Villeinage', 19.

[13] Hilton, 'Poem on Disputed Villein Services', 97; 'Et villenagiorum aliud purum aliud privilegiatum', *Bracton Online*, iii. 131.

Adam—when still cheerful—thinks that he can take a written plaint before the king. The abbot—and the poet—work hard to show that his peasant plaint has no legal status. The legal inadmissability of the peasants' plaint is expressed in the poet's representation of the peasants and their speech. Adam's plaint is never heard. The snatch of English ('tel me') in the midst of the pleader's Latin legal vocabulary ('causa', 'reus', 'dominus') suggests a context of social inequalities for William's 'misunderstanding'. When the villagers do speak, instead of presenting a complaint about their lord, they express their servility, lamenting their poverty and blaming their leader. Denied the opportunity to have their written plaint heard, each speaks in the vernacular as a villein, confirming his villein status by saying to Brother Roger 'Do that ti will is' (a vernacular version of the legal formula). These linguistic markers underline the point that Adam's plaint has no legal status; it is not admissible for a hearing in a royal court as a plaint from a free man would be. Unlike such plaints, it has no legal standing.

The poem dates from a time of new developments in law: a time of the definition of who could complain in a royal court, and of changes in the form and processes of legal complaint. The context for these changes was judicial reform. Judicial changes initiated in the reign of Henry II extended the kinds of grievances for which the royal courts could give redress, with the consequence that the numbers and social diversity of litigants increased. The Stoughton villagers' awareness of royal justice is one example of the impact on peasants.[14] At the same time, there were also hardening definitions of who could and could not access royal justice.[15] Under the coronation oath, the king swore to uphold justice for all. The revision of Magna Carta in 1217 sought to clarify the position of lords, protecting their interests by confirming the exclusion of villeins and their holdings from royal jurisdiction, 'justice for all' notwithstanding. A villein could not pursue a grievance about labour service in the royal courts, because royal justice did not recognize the unfree as legal subjects with interests of their own that could be damaged.[16] Whereas in the eleventh century, *villein*

---

[14] Visits of itinerant courts to the shires gave villagers access to royal justice, while measures were taken to reduce financial barriers to litigation (Musson and Ormrod, *Evolution*, 129–30; Bolland, (ed), *Select Bills*, pp. xx–xxvi). The corollary of the extension of reach of the royal courts was the decline of the seigneurial courts, and their procedural and administrative alignment with royal justice (see Brand, *Origins*, 18–19, and on procedural impacts see Razi and Smith, 'Manorial Court Rolls'.) The incorporation of common law procedures in manor courts also brought both free and unfree peasants within the ambit of royal justice (Smith, 'English Peasantry', 350–5). The decentralization of estate administration to local bailiffs and reeves from the 1260s and 1270s generated 'a small array of jobbing clerks' trained in business and legal affairs such as court-keeping and accountancy, such as the fourteen clerks recorded at Halesowen in the early fourteenth century, some of whom would have been part-time agricultural workers as well as clerks (Razi and Smith, 'Manorial Court Rolls', 60–1).

[15] The discussion which follows is based on Hyams, *Kings, Lords and Peasants*, 125–60.

[16] The theoretical exceptions were cases of sedition, and death or serious injury. See Hyams, *Kings, Lords and Peasants*, 125–60.

meant 'peasant', by the late thirteenth century it meant someone with no access to the royal courts.[17] The Stoughton villagers' case is that they are 'sokemen' (an allusion to the social structures under the Danelaw, Hilton suggests) rather than pure villeins, and that therefore they are protected from arbitrary increase of labour services.[18] Hilton proposes that cases on new grounds such as these are signs that the dividing line between the unfree villein and the free had finally hardened—hence villagers were forced to find new ways of disputing their status. Besides claiming to be 'sokemen', another possibility was for tenants to prove—usually by producing Domesday Book entries—that their lands were once royal estate ('ancient demesne') and so should have special legal privileges and protections.[19]

It was not just that the definition of *who* might bring a case was arrived at; changes were made in the *way* that subjects might access justice. *Poem on Disputed Villein Services* dates from a time when the way in which a lawsuit might be initiated was changing. In the reign of Edward I, written complaint—the *bill*—became a legitimate means of instigating a legal action. From this period plaintiffs were encouraged to sue by plaint or by bill, rather than, as previously, having to go through the difficult and costly process of purchasing a writ. This is precisely what 'wretched Adam' in *Poem on Disputed Villein Services* does: 'Coram rege cadam, causam scriptam sibi tradam'—he takes a written case to the king's court. The legal historians H. G. Richardson and G. O. Sayles describe *Poem on Disputed Villein Services* as among the earliest evidence for written plaints of this kind in the royal courts of England. This brought the courts into line with developments in continental procedure, and with the procedures used in the ecclesiastical courts.[20] Bill procedure meant a change in the means of and opportunities for access to royal justice. Cases which would previously have gone to local courts were taken to the king's itinerant court of eyre.[21] From the reign of Edward I, the crown instituted many new opportunities for complaint in this way. This extension of access to royal justice is manifested above all in the crown's creation of special commissions of inquiry to solicit complaints about royal officials and to give redress for abuses at intervals throughout this period. Parliament afforded another opportunity for the submission of complaints. This was another practice instigated and promoted by Edward I. Whereas only a few

[17] Hilton, 'Freedom and Villeinage', analyses the evidence for the chronology of this change, showing that it was clear by the mid thirteenth century and complete by the late thirteenth century; cf. Dyer, 'Attitudes towards Serfdom'.

[18] Hilton, 'Peasant Movements', 81.

[19] Hilton, 'Freedom and Villeinage', 19; McIntosh, 'Privileged Villeins'.

[20] Richardson and Sayles (eds.), *Rotuli ... Inediti*, p. lxiv, and for parallels with the libels of the ecclesiastical courts see p. lix. For earlier, continental examples see Harding, 'Plaints and Bills', 67–70 and cf. Harding, *Law Courts*, 121.

[21] Harding, 'Plaints and Bills', 74–5; Harding, *Law Courts*, 121–2; Bolland (ed.) *Select Bills*, 156; Musson, *Medieval Law*, 159; Bellamy, *Criminal Trial*, 19–56.

petitions to parliament survive from the reign of Henry III, hundreds survive from the reign of Edward I, and thousands from subsequent reigns.[22]

Poem on Disputed Villein Services sees peasant plaint in the light of the new judicial complaint. Of crucial and uncertain status between admissibility and inadmissibility in relation to the developing process and definitions, and the new opportunities, flexibilities, and restrictions, peasant plaint becomes a focus for the working out of what constitutes a complaint recognizable in law. For the poet it becomes a tradition newly charged with possibilities—and dangers. The poem is one of many writings whose engagement with peasant plaint, I shall suggest in this chapter, registers most acutely the immense literary and cultural impact of the new judicial process by bill. My purpose in this chapter is to illustrate the variety of responses to the tradition of peasant plaint that are shaped by the new judicial procedure, looking first at plaints in legal records, then at a range of Anglo-Norman and Latin literary texts, and finally at some vernacular poems from London, British Library, MS Harley 2253.

I want to stress at the outset that my concerns are rather different from those of previous scholars who have discussed this material. I shall offer a quite different interpretation of peasant plaint sources in the period from those offered previously, and one quite different from what many readers, familiar with this previous work, might expect. Recent analysis of medieval complaints against servitude and its injustices has been of several kinds. The major factor underlying the differences of methodology is the view taken of the relationship between complaint (written, inevitably) about peasant servitude and the 'voices' of the peasants themselves. Georges Duby analyses peasant laments in relation to lord–peasant power relations, reading them as in fact legitimizing and perpetuating the status quo.[23] Others, however, claim that the 'voices' of peasants can be rendered audible from the written record. English social and economic historians have viewed certain poetic complaint texts, such as *The Song of the Husbandman* and *Against the King's Taxes*, and even Middle English chronicles, as expressions of protest that reveal the viewpoint of the peasant.[24] Others have experimented with methodologies of reading in attempts to make peasant voices audible even where there is plainly ideological bias in the literary sources.[25] I am not concerned here with the question of whether and how we

---

[22] Richardson and Sayles (eds.), *Rotuli … Inediti*, p. viii.

[23] Duby, *Three Orders*, 160–1.

[24] See, e.g., Harriss, *Public Finance*, 250–2; Maddicott, 'The English Peasantry and the Demands of the Crown', 12–14; and Maddicott, 'Poems of Social Protest'. For two contrasting ways of viewing peasant feeling in chronicles, see Turville-Petre, 'Robert Manning's *Chronicle*'; and Moffat, 'Sin, Conquest, Servitude'; and see further below.

[25] Bisson's study of peasant complaint in twelfth-century Catalonia lyrically exploits records of peasant loss to redress the Harvard historian's loss (passionately evoked) of the peasant voice and experience: 'it is in their resonant passion, and especially in their misfortunes, that these people speak, or even cry out, to us'. Bisson finesses the problem of written mediation by arguing that the scribes identified with the peasants' experience of power because they shared similar experiences

might hear or recover the 'voices' of medieval peasants. I am concerned rather with the ways in which peasant plaint registers the impact of the new judicial structures, processes, and procedures, and with what this meant more broadly for literature.

PEASANT PLAINT IN THE ROYAL COURTS

Although the Stoughton villagers were denied a hearing for their plaint, and the poet drives the point home, there are plenty of other instances in which peasant plaint was accorded legal standing by the new complaint procedure. The judicial record from this period is full of the grievances of villagers. The grievances of peasants are frequently recorded in the court records that result from royal invitations for complaint. One of the most frequent grievances concerns the administration of purveyance, or prise, and its impact on villagers and peasants. Purveyance was a means by which the royal household and armies were provisioned.[26] The impact of purveyance fell unevenly socially as well as geographically. It affected the peasantry much more severely than the upper classes and clergy. More advantaged social groups could engineer protection or even exemption, by purchasing royal letters of protection, or, of course, by bribing officials.[27] Taking the household first, purveyance was used to provide for the household and subsidiary households on their itineraries around the kingdom. *Precursores* rode ahead of the household to get provisions ready. They worked with local royal officials and valuers, arranging to have foodstuffs, stabling, and other necessities ready for the household's arrival. The provisioning of armies took place on a national scale. In each county the sheriff was responsible for meeting royal requirements. In the period I am discussing in this chapter, purveyance was particularly intensive in 1294–7 (for campaigns in Scotland and Gascony), 1314–16 (Bannockburn), and 1333 onwards, for campaigns in Scotland and France.[28] Provisions might be obtained in a number of ways, ranging from house-to-house collections, to bulk procurement at markets and ports. Theoretically, all

of power and an interest in 'reserving the subjective orality of lordship against the encroachment of written official action' (Bisson, *Tormented Voices*, 2, 20, 117, 137–8. I am grateful to Chris Wickham for drawing this study to my attention.) Christopher Dyer has exploited records of peasant litigation in the royal courts in an effort to 'glimpse, however imperfectly, the mental world of the illiterate and underprivileged' (Dyer, 'Attitudes Towards Serfdom', 279). Bisson is explicitly subjective; Dyer carefully uses forensic procedures to analyse the evidence. Despite these differences, both seek to understand peasant plaint from the viewpoint of the peasant. For further examples, see Freedman, *Images*; Justice, *Writing and Rebellion*; and Strohm, *Hochon's Arrow*, 33–56.

[26] The following outline of purveyance is based on Given-Wilson, 'Purveyance'; Harriss, *Public Finance*, 49–57, 67–9, 101–4, 111, 121–4, 179–80, 247–8, 376–417; Hewitt, *Organisation of War*, 109–72; Maddicott, 'The English Peasantry and the Demands of the Crown'; Thomson, 'Lincolnshire Assize Roll', pp. lii–lxxxviii; and Prestwich, *War, Politics and Finance*, 114–36.

[27] Maddicott, 'The English Peasantry and the Demands of the Crown', 19–21.

[28] Ibid., 16–17.

goods, services, and labour provided must be paid for. But *prise* (from *prendre*) implied taking rather than buying, and shortfalls and losses could occur in various ways.[29] Payment might never be made, or it might not reflect the true value of the goods supplied. Purveyors might insist on buying at a discount.[30] And where payment was made by credit instrument, such as a tally, it could be hard for the creditor to get what he was owed.[31] In 1298 Edward I instigated an inquiry in Lincolnshire in which prise is the commonest topic of complaint.[32] Some forty years later, Edward III instigated the Inquisition of the Ninth (*Nonarum Inquisitiones*), a parish-by-parish investigation of the shortfall in tax revenue from the ninth levied in 1340, which was another occasion on which villagers expressed complaints about prises.[33] Further royal inquiries in Lincolnshire in 1340–42 heard complaints from many villages about royal officials.[34]

The little-known *Nonarum Inquisitiones* records offer particularly good examples of peasant plaint in the judicial record. Edward III levied the ninth (so called because every ninth sheaf was set aside for the king) to fund his military campaigns in France and Scotland. The levy took place amid tension between the crown and lay and ecclesiastical lords, and the eventual yield was too low to meet the debts run up, meaning that the crown had to levy a loan in wool in 1340. The Inquisition of the Ninth called on villages to explain why their payments of the ninth were lower than expected. The royal inquiries were answered with a barrage of peasant complaint. Frequently natural disasters were blamed for reduced productivity. The villagers of Lym cum Halghestok, Dorset, claimed that a sea flood had ruined a great part of their land holdings.[35] The parish of Remesbury, Wiltshire, explained that the lambs were small and the majority of the sheep died because of the hard winter, and the price of wool was low because of lack of money.[36] Another Wiltshire parish listed a string of climatic disasters as well as animal diseases as the reason for their low tax yield:

… propter forte gelu longo tempor' durans … tercia pars terre ejusdem paroch' jacuit incult' et terr' que colebatur ad semen quadragesimal' propter sol' fervore' & siccitatem in estate non debito modo fructificaverunt. Et similiter regnabat maxima ovium mortalitas …[37]

[… on account of a long-lasting heavy freeze … a third of the land of the parish lay uncultivated, and the land which was sown produced a fortieth part on account of fierce sun and drought in summer. And similarly there was great mortality among the sheep …]

The inquiries also elicited complaints against royal officials. In some counties, many villages took the opportunity to explain that their productivity and

---

[29] Thomson, 'Lincolnshire Assize Roll', p. lxvi.   [30] Given-Wilson, 'Purveyance', 161.
[31] Ibid., 155–61.   [32] Thomson, 'Lincolnshire Assize Roll'.
[33] For the records, see *Nonarum Inquisitiones*. For the context, see Fryde, 'Removal'.
[34] Maddicott, 'The English Peasantry and the Demands of the Crown', 62.
[35] *Nonarum Inquisitiones*, 44.   [36] Ibid., 175.
[37] Ibid., 180. The earlier famine of 1315–22 was, however, of much greater severity: see Jordan, *The Great Famine*, 182–8.

prosperity had been ruinously afflicted by the abuses and depredations of royal purveyors, in some cases, on top of climatic and other natural disasters. For example, the villagers of Gamelyngeye, Cambridgeshire, testified to the poverty and oppression of tenants:

... ccccxl acr' terre jacuerunt frisce propter inopiam & paupertatem tenencium ... & propter diversas taxaciones & tallag' que eveniunt de anno in annum ... [38]

[... 490 acres of land lay fallow on account of the destitution and poverty of the tenants ... and on account of the various taxes and tallages imposed year after year ...]

The villagers of Long Stowe, Cambridgeshire, testified similarly to the lamentable condition of tenants and their holdings as a consequence of taxation:

... magna pars terre ejusdem ville jacet frisca & inculta & plura mesuag' existunt vacua in enervacione valoris ejusdem none eodem anno xx et eciam terra ejusdem ville fere inculta propter inpotenciam tenencium qui vexati & destructi sunt per frequent' taxaciones & tallag' reg' ... [39]

[... a great part of the land of the vill lies fallow and uncultivated and many holdings are empty, reducing the value of the ninth from twenty years ago, and even the land of the village is nearly uncultivated on account of the impotence of the tenants who are afflicted and destroyed, through frequent royal taxes and tallages ...]

Such complaints were not confined to Cambridgeshire. The villagers of the manors of Alansmore and Clehonger in Herefordshire complained that ten virgates of land lay fallow because the tenants were poor 'on account of divers taxes and levies imposed upon them' ('propter diversas taxaciones & colleciones eis imponitas').[40]

The royal inquiries of 1340–1 provide other examples of peasant plaint in the judicial record. These inquiries were instituted by Edward III on account of his shortfall in tax revenue when he returned from campaigning in France. The Lincolnshire inquiry of 1341 heard that John de Kele seized wool and silver from the village of Skegness to help the war effort ('ad opus domini Regis'), but none of it went to the king.[41] Ralph Swallow and Stephen Radcliffe did not pass on the profits from the sale of the livestock they had seized ('ita quod non devaluerunt ad proficium domini Regis').[42] The Lincolnshire inquiry of 1341 also heard that William of Wallingford, formerly a king's purveyor, Ralph Swallow, and Stephen Radcliffe seized twenty cattle and oxen from the village of Claypole and sold them.[43] Another complaint was that Roger le Draper had seized corn and oats, spending the money on himself.[44] Yet another was that Hugo de Wygthorpe had attached various men of Waynfleet and extracted thirteen shillings and four pence

---

[38] *Nonarum Inquisitiones*, 208. [39] Ibid., 208.
[40] Ibid., 143. Cf. Maddicott, 'The English Peasantry and the Demands of the Crown', 4.
[41] TNA (PRO), JUST 1/521/9. [42] TNA (PRO), JUST 1/521/4.
[43] TNA (PRO), JUST 1/521/3. [44] TNA (PRO), JUST 1/521/3d.

from them illegally ('per extorsionem').[45] An inquiry in Hertfordshire in the same year heard that Philip, bailiff, and Roger Hurt, his deputy, came to the house of Stephen Wallis and broke down the door of his granary, seizing six quarters of oats, while William King, formerly a bailiff, had seized a cart and two horses against the will of ('contra voluntatem') Robert de Syward.[46] William King of Hertfordshire had no commission to seize a cart and horses (in other words, was not doing it on behalf of the crown).[47] An inquiry in Suffolk in 1314 heard that Robert Halliday unjustly ('iniuste') seized a horse worth fifteen shillings from Thomas de Cressingham and kept the money for fifteen days, and also that he maliciously ('maliciose') came to William's house and seized animals.[48]

On first reading the remarkable, parish-by-parish records of testimony from named peasant jurors who testified to the Inquisition of the Ninth, and the testimony of those who complained to the inquiries, it is tempting to interpret these complaints as the peasants' own strategic exploitation of the old tradition of 'peasant lament'. Invited to explain themselves, the villagers take the opportunity to have peasant complaint heard in court. Such materials have indeed been read as evidence for the voice of peasant complaint. Maddicott, for example, sees the records of inquiries as giving us 'the taxpayer's side of the case'.[49]

However, tempting as it may be to treat such documents as evidence for the legitimizing of peasant complaint by the new complaint procedure, it is as well to consider the diplomatic evidence and the judicial context in which these complaints were expressed. Why was it these points that the inquisitors chose to note in their laconic accounts of the peasants' depositions? And why do they occur so commonly, in the depositions of village after village, even in those of villages as geographically dispersed as Herefordshire and Cambridgeshire? Arguably, peasant plaint is so prevalent in the records because such traditional grievances were what the clerks were primed to hear and record. Evidence that this is the case is provided by the commissions and mandates themselves. For example, returning from campaign in France, Edward III immediately issued a proclamation acknowledging that he had made heavy demands on the people and announcing an inquiry into corruption and abuses among royal officials who had been too quick to levy from 'our poor people' ('notre povere poeple'), becoming rich and powerful with respect to 'their poor neighbours' ('lur povere veysines') to the detriment also of the crown's revenues. He invited the submission of written bills of complaint, in secret if necessary.[50] The mandate commissioning the Hertfordshire inquiry explicitly says that it is set up to hear about 'diuersas oppressiones, extorsiones, dampna, grauamina et excessus per subtaxatores et eorum clericos…' ('various oppressions, extortions, injuries, grievances, and

---

[45] TNA (PRO), JUST 1/521/9.   [46] TNA (PRO), JUST 1/337/4.

[47] TNA (PRO), JUST 1/337/4.   [48] TNA (PRO), JUST 1/850/4d.

[49] Maddicott, 'The English Peasantry and the Demands of the Crown', 12.

[50] For the political context, see Fryde, 'Removal'; and for the proclamation 149 and n. 4.

outrages by tax officials and their clerks ... ').[51] The crown framed invitations to complain in the terms of peasant plaint, and the complaints echoed peasant plaint back to the king.

The key point is that these plaints were designed to achieve redress for the crown. It was only incidently, if at all, that the villagers would benefit from these hearings (though we should not exclude the possibility that they tried to do so).[52] It was because the king had been robbed or defrauded of tax that these traditional peasant grievances against taxation were given the status of legal plaint. Hence the repeated allegations, in the examples quoted above, that the king's purveyors have kept what they have seized for themselves, or have sold their pickings and not passed on the profit to the crown. These complaints work especially in the interests of royal government's control over administration in the regions. The old tradition of peasant plaint takes on new legal validity for the reason that the interests of the crown are involved.

Another kind of plaint where grievances about taxation and prise are expressed is the commons' petition (sometimes called the 'commune petition' or 'common petition') to parliament. Like continental parliaments, the English parliament's function was to dispense justice.[53] Complaint could be made to parliament, particularly in cases where a remedy was not available in the common law courts.[54] Commons' petitions to parliament related private grievances to the royal interest.[55] Emerging between 1316 and 1327, commons' petitions were those guaranteed or sponsored by the parliamentary commons.[56] The commons' petition invoked the concept of the public interest, as distinct from the interests of the crown, or of the individual. Peasant plaint is deployed in many petitions that originate from the 'commons' or from a community. Some petitions are presented in the names of the people of a region. For example, in 1320 the 'men of Holderness' brought a complaint about the purveyors John Goldeneye and Robert Romeyn, complaining that various people had never been paid for the

---

[51] TNA (PRO), JUST 1/337/1.

[52] It is possible to read these complaints as serving the interests of the peasants themselves as well. The villagers may have been, in effect, seeking to offset losses to prise against their tax liability. Compare other uses of local tax collection structures in the interests of peasants themselves, for example, in a case in Wiltshire, 1348, when some villagers used the structure in place for assessing and gathering the lay subsidy to accumulate funds for an action to prove ancient demesne; see Müller, 'The Aims and Organisation of a Peasant Revolt'.

[53] Sayles, *Medieval Parliament*, 40–1.

[54] Richardson and Sayles (eds.), *Rotuli ... Inediti*, p. viii.

[55] Harding, 'Plaints and Bills', 80.

[56] It looks as if this kind of petition developed as a way of negotiating the petitioning process. There were procedural advantages: once the number of private petitions became much larger, it could be difficult to get a reply. Gradually a procedure emerged whereby commons' petitions were treated differently from private petitions. Commons' petitions went straight to the clerk of the parliament, whereas private petitions were screened and processed by receivers of petitions. For the development of the commons' petition and associated procedures, see Harriss, *Public Finance*, 118–24; Myers, 'Parliamentary Petitions', 396–8; Rayner, ' "Commune Petition" '; and Richardson and Sayles (eds.), *Rotuli ... Inediti*, p. xiii.

goods seized from them.[57] The basis for the petition is that this abuse wrongs both the king, and the people of Holderness. The 'commonalty of Lincolnshire' presented a petition concerning grievous sufferings in their region in the same period:

A nostre Seignur le Roi & a son Conseil monstre la Comunalte du Conte de Nicole [i.e. Lincoln], en priaunt q'il voille avoir regard a les meschefs & perdes q'il ont eu, & uncore ont, c'este asavoir de morayn de bestes, & de bas terres surundez par cretm de ewe, & ble failli, & des gentz pris & mis a raunzon par les enemis & rebelles nostre Seignur le Roi, & plusours ont voidez terres & mesons, pur malice & doute des enemis avantditz: Par quoi grant partie des terres du dite Conte gisent desenez … Vos Baillifs & Ministres venont, & ont pris a grant some des quartres de ble & de bres, a vostre oeps, a grant meschef du Counte avantdite …[58]

[To our Lord the King and his Council, the commonalty of the county of Lincoln complain, praying that he pay heed to the troubles and losses which they have had, and still have, that is to say, disease of livestock, lowlands flooded with water, failed corn, and people taken and held to ransom by enemies and rebels of our lord king, and many have left their lands and houses for malice and fear of these enemies. For this reason a great part of the land of the said county lies fallow … Your bailiffs and agents have come, and have taken a large number of quarters of corn and malt, to your service, to the great affliction of the said county …]

Other petitions are presented simply in the name of 'la commune'. One example comes from a parliament held at York in 1334:

Et pur ce qe le poeple est molt greue par diuerses prises des autres qe des gentz nostre seignur le roi, si prie la commune qe totes prises soient defenduz sauue les prises le roi, et qe celes prises soient faitz selonc ceo qi ordine fust par estatut.[59]

[And because the people are greatly aggrieved by various prises of others than the people of our lord king, the commune prays that all prises be forbidden except prises of the king, and that those prises be taken in the manner ordained by statute.]

The petitions from Lincolnshire and the men of Holderness clearly serve interests in the shires. Differences between the form of these petitions and that of instruments drafted by parliamentary clerks suggest that these complaints were drafted beyond parliament; it seems likely that provincial lawyers were involved, and that the county courts may have provided a structure within which provincial political society could formulate petitions.[60] In these examples, therefore, it is likely that we see the county communities exploiting peasant complaint in the complex negotiations with the crown enabled by the new petitionary structure.

---

[57] *PROME*, parliament of Edward II, 1320 October, item 46.

[58] *RP*, i. 400. This petition does not appear on the parliament roll. It is TNA (PRO), SC 8/6/259; see *PROME*, 'Appendix of Unedited Petitions, 1307–1337'.

[59] Richardson and Sayles (eds.), *Rotuli … Inediti*, 237.

[60] Harriss, *Public Finance*, 123, 260; Maddicott, 'County Community'; and Maddicott, 'Parliament and the Constituencies'.

The commons' petition provided another way in which the lament of the peasant could be appropriated and mobilized for new political ends in the new judicial context.

PEASANT PLAINT AND NEW 'VILLEINS'

We have been exploring the ways in which peasant plaint was mobilized as complaint that had legal standing and force. In the next section I shall illustrate a rather different use for peasant plaint. We shall look at texts in which peasant plaint is used with all of the loading of inadmissible complaint, as plaint that has no legal recognition, in other words, as a discourse that is marked with disenfranchisement. The texts that we shall be looking at are not the utterances of villeins, or of advocates for villeins, against their lords. They are texts that engage with the legal and constitutional relations of the crown with the barons, and with the Church. They are texts where we would not expect any identification with villeinage. However, I shall argue that these bodies claim that peasant plaint is, or soon will be, the only means of complaint left to them.

The starkest, clearest, example comes from a petition issued by the Earl of Hereford in 1297. The Earl of Hereford petitioned the exchequer on behalf of himself and others against the levy of an eighth. He complained about the wording of the writs authorizing this levy. The writs said that the eighth had been granted by earls, counts, barons, and the community of the realm. The earl objected that the levy had never been 'granted' ('ne feut graunte'), adding that nothing put a man in serfdom more than 'redemption of blood and being tallaged at will' ('nule chose ne met plu tot homme en servage qe rechat de saunc e estre taille a volunte') and that if the eighth were levied it would disinherit them and their heirs.[61] The earl was making the point that the taxation of free men was subject to consent, whereas the crown was taking at will and thereby conferring the status of villeins on those so taxed.

In the same year a petition known to modern historians by its opening word *Monstraunces* (from *moustre*, 'to show', an Anglo-Norman verb often used in formulas at the opening of plaints) was presented to the king. This complaint is presented in the name of 'archbishops, bishops, abbots, priors, earls, barons, and all the community of the land' ('erceveskes, eveskes, abbees, priours, countes, et barounes et tout la communiaute de la terre')—though, in fact, it aligns with baronial interests.[62] It sets out grievances concerning royal financial and military demands. The petitioners complain that they cannot perform military service, or

---

[61] Edwards, *'Confirmatio Cartarum'*, 156.
[62] Ed. Edwards, *'Confirmatio Cartarum'*, 170–1, quotation from 170.

give financial aid to the king, because they are oppressed by 'diverses talliages et diverses prises' ('various tallages and prises') as a consequence of which they are so poor they can scarcely sustain themselves, let alone pay taxes. The petitioners complain that the laws and customs of the land have been infringed, and they no longer enjoy the liberties ('fraunchises') which they used to have.[63] Both clergy and laity are aggrieved because the points of Magna Carta and the Charter of the Forest are no longer observed.

Tallage, like prise, was not simply 'taxation'. The word covered a broad range of meanings, including the kinds of taxation associated with villeinage. In these latter meanings, it was associated with servility. *Tallage* was related to *taille* ('count up'), being a head (i.e. arbitrary) tax.[64] The vocabulary associated with taxation became a sensitive issue from the early decades of the thirteenth century, when royal writs began to distinguish between *tallage* of peasants and *aid* from freemen.[65] Whether a peasant was subject to *tallage*, to making payments 'high and low, at the will of the lord' was one of the criteria applied by courts to determine whether an individual was a villein. For example, the jury summoned in the case of the villagers of Stoughton testified that the villagers' ancestors 'did villein customs as in the redemption of flesh and blood, tallages and other works with forks and flails as villeins do … they were villeins of the abbot's predecessors and performed villein customs at the will of those abbots as in tallages, redemption of flesh and all other villein conditions'.[66] The key point was that tallage could be exacted 'at the will of' the lord. According to Bracton's definition, to be 'able to be tallaged at the will of the lord high and low' ('talliari … potest ad voluntatem domini ad plus et ad minus') was a mark of 'purum villenagium'.[67] J. G. Edwards surmises that the phrase 'diverses talliages et diverses prises' in the *Monstraunces* refers to a *variety* of different kinds of levy; he argues that it cannot refer literally to what the *law* recognized as *tallage*. Given the broad range of meanings available, one cannot press the point too far. But the context suggests that the petitioners may have been using the word *tallage* with the connotations of unfreedom: as we have seen, in the same year the Earl of Hereford wrote that 'estre taille a volunte' ('to be tallaged at will') led to 'servage'. Arguably, by using the word 'tallage', the petitioners were making a point about the implications of taxation for their legal status. By describing the burdens they suffered as 'tallage', they may have been asserting that the financial and military prosperity of the realm, and their own status as legal subjects, were both imperilled by the king's taxation. The petitioners' echoing of peasant plaint would have asserted the contrasting

---

[63] Edwards, '*Confirmatio Cartarum*', 170, 171. Cf. Rothwell (ed.) *Chronicle of Walter of Guisborough*, 292–3.

[64] Freedman, *Images*, 244.   [65] See Hyams, *Kings, Lords and Peasants*, 191–2.

[66] Farnham, *Leicestershire*, 153–4; for discussion of the meaning of *tallage*, see Hyams, *Kings, Lords and Peasants*, 191.

[67] *Bracton Online*, iii. 131.

legal validity of their own complaint, and in this way they would have been able to emphasize that it would be unjust to regard it in the same way as the plaint of the unfree peasant.

The *Confirmatio Cartarum*, a royal letter patent issued in 1297, explicitly addresses the grievances expressed in the *Monstraunces*.[68] It suggests that these connotations had been heard by the crown. Noting the fear that the levies (here carefully called 'les aides e les mises', not 'tallages') could become bondage ('servage') for the petitioners and their heirs ('pussent turner en servage a eus, e a leur heirs'), it guaranteed that such payments would not be added to custom ('ne treroms a custome'), and that, henceforth, such levies would only be taken with the common consent of the realm, and for the common profit, with the exception of ancient and accustomed aids and prises.

It was not only the barons who claimed that they were in danger of being reduced to complaining like oppressed peasants. Ecclesiastics too appropriated peasant complaint to show that the Church was being excluded from access to justice. It is not that the Church was against villeinage. We have seen that the monks of Leicester Abbey disputed their villeins' bid for freedom. But it was against its own potential legal disenfranchisement, and mobilized peasant plaint to make the point. An early example of a text that demonstrates this well is an Anglo-Norman poem entitled by Isabel Aspin *Song of the Church*.[69] The poem survives in two versions, each in one manuscript only.[70] The earlier manuscript, London, British Library, MS Cotton Julius D. vii, is a book associated with St Albans; the poem, written (?as a filler) on the second to last leaf, along with Latin anticlerical verse and maxims, is the only Anglo-Norman item. A rubric records that the poem was written in 1255 on the desolation of the English Church. The second manuscript is Oxford, Bodleian Library, MS Douce 137, a volume of Latin and French legal materials, some of which suggest a connection with Abingdon Abbey. The poem must have been copied in this book between 1262 and *c*.1290, and Aspin has argued that adaptations in this version suit circumstances around 1290.[71] I shall concentrate first on the material common to both versions (quoting from the later version), and then later in this chapter I shall discuss the material that occurs only in Douce 137.

The poet describes the distress and lamentation of the Church. The complaint of the Church has been foreshadowed by the 'plente Jeremie' (l. 3), the *Lamentations of Jeremiah*. In the *Lamentations*, Jerusalem laments because she is subjected to paying tribute to her enemies. Jerusalem, formerly mistress of her

---

[68] Stubbs (ed.), *Select Charters*, 487–94; for discussion, see Edwards, '*Confirmatio Cartarum*'. Cf. *De Tallando non concedendo* (Stubbs (ed.), *Select Charters*, 497–8), whose relation with the *Confirmatio* is unclear.

[69] Aspin (ed.), *Anglo-Norman Political Songs*, 36–48. Passages and translations below are quoted from this source except where explicitly noted.

[70] Ibid., 36–7.   [71] Ibid., 37.

people, is now like a weeping widow; just so Holy Church groans and weeps, ('ele se gient e plure', l. 15). The poet develops the comparison between the Church and the widow:

> Jadis fu saynt' eglise
> Franche et desus,
> Amee e cherie,
> Nule rien plus.
> Mes ore est enservie.
> E tant avilie,
> E abatu jus.
>
> (ll. 21–7)

[Formerly holy church was free and uppermost, loved and cherished, nothing more so. But now she is in servitude and so much despised and brought low.]

The poet is drawing on the tradition in which Jeremiah's lament about the subjugation of the Israelites is interpreted as a prophecy about the Church.[72] Isabel Aspin's translation, quoted here, does not quite convey the loading of the poet's vocabulary. The poet is aligning the tradition of biblical lament against slavery with the vocabulary of legal freedom and unfreedom. It is not just that the Church has been 'brought low'. Formerly the clergy were *franche*, of free status; now they are *enservie*, brought to the condition of serfdom, and *avilie*, perhaps, 'made into villeins'.

The cause of disenfranchisement is that the Church is subject to financing the crown to fund foreign wars:

> Le rei vet a Surie
> Par bon entendement;
> Vivera de rubberie
> Ke la clergie li rent.
> Ja ne fra bone emprise
> Pur reyndre saynt' eglise,
> Jo quid certaynement.
> Ke veot aver ensample
> Regarde le rei de France
> E sun achiefement.
>
> Grevus est li tallage
> Mes y nus cuveynt suffrir.
>
> (ll. 41–52)

[The king is going to Syria with good intent; he will live on stolen goods which the clergy hand over to him. He will never accomplish a successful enterprise to redeem holy church, it is certainly my opinion. Whoever wants to have an example may look at the king of France and his achievement. The tax is grievous but we must suffer it.]

---

[72] For the tradition, see Freedman, *Images*, 78.

Once again, Aspin's translation, quoted above, does not quite convey the loading of the vocabulary. It is not just 'tax', but 'tallage', that is at issue. As we have seen, *tallage* was not simply 'taxation'. The poet is using an Anglo-Norman legal word with broad meanings that included various kinds of taxation, including impositions on the unfree. Jerusalem's lament becomes aligned with the plaint of the peasant. The poet's point is that the Church is forced to complain like a slave or a villein.

The implications of the distinction between *tallage* and *aid* were discussed by theologians. At stake was the relation between the Church and secular power. The Fourth Lateran Council of 1215 decreed that the clergy must not agree to royal demands without first consulting the pope.[73] The papal bull 'Clericis laicos', issued by Boniface VIII in 1296, forbad clergy to pay tax to laymen from the revenues of their churches. The competition between royal and papal power generated a range of writings, from treatises in political theory to polemical pamphlets.[74] Continental writers theorized relations between the Church and secular authority using the model of the relation between lord and villein. For example, some Parisian *quodlibeta* from the 1280s distinguish between the purposes to which taxes might be put. A lord might tallage his serfs for his own purposes, but taxes exacted from freemen were to be used for the common good. These principles were adapted to discussion of taxation of the clergy. For example, in *Disputatio inter Clericum et Militem* (?1296–7), both disputants discuss taxation of the clergy using the language of villeinage. The Knight defends taxation using an analogy with his own position as a landlord: just as the knight as a landlord 'has the right to collect certain rents from certain farms, so, by the judgment of his own will, the emperor may levy tribute upon the world in general when it is appropriate to do so for the defence of the commonwealth'. In a passage redolent of the *Song of the Church*, the Clerk complains that the liberties of the Church are infringed because goods are snatched from them by kings, princes, and nobles:

Aetate mea, vidi Ecclesiam in honore magno apud reges et principes et nobiles universos haberi; et nunc video econtra miserandum. Ecclesia facta est vobis omnibus praeda; exiguntur a nobis multa; dantur nulla; bona nostra, si non damus, rapiuntur a nobis; conculcantur iura nostra; libertantes infringuntur.

[In my time, I have seen the Church held in great honour among kings and princes and nobles everywhere; yet now, by contrast, I see her wretched. The Church is made a prey for you all; many things are taken from us, and none given. If we do not surrender our goods, they are snatched from us; our rights are trampled upon; our liberties infringed.][75]

---

[73] Nederman (ed. and trans.), *Political Thought*, 142.   [74] Dyson (ed.), *Royalist Tracts*.
[75] Ibid., 12–13. The text is usually dated 1296–7; however, this date is not beyond question: the text's earliest surviving appearance is in the *Somnium viridarii*, a political compendium of 1376 or 1377, and surviving manuscripts are all of a later date. It was translated into French as *Le Songe du Vergier*, and into English by John Trevisa *c.*1380 (Dyson (ed.), *Royalist Tracts*, pp. xviii–xxii).

The Clerk's claim is that taxation puts ecclesiastical and monastic lords in a position analogous to that of the oppressed peasant. He appropriates peasant complaint to show loss of legal subjecthood.

Two treatises addressed explicitly to Edward III show peasant plaint put to the defence of the Church. The *Epistola ad Regem Edwardum III* and the *Speculum Regis Edwardi III* are now both attributed to William of Pagula (d. 1332), an Oxford-trained canon lawyer and secular priest. Both the *Epistola* and the *Speculum* advise the king on issues of taxation. The treatises are closely related in content, though somewhat distinguished in style.[76] Both texts devote a great deal of space to the laments of the poor and the enslaved against unjust treatment. The author begins the *Epistola* by announcing that he will advise the king so that he 'may do justice to each individual'. The most important duty of a king is to ensure justice to all. However, today exactions are transgressing common law, and the victims lament:

Et ideo a quibus bona sic capiuntur clamant ad Deum. Quid autem clamant, non exprimo. Immo, Deus novit et illos pauperes libenter audit Deus; unde psalmista: *Desiderium pauperum exaudivit Dominus, speracionem cordis eorum audivit auris tua* … Et Ecclesiasticus xxj: *Deprecacio pauperis ex ore usque ad aures Dei pervenit et clamor innocencium pervenit ad Deum.* Exod. ij: *Clamor filiorum Israelis ascendit ad Deum quos gravabant Egypcii sub labore et audivit Deus gemitus eorum.* Unde Job xxiiij: *Anime vulneratorum clamant ad Deum et Deus inultum abire non patitur.*

[And therefore, those from whom goods are taken cry to God. What they cry to God, I cannot express. Indeed, God knows and God freely hears those paupers; wherefore, the Psalmist says, 'The Lord has heard the desire of the poor, your ear has heard the hope of his heart' (Psalms 9: 17) … and Ecclesiasticus 21: 6 proclaims, 'A plea from a poor man's mouth goes straight to the ear of God and the cry of the innocent rises to God.' Exodus 3: 9 says, 'The cry of the Israelites, who have been weighted down under burdens by the Egyptians, ascends to God, and God hears their groans.' Wherefore it is read in Job 24: 12: 'The souls of the wounded cry out to God and God does not allow them to go away unavenged.'][77]

The complaints of the king's subjects are explicitly expressed using the language of biblical lament of the poor and enslaved Israelites. This is similar to the use of the *Lamentations of Jeremiah* in the *Song of the Church*. The *Epistola* and the *Speculum* use a range of devices of this kind for representing complaint against

---

[76] Moisant (ed.), *De speculo regis Edwardi III*. I follow Boyle, 'William of Pagula', in calling recension A the *Epistola* and recension B the *Speculum*. For translations (from which I quote below), and recent discussion of the authorship issue and of the relationships of the texts see Nederman (ed. and trans.), *Political Thought*, 65–8; and Nederman and Neville, 'Origins', 317–29. William was the author of several treatises on canon law and pastoral theology, the most well known of which is the *Oculus Sacerdotis*.

[77] Moisant (ed.), *De speculo regis Edwardi III*, 84; Nederman (ed. and trans.), *Political Thought*, 74.

the king's injustices. The *Epistola* uses the language of widows' and orphans' supplications, quoting Ecclesiasticus 35: 17–19: 'Non despiciet Dominus preces pupilli nec vidue, si effundat loquebam gemitus. Nonne lacrime vidue et clamor ejus ascendunt ad Deum et Dominus exauditor est?' ('The Lord does not ignore the orphan's supplication nor the widow's as she pours out her story with groans. Do the widow's tears not run down her cheeks as she cries to God and the Lord listens?')[78] The author also describes how complaints are brought in the courts. Those responsible are allowed by the royal courts to go unpunished, and so justice is not done:

Sed, si ad curiam tuam conqueratur de hujusmodi garcionibus, ille garcio qui predicta bona rapuit, absentabit se, neque tunc invenietur et alii garciones totaliter se excusant, cum tamen, omne, de hujusmodi rapina communicabant.

[But if a complaint be made in your court concerning this sort of servant, that servant who has taken the aforesaid goods will absent himself and then he will not be found, and the other servants will excuse themselves completely, since all of them have been taking a hand in robberies of this kind.][79]

In another injustice, described in the *Speculum*, many creditors go unpaid, and their cases unanswered:

Si quis habet querelam contra te, sis pocius pro causa illius donec tibi constet de veritate, sic debent illi de consilio tuo stare citius pro justicia. Sed intellige, domine rex, quod mille et mille homines habent causam contra te pro debitis tuis non solutis.

['If someone has a quarrel with you [i.e. brings a complaint], you should be more concerned for their case until there is agreement between you concerning the truth, and thus your counselors should stand up immediately for justice.' But understand, Lord King, that thousands and thousands of people have cases against you for the debts you have not paid.][80]

God's justice, where plaintiffs are heard, is contrasted with that in the king's courts, where they are not. In the *Speculum*, William claims that the king's subjects 'engage in sighs and tears' when the king arrives in their neighbourhood. One cause of this sorrow, he says, is that the *precursores*—the outriders who went ahead of the king's purveyors—and other servants of the household impose labour services on the people:

Alia causa est quia precursores tue curie garciones et alii capiunt homines et equos laborantes circa agriculturam; et animalia que terram arant et semina portant ad agrum, ut laborent per duos uel tres dies in tuo servicio, nihil pro labore percipientes ...

---

[78] Moisant (ed.), *De speculo regis Edwardi III*, 92; Nederman (ed. and trans.), *Political Thought*, 80.
[79] Moisant (ed.), *De speculo regis Edwardi III*, 94; Nederman (ed. and trans.), *Political Thought*, 82.
[80] Moisant (ed.), *De speculo regis Edwardi III*, 155; Nederman (ed. and trans.), *Political Thought*, 127. The quotation is from Jean de Joinville's 'Les enseignements de Saint Louis à son fils'.

[Another cause [of the people's sorrow] is that the scouts for your court, servants, and others seize men and horses working around the fields, and animals that plough the earth and carry seed to the field, so that the men and animals work two or three days in your service, receiving nothing for the work …][81]

The image of imposed labour services occurs again to support the point that seizing the goods of others is illegal:

… tu per tuos ministros, capis bona infinita ab aliis, ipsis invitis, sicut raptor. Quia scire debes quod sicut liberalitas est signum nobilitatis, sic rapina est signum rusticitatis. Unde nobiles multi, qui nobiles reputantur opinione hominum, rusticissimi sunt, cum non cessant capere bona pauperum, ipsis invitis, de quorum laboribus ipsi vivunt.

[… you through your ministers seize infinite goods from others, although they are unwilling, just like a thief. You ought to know that as liberality is a sign of nobility, so robbery is a sign of barbarism. Wherefore many nobles, who are counted nobles by the opinion of men, are barbarians, since they do not stop seizing the goods of paupers, although unwilling, from whose labors they live.'][82]

By applying the language of villeinage to prise, William of Pagula is contributing to debate about the legal basis of purveyance.[83] Like the authors of the *Monstraunces* and the *Song of the Church* he mobilizes the complaints of the poor against servitude as complaints with a relevance and charge for lords as well as peasants. He develops his arguments in ways particularly supportive of ecclesiastical lords. In the *Epistola* he suggests that the king is acting illicitly as lord of the clergy, since the goods of the Church really belong to the poor and the clergy are in bondage to the poor.[84] Purveyance is, therefore, robbery, a felony in common law.[85] Elsewhere in the *Epistola* he argues that purveyance violates the provisions of Magna Carta, and in the *Speculum* he calls for reform of privileges and statutes that permit such injustices to 'the holy churches or the paupers or even to the community of this kingdom'.[86]

William of Ockham, writing a few years later in support of Edward III and his ally the exiled emperor Ludwig, used similar language but this time in support of royal power over the clergy. In *An princeps* he argues that the pope is in bondage to the clergy, and the clergy are free (to pay taxes to the king).[87] He explicitly uses

---

[81] Moisant (ed.), *De speculo regis Edwardi III*, 132; Nederman (ed. and trans.), *Political Thought*, 108.

[82] Moisant (ed.), *De speculo regis Edwardi III*, 154; Nederman (ed. and trans.), *Political Thought*, 126.

[83] For the debate about purveyance and wider issues of public finance, see Harriss, *Public Finance*.

[84] Moisant (ed.), *De speculo regis Edwardi III*, 140–1; Nederman (ed. and trans.), *Political Thought*, 85.

[85] e.g. Moisant (ed.), *De speculo regis Edwardi III*, 100; Nederman (ed. and trans.), *Political Thought*, 77–9, 86. Cf. the claim in *Song of the Church* that the king lives by robbery ('Vivera de rubberie').

[86] Moisant (ed.), *De speculo regis Edwardi III*, 89, 145; Nederman (ed. and trans.), *Political Thought*, 78, 118–19.

[87] For the date (1338–9) and political context of this treatise, see Nederman (ed. and trans.), *Political Thought*, 145–8; and Offler (ed.), *Guillelmi de Ockham, Opera Politica*, i. 220–3.

rural labour service as a figure for the position of the papacy, quoting Bernard's letter to Pope Eugenius, *De consideratione*:

Item, idem [i.e. Bernard] ad eundem [i.e. Eugenius]: *Loquere tibi: 'Abiectus eram in domo Dei mei'. Quale est hoc de paupere et abiecto: 'Levor super gentes et regna'. Et infra: Nam et propheta, cum similiter levaretur, audivit: 'Ut evellas et destruas, et disperdas et dissipes, et aedifices et plantes'. Quid horum sonat? Rusticani magis sudoris schemate quodam labor spiritualis expressus est. Et nos igitur, ut multum sentiamus de nobis, nobis impositum sentiamus ministerium, non dominum datum. Et infra: Disce sarculo tibi opus esse, non sceptro, ut opus facias prophetae.*

[And again [Bernard] to Eugenius, 'Say to yourself, "I was an abject in the house of God" ⟨Psalms 83: 11⟩. How then am I "lifted over peoples and kingdoms" from poverty and abjectness?' And further on, 'When the prophet was similarly elevated, he heard, "Root up and pull down, and lay waste and destroy, and build and plant" ⟨Jeremiah 1: 10⟩. What is there of haughtiness in this? Rather, spiritual labour is here expressed in the figure of rustic toil. Let us likewise, highly as we regard ourselves, feel that a service has been imposed on us, not that we have been granted a power.' And further on, 'Learn that you need a hoe, not a scepter, to carry out the work of a prophet.']⁸⁸

He marshalls proofs from scripture to show that the Church is not in 'bondage' to the papacy.⁸⁹

Another genre which makes prominent use of peasant plaint in this period is the chronicle. The St Alban's monk Matthew Paris (d. 1259) describes the English in 1085 as lamenting slaves: 'omnesque in moerorem et servitutem redacti fuissent' ('and all [English people] were reduced to lamentation and servitude'); their condition is worse than that of the Egyptians' slaves (note that Latin *a servitute* could be translated as *de villenage* in Anglo-Norman).⁹⁰ He suggests

---

⁸⁸ Offler (ed.), *Guillelmi de Ockham, Opera Politica*, i. 239; Nederman (ed. and trans.), *Political Thought*, 165.

⁸⁹ 'Lex enim Christiana ex institutione Christi est lex libertatis, ita quod per ordinationem Christi non est maioris nec tantae servitutis quantae fuit lex vetus. Hoc namque ex auctoritatibus scripturae divinae colligitur evidenter. Beatus enim Iacobus in canonica sua c.i vocat eam legem perfectae libertatis, dicens: *Qui autem prospexit in lege perfectae libertatis, et permanserit in ea,* etc. ... Et c. iv: *Non sumus ancillae filii, sed liberae, qua libertate Christus nos liberavit* ... Et beatus Petrus, ut habetur Actuum xv, ait: *Quid temptatis ⟨Deum⟩ imponere iugum super cervices discipulorum, quod neque patres nostri nec nos portare potuimus?* ... Ex quibus aliisque quampluribus colligitur quod Christiani per legem evangelicam et instructionem Christi sunt a servitute multiplici liberati, et quod non sunt per legem evangelicam tanta servitute oppressi quanta Iudaei per legem veterem premebantur.' ['The Christian law from Christ's institution is a law of freedom (*lex libertatis*), so that by the edict of Christ it is not of greater or equal servitude as the old law. This is clearly evident from Scripture. James calls it the law of perfect freedom, saying: "For whoever looks forward in the law of perfect liberty and remains in it," etc. (James 1: 25) ... And in ⟨Galations⟩ 4: 31: "We are not children of the bondwoman but of the free, in which liberty Christ has freed us" ... And Peter, according to Acts 15: 10, says: "Why do you tempt God to put a yoke on the necks of his disciples which neither our fathers nor we could bear?" ... It can be gathered from these and many other examples that Christians have been freed from various servitudes by the law of the Gospels and the teachings of Christ, and that they are not as oppressed by the law of the Gospels as the Jews were by the old law.'] (Offler (ed.), *Guillelmi de Ockham, Opera Politica*, i. 230–1; Nederman (ed. and trans.), *Political Thought*, 156–7.)

⁹⁰ Madden (ed.), *Matthaei Parisiensis ... Historia Anglorum*, i. 28–9; for the Anglo-Norman usage, see *The Anglo-Norman Dictionary*, entry for *vileinage*.

analogies between the history of the peasants and the history of the religious houses. Matthew describes William's treatment of the monasteries in 1071:

Anno Domini M°.LXX° rex W⟨illelmus⟩, diabolico excitatus spiritu, vel malorum hominum consilio fascinatus, omnia Anglorum monasteria, quae sub temporibus regum Angliae piissimorum pace et libertate gratulabantur, auro spolians et argento insatiabiliter apporriavit, sanctorum patrum non deferens sanctionibus, cartis aut statutis; immo etiam nec feretris pepercit aut calicibus. Episcopatus autem et abbatias omnes, quae baronias tenebant, et eatenus ab omni servitio seculari libertatem habuerant, sub servitute statuit militari; inrotulans episcopatus et abbatias pro voluntate sua, quot milites sibi et successoribus suis, hostilitatis tempore, voluit a singulis exhiberi.[91]

[In the year of our Lord 1070 king William, stirred by a devilish spirit, or bewitched by the counsel of evil men, acquired all the monasteries of the English (which in the times of most pious English kings rejoiced in peace and liberty), insatiably despoiling them of gold and silver, not mindful of the sanctions, the holy fathers, of charters, or of statutes; moreover he did not even spare their chalices or reliquaries. But all episcopacies and abbacies, which held baronial tenures, to such a degree that they had freedom from all secular services, he subjected to military service, enrolling episcopacies and abbacies at his own will, how many knights he wished each of them to produce for him and his successors in time of war.]

Matthew describes the conquest as a loss of liberty for the Church. Previously free from any servitude to lords ('ab omni servitio seculari'), now ecclesiastics are obliged in perpetuity to provision the king in times of war. The monasteries are placed under a different kind of 'servitio' from that of villeins, but again the burdens imposed are arbitrary, 'pro voluntate sua', at the will of the king. Under 1073 Matthew describes how this arbitrary exercise of lordship affected his own house of St Albans, when William arbitrarily deprived St Albans of possessions and treasures and gave them to Westminster.[92]

Peter Langtoft traces the colonization, and loss, of the lands of the English using similar language in his Anglo-Norman verse chronicle:

> La quinte an donayt William le Conquerour,
> Quant Engleterre conquist, e se fist seygnur.
> Le ray Harald tuayt, ke perdist le honur;
> Countes et barouns morirent en l'estour.
> Les Englays unt vesquy jekes en çà tuz jour
> Desuthe estraunge garde, en servage et langour.
> En la geste après troverez la dolur.
>
> [The fifth wound William the Conqueror gave,
> When he conquered England, and made himself its lord.

---

[91] Madden (ed.), *Matthaei Parisiensis ... Historia Anglorum*, i. 12–13.

[92] Ibid., i. 18. The phrase 'est pro ratione voluntas' ('[the ruler's] will is held to be reason', based on Juvenal, *Satire* 6. 223) and the effect of the ruler's will were debated in this period. Matthew Paris was among those who argued that an unjust law could not be made into a just one simply because it was willed by the prince; see Pennington, *Popes, Canonists and Texts*, iii. 6–26.

He slew king Harold, who lost the honour;
Earls and barons perished in the battle.
The English have lived till now always
Under foreign rule, in serfdom and suffering.
You will find their grief in the history which follows.][93]

Like Matthew Paris, Langtoft describes the position of the conquered English in terms of grievous villeinage. Having seized the land from the Britons, following the Norman conquest the English have, henceforth, lived in 'servage' and in suffering which is related in the chronicle. Peter Langtoft handles the narrative of William's rule by focusing on its impact on ecclesiastics in the north-east of England. He describes how William puts down a rebellion, laying waste to the land so that between York and Durham no sod is turned, no corn sown, for nine years; churches are destroyed and plundered by the Normans like robbers ('en guise de laroun'). However, when William learns of this he requires redress:

Kaunt le ray William seet la verité,
Coment saint eglyse est si mal mené,
Ad tuz ses ministres tost ad comaundé
Ke chascun trespas sait ore amendé,
Et ke saint eglyse sait playnement feffé
Denz les fraunchises dount ele fu dowé,
Et ke la reverye là sait restore.
Mès nes un des robbeurs de plus ne fu chargé,
Ne portayt penaunce de ⟨l'⟩iniquité.

[When king William knows the truth,
How holy church is so ill treated,
He has immediately given command to all his officers,
That amends be at once made for every trespass,
And that holy church be fully infeoffed
In the fraunchises with which it was endowed,
And that the plunder be there restored.
But not one of the plunderers was further punished,
Nor underwent penaunce for his wickedness.][94]

The language and detail make this episode a historical antecedent for the exaction of prises. Langtoft was a canon of Bridlington in east Yorkshire, part of an area particularly vulnerable to purveyance.[95] Abuses of purveyance are the injustices most frequently complained about in an inquiry instituted in Lincolnshire by Edward I in 1298.[96] The region suffered because it was on the road north, a route frequently taken by the royal household and armies, often in connection with military campaigns against the Scots. It also suffered

---

[93] Wright (ed.), *Chronicle of Pierre de Langtoft*, i. 288–90. Cf. Freedman, *Images*, 128.
[94] Wright (ed.), *Chronicle of Pierre de Langtoft*, i. 413–21 (episode), 420–1 (extract).
[95] Maddicott, 'The English Peasantry and the Demands of the Crown', 24–6.
[96] Thomson, 'Lincolnshire Assize Roll'.

because, as corn-growing land, it produced a staple foodstuff important for provisioning the household and armies. The Normans' pillaging of the north-east results in failure to till the land, runs counter to law, and disenfranchises its ecclesiastical victims. William's dispensation of justice (giving redress to victims, if not punishing offenders) provides a model for legal process with regard to purveyance.[97]

Robert Manning follows Langtoft closely in his *Chronicle*, a text written in Middle English and completed by 1338:

> Siþen he & his haf had þe lond in heritage
> Þat þe Inglis haf so lad þat þei lyue in seruage.
> He sette þe Inglis to be þralle þat or was so fre.
> He þat bigan it alle, in þe geste may ȝe se …
>
> & sette vs in seruage, of fredom felle þe floure;
> Þe Inglis þorgh taliage lyue ȝit in sorow fulle soure.[98]

Here Manning adds to Langtoft's term 'servage' the loaded term 'taliage'; William's enslavement of the English finds its contemporary fulfilment in the exaction of tallage, to the continued sorrow of the people. The description of this period in *Castleford's Chronicle* (or the *Boke of Brut*, ? *c*.1327) goes further:

> Alle þe Englissemen, þe soȝ to spelle,
> Þat forth wiȝin Englande walde duelle,
> Trauaile þai salle, so þam nede stode,
> On oþer mennes soile to win þar fode,
> Duelle þai salle alls bondes and thralles
> And do alle þat to thraldum falles,
> Lif forth and trauaile in bondage—
> Þai and þar blode euer in seruage.[99]

This passage characterizes the condition of the English using other markers of legal serfdom: landlessness, labour service, and heredity.

Recently scholars have asked why chroniclers, members of religious orders, should wish to align themselves with the complaints of peasants. Thorlac Turville-Petre has argued that Manning sought to reflect the resentment felt by 'lewed' people because his order, the Gilbertines, had reasons to side with the peasantry against their lords, as they sought financial support from the wealthier peasantry and found themselves in competition for labour with the

---

[97] Wright (ed.), *Chronicle of Pierre de Langtoft*, i. pp. xix-xx, and subsequent critics (e.g. Turville-Petre, 'Robert Manning's *Chronicle*', 9) have seen Langtoft as concerned to show the justice of the wars of Edward I against the Scots, arguing that the canon of Bridlington was an enthusiast for the royal cause because the north-east suffered badly from Scottish raids. However, in the light of his alignment of Norman history with contemporary complaints about prise, it is arguable that he was also concerned to demonstrate the *injustices* perpetrated, especially on ecclesiastics, in connection with these wars.

[98] Sullens (ed.), *Robert Mannyng*, part 2, ll. 139–42, 1620–1.

[99] Eckhardt (ed.), *Castleford's Chronicle*, ll. 31931–8.

great landowners.[100] Moffat rejects this argument, preferring instead to read this alignment between monastic lords and peasants as having a racial basis: these chroniclers are not revealing the 'legal reality' of servitude 'but rather an idea of racial servitude'. The chronicles therefore, for Moffat, are evidence of racial disharmony, and racial identities that preachers and peasants would have agreed upon.[101] Paul Freedman agrees with Moffat that Turville-Petre's arguments are not convincing, but also finds wanting Moffat's suggestion that the chroniclers were appealing to a common racial identity with the peasants. He argues that these passages have little to do with serfdom and its justification. Adducing peasant appeals to 'ancient demesne', he suggests that the peasants had a very different—much more favourable—view of early Norman lordship, and that the chroniclers are really complaining about immediate issues: the barons' wars, foreigners, and taxes.[102] Gillingham too disputes the racial identity thesis. He argues that when Gerald of Wales speaks of the English having been reduced to 'servitutem', Gerald is referring to the tyranny of kings, not to the racial superiority of Norman lords.[103] But recognition of the political implications of peasant complaint for the position of the monks, as detailed above, provides a new framework in which to read the chroniclers' laments about the subjection of the English. The English subjected to enslavement by their Norman rulers are the historical antecedents of villeins *and* of the monasteries. These chronicles are among many texts that find in peasant plaint a genre whose legitimacy and uses have been made volatile and contestable by the new legal frameworks.

The last text to be discussed in this section is the macaronic (Anglo-Norman and Latin) poem *Against the King's Taxes*.[104] The association of this poem with the other texts discussed in this chapter might at first sight seem unpromising. *Against the King's Taxes* has frequently been read as reflecting the point of view of the peasant. There has been no suggestion that it might chime with the interests of ecclesiastical or noble lords. Harriss says that it 'reflects the mood of the lesser landowning classes'.[105] Maddicott classes it with 'a new literature of protest' that emerged 'because there was more to protest about … [it is] verse which has some claim to be popular'.[106] Scattergood finds that the poem has 'a populist agenda', noticing that the poet insists that 'the voice of the "commune" be heard in shaping national policy'.[107] But in the light of the analysis of peasant plaint in this chapter, we are now in a position to add to, refine, and revise these analyses.

---

[100] Turville-Petre, 'Robert Manning's *Chronicle*'.
[101] Moffat, 'Sin, Conquest, Servitude'; quotations from 151.
[102] Freedman, *Images*, 128–9.   [103] Gillingham, 'Slaves of the Normans?'.
[104] Aspin (ed.), *Anglo-Norman Political Songs*, 105–15. Passages and translations below are quoted from this source except where explicitly noted.
[105] Harriss, *Public Finance*, 251.   [106] Maddicott, 'Poems of Social Protest',142–3.
[107] Scattergood, 'Authority and Resistance', 163–7, quotations from 167.

In particular, we are in a position to note the similarities between this poem and the appropriation of peasant plaint in texts that defend the Church.

Against the King's Taxes echoes many of the points made in the literary and judicial complaints we have already discussed:

> Ore court en Engletere de anno in annum
> Le quinzyme dener, pur fere sic commune dampnum;
> E fet avaler que soleyent sedere super scannum,
> E vendre fet commune gent vaccas, vas et pannum.
> Non placet ad summum quindecim sic dare nummum.
>
> Une chose est countre foy, unde gens gravatur,
> Que la meyté ne vient al roy in regno quod levatur.
> Pur ce qu'il n'ad tot l'enter prout sibi datur,
> Le pueple doit le plus doner et sic sincopatur.
> Nam que taxantur regi non omnia dantur.
>
> Unquore plus greve a simple gent collectio lanarum,
> Que vendre fet communement divicias earum.
> Ne puet estre que tiel consail constat Deo carum
> Issi destrure le poverail pondus per amarum.
> Non est lex sana quod regi sit mea lana.
>
> Uncore est plus outre peis, ut testantur gentes,
> En la sac deus pers ou treis per vim retinentes.
> A quy remeindra cele leyne? Quidam respondentes
> Que ja n'avera roy ne reygne set tantum colligentes.
> Pondus lanarum tam falsum constat amarum.
>
> (ll. 11–30)

[Now the fifteenth runs in England year after year, thus doing harm to all; by it those who were wont to sit upon the bench have come down in the world; and common folk must sell their cows, their utensils, and even clothing. It is ill-pleasing thus to pay the fifteenth to the uttermost farthing.

One thing (above all) is dishonest, whereby the people are oppressed; not half the tribute raised in the land reaches the king. Because he does not receive the tax in its entirety just as it is granted to him, the people must pay the more, and thus they are cut short. For all that is levied is not surrendered to the king.

Still more hard on simple folk is the wool collection; commonly it makes them sell their possessions. It cannot be that such a measure, crushing the poor under a grievous load, is pleasing to God. The law that makes my wool the king's is no just law.

An even greater offence, as men bear witness, is that they forcibly keep back two or three stones weight in the sack. To whom will this wool go? Some reply that never shall king nor kingdom get it, but only the wool collectors. Such a false weight of wool is a calamity.]

Here the poet emphasizes that taxation is so heavy that it is counter-productive: people are forced to sell their means of livelihood and so become economically inactive. The yield of the tax collection and the wool levy, moreover, are subject to corruption among officials. Thus it is that the poor pay, while the rich go (literally) scot-free. The poet swipes at the practice of paying for prises with tally-sticks which often proved worthless, wittily pointing out that it is better to eat off wooden plates and pay with silver, than to eat off silver plates, and pay with wood (ll. 71–5).

The poet nowhere mentions explicitly the impact of taxation on the Church. Yet the taxation specified, the 'fifteenth', applied to clergy as well as laity. Moreover, the language of the poem chimes with that of other texts that recruit peasant plaint in the service of defences of the Church. Just as *Song of the Church* and William of Pagula suggest that such taxation is robbery, so *Against the King's Taxes* characterizes it as 'rapina', and 'rapta' (ll. 59–60), and against 'lex sana' (l. 25), and calls the tax 'tribute' (ll. 41, 61), a word that links royal taxation with the subjection and enslavement of conquered peoples. It also hints at the impact on classes above the poorest: those who used to sit in comfort are brought low ('avaler', l. 13). In addition, the management of point of view hints at the wider implications of injustice to peasants. For the most part injustices to the poor are couched in the third person, the poet witnessing to the testimony of others 'the people are aggrieved' (my translation of 'gens gravatur', l. 16; Aspin translates 'oppressed'), 'it is grievous to simple people' ('greve a simple gent', l. 21, my translation). But from time to time the poet switches into the first person: 'The law that makes my wool ['mea lana'] the king's is no just law' (l. 25), 'I see' ('Je voy', l. 51), 'I doubt' ('Je me doute', l. 64), 'I do not know' ('Je ne say', l. 78), suggesting identification with the plaints of the poor. We may compare a passage in William of Pagula's *Speculum*, where, deploring the lamentation that attends the king's arrival in the countryside, William expresses fear of predation in the first person:

Nec mirum, quod lamentaciones et suspiria sunt in adventu tuo: quia in veritate, que Deus est, dico quod pro persona mea, quandocumque audierem rumores de tuo adventu et audio vestrum cornu, totum contremisco, sive fuerim in domo, sive in campo, sive in ecclesia, sive in studio, seu etiam in missa. Quando vero aliquis de tua familia pulsat ad portam, tunc magis contremisco. Sed quando ad ostium, tunc multo magis.

[And it is no wonder that there are sighs and lamentations upon your arrival, since in truth, which is God, I say that for my own person, whenever I hear rumors of your arrival and I hear your horn, I tremble all over, whether I am at home, or in the field, in church, or in the study, or even at mass. For when someone of your household beats on the gate, I tremble even more. But when he beats on the door, then I tremble most of all. And thus, the closer he approaches, the more I tremble and am very fearful.][108]

The later, variant version of the *Song of the Church* similarly suggests first-person experience of suffering:

> Grevus est li tallage
> Mes y nus cuveynt suffrir.

---

[108] Moisant (ed.), *De speculo regis Edwardi III*, 134; Nederman (ed. and trans.), *Political Thought*, 110.

> Mes ceous nus funt damage
> Ky le devyent cuillir.
> Mes que ke nus die,
> Chescun en sun quer prie,
> Si Deu le veut oyr,
> Ke Dampnedeu les maudie
> Tut ceous ke mettent aye
> Pur nostre tolir.
>
> (ll. 51–60)

[The tax is grievous but we must suffer it. But those who ought to collect it do us harm. But whatever anyone may say [to us, 'nus'], let each pray in his heart, if God wills to hear him, that the Lord God may curse them, all those who lend aid to take away what is ours.][109]

Here, in the later version of the poem only, the poet shifts in an additional final stanza to the first-person plural. Yet another example of this device occurs in Robert Manning's *Chronicle*. Discussing the historical origins of contemporary servitude, Manning shifts from the third to the first person: '[William] sette vs in seruage'.[110] These are all instances in which the first person is used to appropriate peasant plaint in the service of ecclesiastical interests.

The language of *Against the King's Taxes* also suggests the appropriation of peasant plaint in the interests of other groups. The poet skilfully intercuts Anglo-Norman and Latin, deploying peasant plaint in both of the languages of authority in the period, and making complex metrical links between the two. In a further appropriation, he addresses these plaints not to the king, fount of common law justice, but to God:

> Quant vendra le haut juggement, magna dies ire,
> S'il ne facent amendement tunc debent perire.
> Rex dicit reprobis 'ite', 'venite' probis.
>
> Dieu que fustes coronee cum acuta spina,
> De vostre pueple eiez pitee, gracia divina,
> Que le siecle soit aleggee de tali ruina …
>
> (ll. 53–8)

[When the last judgement comes, that great day of wrath, if they [the corrupt rich] do not mend their ways they must surely perish. The King shall say to the unrighteous: 'depart from me', and to the righteous: 'come'.

God who wast crowned with piercing thorns, by thy heavenly grace take pity on thy people so that this world may have respite from such affliction; to state the substance of the case it is like robbery …]

---

[109] Aspin (ed.), *Anglo-Norman Political Songs*, 46; 'to us' is my addition to Aspin's translation.
[110] Sullens (ed.), *Robert Mannyng*, part 2, l. 1620.

In the absence of the king, and during the reign of corrupt royal agents, the poet must plead in the divine court on behalf of his plaintiffs. He hopes not in royal justice, but in the judgement of God at doomsday.

The manuscript transmission of *Against the King's Taxes* provides some support for this interpretation of the poem as having an appeal to ecclesiastical interests. The poem survives (in a shorter version) in London, British Library, Additional MS 10374, an early fourteenth-century cartulary from the Cistercian house at Whalley, Lancashire.[111] The other materials in this book date from 1306 to 1346. This suggests that the poem attracted the interest of monks, and its inclusion in the cartulary might suggest that it was associated in the minds of the cartulary's compilers with other writings concerned with the monastery's legal interests. The poem also survives in London, British Library, MS Harley 2253 (now dated 1340).[112] Identifying the provenance of this book is much less straightforward. But the exhaustive researches of Carter Revard into the activities and connections of this manuscript's scribe suggest that there were ecclesiastical and monastic dimensions to this manuscript's provenance.[113]

PEASANT PLAINT AND VERNACULAR POETRY

We have been exploring the ways in which the relations between peasant plaint and legal plaint are negotiated in Anglo-Norman and Latin literary and judicial writings. In the final section of this chapter I shall explore engagement with peasant plaint in vernacular lyric poetry. Two early Middle English peasant plaint poems in particular helpfully focus issues of the relations between vernacular writing and the judicial plaint of the royal courts. These are two poems from MS Harley 2253, *Satire on the Retinues of the Great*, and *Song of the Husbandman*. I shall suggest that when these poets see peasant plaint in the light of the new judicial process, they shape ideas about the place of the English language in legal process, and about the vernacular as a medium for literary composition.

Satire on the Retinues of the Great is not immediately obviously related to peasant or judicial plaint. At first sight it is set apart both stylistically, and in subject-matter. Its subject is horsemen, grooms, stable-boys and their hangers-on. Its language is vigorous, plain-speaking, and earthy:

> þe knaue crommeþ is crop er þe cok crawe;
> he momeleþe & moccheþ ant marreþ is mawe.
> when he is al for-laped ant lad ouer lawe,
> a doseyn of doggen ne myhte hyre drawe.

[111] Maddicott, 'Poems of Social Protest',137; cf. Scattergood, 'Authority and Resistance', 166.
[112] Internal and palaeographical evidence point to completion of Harley 2253 after 1338–40; see Revard, 'Scribe and Provenance', 21–107.
[113] Revard, 'Scribe and Provenance'; see also Corrie, 'Kings and Kingship', 77–9.

> þe rybaud₃ a-ryseþ er þe day rewe.
> he shrapeþ on is shabbes ant draweþ huem to dewe;
> sene is on is browe ant on is e₃e-brewe,
> þat he louseþ a losynger, & shoyeþ a shrewe.
>
> (ll. 17–24)[114]

The poet's obsession with the lower forms of life associated with the stables has bemused critics (though they have celebrated the poem's linguistic vigour).[115] However, Thomas Wright long ago suggested that the poem is a satire on the 'idle attendants and servants [who] preyed upon the produce of the industrious peasantry', and Thorlac Turville-Petre's edition explains that the reason for the focus on grooms is: 'the demands made on farmers by the king's and nobles' horsemen as they travelled through the country'.[116] This concern with predatory horsemen represents a common topic in complaints against prise. In denouncing horses and horse-attendants, the poet is attacking a popular target often mentioned in peasant plaints. Royal horses and their attendants were a burden on the countryside both because they required provisions, and because they sometimes required stabling, accommodation, and sustenance on their travels. For example, John Sutton petitioned the king and council in parliament about the losses incurred when Gyles de Beauchamp lodged men and horses without paying when the king travelled to Pontefract.[117] The royal inquiry into maladministration in Hertfordshire commissioned in 1341 specifically invited complaints about 'our horse-keepers and their servants'.[118] William of Pagula's *Epistola* and *Speculum* are notable for their use of predations of poor peasants by royal horsemen as images of the injustices of royal taxation policy. The charges against the horse-attendants in *Satire on the Retinues of the Great* can all be paralleled in William of Pagula and many other texts of the complaint literature we have already examined—there are too many grooms (they are as numerous as flies hatching from dung); they are attended by women and dogs (ll. 13 and 20); they need to be fed and feed to excess.[119] The poet expresses one of the common points of complaint by commenting that the horse-attendants wear fine clothes:

> hue boskeþ huem wyþ botouns, ase hit were a brude,
> wiþ lowe lacede shon of an hayfre hude,
> hue pykeþ of here prouendre al huere prude.
>
> (ll. 26–8)

---

[114] Robbins (ed.), *Historical Poems*, no. 7, pp. 27–9.

[115] See, e.g., Turville-Petre, *England the Nation*, 200–1; Scattergood, 'Authority and Resistance', 194.

[116] Wright (ed.), *Political Songs of England*, 237; Turville-Petre (ed.), *Alliterative Poems*, 34, headnote.

[117] *RP*, i. 401. This petition, TNA (PRO), SC 8/6/265, does not appear on the parliament roll; see *PROME*, 'Appendix of Unedited Petitions, 1307–1337'.

[118] TNA (PRO), JUST 1/335/1.

[119] For other examples, and a fuller discussion of the links with purveyance complaints, see Scase, ' "Satire on the Retinues of the Great" ', 309, 313–15.

With the comment in the last line 'they take all of their finery from their providers', the poet turns the image of the dandy into a succinct image of the private profiteering so often imputed to royal officials.[120]

As well as including the topics associated with peasant plaint against prise, *Satire on the Retinues of the Great* positions itself in relation to the forms and language of judicial complaint. As we have seen, victims of prise could attempt to get redress in a number of ways, from presenting tally-sticks for payment, to petitioning royal inquiries or parliament for redress of their losses. Just so, the poem itemizes 'arrerage' (l. 32), the losses incurred:

> whose rykeneþ wiþ knaues huere coustage,
> þe luþernesse of þe ladde, þe prude of þe page,
> þah he ʒeue hem cattes dryt to huere companage,
> ʒet hym shulde a-rewen of þe arrerage.
>
> (ll. 29–32)

The poem is a comic inflection of the complaint. The language and form of the poem suggest the account roll ('y ... rede o mi rolle', l. 1; 'coustage', 'arrerage') presented to demonstrate loss and demand payment, while the listing of malefactors 'colyn' and 'Colle' (l. 2) imitates the naming of offenders in forensic complaints.

Song of the Husbandman echoes many of the complaints about injustices to peasants that we have explored in this chapter.[121] Taxes are heavy ('euer þe furþe peni mot to þe kynge', l. 8). Tax collectors are corrupt ('mo þen ten siþen y told my tax', l. 40) and profiteering:

> ... al is piked of þe pore, þe prikyares prude.
> þus me pileþ þe pore and pykeþ ful clene,
>
> (ll. 24–5)

The horsemen ('prikyares') have finery gained from the profits of extortion from the poor. Farmers are forced to sell their means of livelihood, their tools ('mi bil & my borstax', l. 44), animals ('mi mare', l. 54), and even their seed ('to seche seluer to þe kyng y mi seed solde', l. 63), so that the land lies fallow: 'forþi mi lond leye liþ & leorneþ to slepe' (l. 64). With natural disasters on top ('gode ʒeres & corn boþe beþ agon', l. 3, and 'wickede wederes', l. 70), people are reduced to idleness and beggary: 'ase gode in swynden anon as so forte swynke' (l. 72).

Many critics and historians have mined *Song of the Husbandman* as vernacular testimony to the injustices felt by peasants in early fourteenth-century England, but as in many of the other texts we have looked at in this chapter, the peasant's

---

[120] There is no need to go to the lengths of Turville-Petre's ingenious interpretation, 'their fancy shoes are made of the skin of the heifer they have just eaten' (Turville-Petre (ed.), *Alliterative Poems*, 35, n. *ad loc.*).

[121] Robbins (ed.), *Historical Poems*, no. 2, pp. 7–9.

plaint here is accorded a relevance beyond his own class.[122] The peasant speaker
aligns the lot of the oppressed rustic with that of other social groups:

> þus me pileþ þe pore and pikeþ ful clene,
> þe ryche me raymeþ wiþ-outen eny riht;
> ar londes & ar leodes liggeþ fol lene,
> þorh biddyng of baylyfs such harm hem haþ hiht.
> Meni of religioun me halt hem ful hene,
> baroun & bonde, þe clerc & þe knyht.
>
> (ll. 25–30)

The peasant laments that *all* orders and degrees are oppressed. As George Kane
points out, the poor are fleeced, and so are the wealthy.[123] The rich are unlawfully
subject to extortion, and their lands and labourers are impoverished. But it is
important to notice that, like many other complaints that mobilize peasant
plaint, the poem focuses on *reduction in social status*. The rich are *reduced* to
the condition of the peasant, and not merely economically but also socially.
All are degraded to the condition of the socially despised ('me halt hem ful
hene')—religious orders, barons, bondsmen, clerks, and knights. The peasant's
lament against servitude ('Nou we mot worche', l. 5) is a lament on behalf of
all who have been *reduced* by royal taxation to a position analogous to that of
the villein. The poem is a plaint for those whose lands and tenants have been
afflicted, and for those who have been fleeced of their wealth ('þat er werede
robes, nou wereþ ragges', l. 36). The speaker himself is threatened with being
reduced to the condition of a villein:

> ȝet comeþ budeles, wiþ ful muche bost:
> 'greyþe me seluer to þe grene wax;
> þou art writen y my writ, þat þou wel wost!'
> …
> ȝet I shal be foul cherl, þah he han þe fulle …
>
> (ll. 37–9, 47)

The bailiffs with their exchequer writs (typified by the green wax) threaten the
reduction of the speaker to a 'foul cherl'. The poet exploits the alliterative line to
point up the intimate connection between the writ and villeinage: the fulfilling

---

[122] My analysis opposes that of most commentators. *Song of the Husbandman* has frequently
been read as an expression of peasant protest, with critical debate focusing on questions of topical
reference (is the poem topical and, if so, to exactly which taxes and natural disasters does the poem
refer?) and on the precise echelon of the peasantry the speaker belongs to (is he a simple peasant,
prosperous tenant farmer, a lowly cotter?). For example, Scattergood, 'Authority and Resistance',
188, suggests that the poet 'claims to speak on behalf of a whole class of poor tenant farmers'; while
Newhauser asserts that the poem 'does not merely depict the plight of the oppressed rural worker;
in one fashion or another, it actually takes his point of view'. For a survey of critical approaches, see
Newhauser, 'Historicity and Complaint', 205–6, and for this citation, see 210.

[123] Kane, 'Some Fourteenth-century "Political" Poems', 86.

of the writ (or the 'filling' of the bailiff) collocates with the making into a 'foul cherl' of the complainant.[124] The mobilization of the peasant plaint in *Song of the Husbandman* is, therefore, closely comparable with its exploitation in the Latin and Anglo-Norman literary and judicial texts discussed above. While these texts use peasant plaint to voice the complaints of lay and ecclesiastical lords, here too peasant plaint works on behalf of other social groups.

Song of the Husbandman carefully positions itself in relation to the processes of judicial complaint. Its references to judicial process have not previously been noticed. They have been somewhat obscured by certain traditions of editing and glossing. Two lines in particular are crucial, both of them in the opening lines of the peasant's first-person speech:

> Nou we mote worche, nis þer non oþer won,
> mai ich no lengore lyue wiþ mi lesinge;
>
> ʒet þer is a bitterore bid to þe bon,
> for euer þe furþe peni mot to þe kynge.
>
> þus we carpeþ for þe kyng, & carieþ ful colde,
> & weneþ forto keuere, & euer buþ a-cast ...
>
> (ll. 5–10)

MED glosses 'carpeþ' (l. 9) under *carpen* 1(a) 'to talk, chat, converse, discourse'. But another possible meaning is 'cry out, wail, complain' (*carpen* 3(b)). If the sense is 'complain', how should we construe 'for þe kyng'? Thomas Wright translates 'Thus we complain for the king'.[125] But it is hard to see in what sense the speaker could be complaining on behalf of the king. An alternative would be to read 'for' as an example of *MED for(e* 1 'Before (in space), in front of ... in the presence or sight of'. If read in this way, 'for þe kyng' is the vernacular equivalent of *coram rege*, 'before the king', a legal term denoting the royal status of a court.[126] Interpreted this way, the whole phrase means 'thus we complain in the royal court'. The rest of the sentence can be construed in relation to judicial complaint. *MED* glosses 'keuere' here as an instance of *coveren* (v. (2)), 5(b) 'to make an acquisition'. But in a judicial context, a more appropriate meaning would be sense 3 'to recover, regain, get back (something lost or taken)'. Construed in this way, the lines refer to a failure of justice in the royal courts: 'Thus we complain *coram rege*, and are severely aggrieved [*MED carien*, (v.) 1], and expect redress of our losses, and always lose [our cases].'

---

[124] According to *MED cherl* 1(a), this word can denote 'freeman or bondsman'; however, given the shifting and ambiguous meanings of the language of villeinage, I think it questionable that *cherl* could denote legal freedom unambiguously at this date. With the changes and redefinitions of legal status, OE *ceorl* had reduced in social status and could now mean 'unfree'; probably it now always connoted unfreedom: none of the examples quoted in *MED* seems to me unambiguously to denote 'freeman', while the example from *Piers Plowman* B xi. 22 clearly denotes 'bondsman'.

[125] Wright (ed.), *Political Songs of England*, 149.

[126] For the term, see Bolland (ed.), *Select Bills*, p. xviii.

If we read these lines as referring to a judicial context, then we have grounds for revisiting a textual crux in l. 7: 'ʒet þer is a bitterore bid to þe bon'. This line is problematic partly because 'bid' makes no sense in this context: clearly it requires emendation. *MED* glosses the line as an instance of the saying 'to the [bone]' (*bon* n. (1), 4c), emending 'bid' to 'bit' ('bite'). Turville-Petre follows, glossing 'There is yet a more grievous cut to the bone'.[127] But this emendation is questionable: *MED* cites no other instances of 'bite to the bone'. Others suggest that 'bon' refers to 'boon-work', that is, the work required ('bid') by lords from their tenants.[128] However, this is unsatisfactory syntactically; the 'bitterer bid' is identified as the heavy taxation exacted by the king (the 'fourth penny'), not work exacted by lords. Yet there is a further possibility. If we interpret 'bon' as 'petition' (*MED bon* n. (2), 1a and 2), and view it as the petition brought before the king's court, then 'bitterer bid' is part of that petition. A Middle English word denoting such an item is *MED bed(e* (n.) 1b, whose meanings include 'request', and one of the petitions in the Lord's Prayer. Judicial petitions, especially commons' petitions in parliament, were customarily structured as a list of grievances, following the pattern in which clergy presented lists of complaints (*gravamina*).[129] The 'fourth penny' would therefore be the greatest grievance in the peasant's petition to the court, and we would translate 'Yet there is a more grievous item in the petition: always the fourth penny must go to the king'.

Both *Satire on the Retinues of the Great* and *Song of the Husbandman* define English poetry in relation to judicial plaint.[130] Unlike the other texts we have discussed, *Satire on the Retinues of the Great* is complaint inflected in a markedly vernacular register. Language mixing was not uncommon in legal and business

---

[127] Turville-Petre (ed.), *Alliterative Poems*, 17.

[128] Newhauser, 'Historicity and Complaint', 214; cf. Wright (ed.), *Political Songs of England*, 149, 'yet there is a bitterer asking for the boon'.

[129] Harriss, *Public Finance*, 74. This is how the petitions were *enrolled*; there is some doubt as to when in the process this structure was imposed (i.e. whether articles of complaint were consolidated into one petition by the plaintiffs, or once they had been received, by clerks); see Myers, 'Parliamentary Petitions', 606; Sayles, *Medieval Parliament*, 49–50.

[130] Other poems in London, British Library, MS Harley 2253 appropriate the discourse of the peasant plaint in various ways. *The Man in the Moon*, for example, satirically exploits the interpretation of the moon's surface as a peasant. In this reading the peasant is a fugitive from seigneurial justice, whose hope of rescue lies in the corruption of manorial officials (Turville-Petre (ed.), *Alliterative Poems*, 32–3. For recent discussion, see Scattergood, 'Authority and Resistance', 189–90.) *Satire on the Consistorie Courts* (Robbins (ed.), *Historical Poems*, no. 6, pp. 24–7) offers the persepective of the 'lewed' defendant in a Church court, in a case in which women are the plaintiffs. This is a version of traditional 'beware of women' antifeminist satire, wittily reversing the usual gender roles (here women complain about men) and social roles. The summoners are hated by 'hyrdmen' and 'hyne' ('hiredmen' and 'servants', l. 40), and in the defendant's eyes, the court officials are like villeins: a court clerk is 'an old cherl in a blake hure' (l. 19), and the court officials who threaten him are like black and perspiring 'þralles' (ll. 69–70) that is, like sun-burned and sweaty bondsmen. In reading the poem as manipulating the discourse of villeinage, I offer an alternative to the interpretation of Turville-Petre, 'English Quaint and Strange', who argues that the poet mocks the vulgarity of the defendant and seeks to appeal to an audience 'contemptuously amused by the vulgarity and meanness of his experiences and attitudes' (83).

documents.[131] The poet takes this to extremes. Alongside the Anglo-Norman legal and administrative words is a whole lexicon of vernacular pejoratives for the stable-lads (*boye* (l. 6), *gedelyng* (ll. 5 and 36), *glotoun* (l. 14), *harlot* (l. 13), *horlyng* (l. 13), *hors-knaue* (l. 3), *knaue* (l. 17), *ladde* (l. 30), *losynger* (l. 24), *rybaud* (ll. 1 and 21) and *shrewe* (l. 24)), and vernacular words for associated objects of disgust (*poste* (l. 7), *ffleh, lous* (l. 12), *shabbes* (l. 22), *cattes dryt* (l. 31)). This vocabulary characterises the voice of the plaintiff. The plaintiff and his roll are the object of ridicule as well as admiration. His complaint is as gross as the abuses complained of. The poet's invective is *like* the stable-boys' vomit: 'spedeþ ou to spewen, ase me doþ to spelle' ('it [excessive consumption] makes you spew, as it makes me narrate/plead', l. 37).

Retinues both celebrates and ridicules the vigour of vernacular plaint. *Song of the Husbandman* also offers a vernacular rendering of the voice of the peasant plaintiff. The poet witnesses to the lamentations he has heard men of the land uttering. The opening lines frame the poem as the complaint of peasants: 'Ich herde men vpo mold make muche mon ... '. The shift in l. 4 to the first person, 'Nou we mote worche ... ', signals a move from the voice of the poet to the voice of the peasant, and the poem brings the vernacular 'mon' of the 'men vpo mold', therefore, into relation with plaint in the royal courts.

In order to analyse how these poems mobilize the vernacularity of peasant plaint in relation to the judicial process, we need to address the difficult issue of the role of English in the law. The role of written English is, for our purposes here, less problematic than that of spoken English. Legal historians have studied the languages in which statutes were written, court rolls were composed, and law was taught, in other words, the literary languages of professional lawyers. We know that in the late thirteenth century the first surviving law reports (informal accounts of cases, made, it is thought, for the purposes of teaching and study), law treatises, and instructional texts were written in French or sometimes Latin, statutes were published in Latin or French, and court rolls were also written in these languages.[132] This points fairly comprehensively (though there are interesting exceptions) to the exclusion of English as a medium for legal literature.

It is much harder to ascertain what language was employed in oral communications, and how English fitted into the overall picture. The evidence of course is far more elusive. Furthermore, scholars have been rather less interested in the linguistic transactions associated with litigants' engagement with the processes of the law. In this area the scholarship is patchy and sometimes contradictory. It is particularly imperfect in respect of the linguistic transactions that took place as part of, or simply to enable, judicial process. It is a matter of debate whether, in the

---

[131] See Wright, 'Bills, Accounts, Inventories'.

[132] Brand, 'The Languages of the Law', 67. I am using the term 'French' in this context as a generic term to cover Anglo-Norman (French developed in England), Law French (specialized lawyer's French), and the language used in the northern continent; cf. Ormrod, 'The Use of English', 753.

early Anglo-Norman royal courts, the language of the oral transactions that took place in court was ever English. It has been argued that the evidence points to the use of French in court.[133] But it has also been argued, on grounds of practicality, that English may have been used, especially in the lower courts, and perhaps in the criminal courts.[134] Patchy consideration has been given to issues of translation into and out of English. It has been suggested that French was gradually preferred to Latin as a medium for writing statutes, because it was easier to paraphrase a French text in English for the purposes of public proclamation of legislation.[135] Translation processes have also been suggested for courts. In court, it has been proposed, formal written documents may have been translated from Latin or French into English when they were read out by the clerk.[136] And lawyers who reported on cases may have translated English proceedings into French written records.[137] However, it appears that technical 'terms and processes' were never translated because they were felt to have no English equivalents.[138] So, although the evidence is patchy, and its interpretation uncertain, it seems less clear that linguistic conventions marked spoken English as they did written English, as a language without legal status, in distinction from Latin and, increasingly from the mid-thirteenth century if not earlier, from French.

The development of the importance of the plaint in the late thirteenth century must have sharpened the ambiguity over the status of English as a vehicle for legal process. In theory, plaint was invited from a wide social spectrum, including, as we have seen, from peasants. It was formally looser than the writ. But like almost all of the other legal texts in this period, bills—written plaints—were written in Anglo-Norman or sometimes Latin. It is not until the late fourteenth century (with one stray exception from 1344) that we find the first bills written in English.[139] As English was neither a language of complaint nor of record, for the monolingual and for the illiterate alike, making a plaint must have involved getting someone to record the grievance in French or Latin writing. Professional lawyers emerged from the middle of the thirteenth century, but their role in the processes of bill writing is not clear.[140] Bolland suggests that plaints could have been drawn up 'by anyone who [could] write or get another to write for him', but the fact that bills follow conventional forms suggests that they must have

---

[133] Brand, 'The Languages of the Law', 64–9.

[134] Hudson, *The Formation of the English Common Law*, 10; Brand, 'The Languages of the Law', 64, 68–70. See Ormrod, 'The Use of English', 770–1, for the suggestion that one of the purposes of the Statute of Pleading of 1362 was to authorize the practice of pleading in English in the criminal courts in the face of pressure for the widespread adoption of French in the courts.

[135] Ormrod, 'The Use of English', 775.

[136] Baker, 'The Three Languages of the Common Law', 226.

[137] Ormrod, 'The Use of English', 774.   [138] Ibid., 772–3.

[139] The exception is a petition to Edward III from John Drayton and Mary King of Gloucestershire, preserved in TNA (PRO), Ancient Petitions, calendared in Chambers and Daunt (ed.), *Book of London English*, 272.

[140] See Brand, *Origins*, 3 *et passim* for the emergence of professional lawyers.

been drafted by those with legal knowledge and training.[141] We know that at the trial of the judges of 1290–3, a clerk was assigned to the job of writing down the complaints made.[142] But some evidence suggests that legal knowledge was perhaps less important that the ability to write French or Latin. Early bills are fairly simple and not rigid in form; even the language of the early commons' petitions to parliament is markedly less professional than that of the statutes based on them.[143] Particularly in the case of peasant plaints, bills must have been marked as English plaint written down. *Poem on Disputed Villein Services* engages with this aspect of the relation of English with the languages of the plaint and the court. Speaking to 'rustic William', the pleader speaks English, the poet signalling this by briefly incorporating into his Latin poem a snatch of the vernacular ('Rustice Willelme, causam, tibi supplico, tel me'). The peasants reply in English, 'Do that ti will is'.[144] English, for this poet, is the language of disallowed plaint.

   Satire on the Retinues of the Great and *Song of the Husbandman* both represent the vernacularity of peasant plaint and its relation to judicial process rather differently from *Poem on Disputed Villein Services*. These poems represent themselves as vernacular written texts that record oral, vernacular plaint. The complaint against the horsemen in *Retinues* is read aloud from a written text: 'Of rybaudȝ y ryme ant rede o mi rolle' (l. 1). *Song of the Husbandman* records complaint heard by the narrator, 'Ich herde men vpo mold make muche mon' (l. 1). The orality of the peasants' plaint is stressed by the fact that their 'mon' replaces their 'song' ('ne kepeþ here no sawe ne no song synge', l. 4). *Retinues*, as we have seen, uses the vocabulary of Anglo-Norman administrative texts ('coustage', 'arrerage') alongside a specialized lexicon of vernacular terms of abuse, and *Song of the Husbandman* alludes to the structure of the written petition as a series of grievances. Neither adopts the form of a bill or petition, but both poems foreground textual form, *Song of the Husbandman* with a complex stanza form that requires alliteration and rhyme, and *Retinues* with a less complex but none the less demanding form of alliterative lines and monorhymed quatrains. These are forms, of course, not of legal plaint but of English literature. In reducing these vernacular, oral peasant plaints to these elaborate forms of vernacular writing, the poets align their practice with that of the bill writers. The new modes of written complaint give these poets and their readers a new framework within which to begin to re-imagine, to theorize, and above all to legitimize, vernacular poetic practice.

---

   [141] Bolland (ed.), *Select Bills*, 158; Musson, *Medieval Law*, 167, n. 165. We know that even quite humble communities had persons among them with skills in business writing and legal affairs (Razi and Smith, 'Manorial Court Rolls', 60–7).

   [142] Richardson and Sayles (eds.), *Procedure without Writ*, p. xlvi.

   [143] Brand, *Origins*, 3–4; Harding, 'Bills and Plaints', 75; Harriss, *Public Finance*, 260. Bolland (ed.), *Select Bills*, pp. xix–xx, contrasts the 'illiteracy' of the texts with the professional quality of the hands and thinks the French of bills is archaic (p. xxx, 156); Richardson and Sayles (eds.), *Procedure without Writ*, p. lix, n. 2 disagree.

   [144] Hilton, 'Poem on Disputed Villein Services', 95, 96.

2

Complaint, Clamour, and Libels

CRIMINAL JUSTICE AND SATIRICAL COMPLAINT

> Beati qui esuriunt
> Et sitiunt, et faciunt
> 　　　Justitiam,
> Et odiunt et fugiunt
> 　　　Injuriae nequitiam;
> Quos nec auri copia
> Nec divitum encennia
> 　　　Trahunt a rigore,
> 　　　Nec pauperum clamore …
>
> *Song on the Venality*
> *of the Judges*[1]

[Blessed are they who hunger and thirst, and perform justice, and hate and flee the wickedness of injustice; whom neither abundance of gold nor the feasts of the rich draw from the straight and narrow path, nor from the clamour of the poor …]

> Sire, si je voderoi mon garsoun chastier
> De une buffe ou de deus, pur ly amender,
> Sur moi betera bille, e me frad atachier,
> E avant qe isse de prisone raunsoun grant doner.
>
> *Trailbaston*

[Sir, if I want to punish my boy with a cuff or two, to correct him, he will [beat me back with a bill] and have me attached, and made to pay a big ransom before I get out of prison.][2]

Song on the Venality of the Judges, found in London, British Library, MS Harley 913 and London, British Library, MS Royal 12. C. xii, and *Trailbaston* from

---

¹ Wright (ed.), *Political Songs of England*, 224–30, 224; the translation is my own.
² Aspin (ed.), *Anglo-Norman Political Songs*, 67–78, ll. 9–12; the passages and translations quoted below are Aspin's, except where noted. In this case the phrase in the inner square brackets is mine: Aspin translates 'he will take out a summons against me', missing, in my view, the implications of 'betera' and the precise legal meaning of 'bille'.

London, British Library, MS Harley 2253, are among several early fourteenth-century poems of satirical complaint that engage with judicial plaint.[3] Echoing and adapting the Beatitudes ('Blessed are they which do hunger and thirst after righteousness', Matthew 5: 6), the speaker in *Song on the Venality of the Judges* blesses those who do right and do not draw back from the 'pauperum clamore', from the 'clamour' of the poor for justice. The *Trailbaston* speaker complains that now even his servants have a hold over him; should he discipline one, the servant can parry his blows with a strike of his own—a *bille* on the basis of which the master can be imprisoned and not released until he pays a ransom.

These poets are offering rather differing perspectives on the implications of plaint culture for criminal justice. The new plaint culture that developed from the late thirteenth century constituted from the first a major change in criminal justice.[4] In Chapter 1 we considered the definition of legally admissible plaints and plaintiffs. Here we shall examine the changes in criminal justice that were brought about by plaint, and the ways in which they were criticized, contested, and developed. Plaint made the initiation of criminal proceedings more flexible and informal. One means of initiating a trial was a private bill put forward by an individual plaintiff. But this was not the only means. A wide variety of kinds of plaint came to constitute grounds for putting someone on trial. Plaints were not restricted to individual complainants but could be put forward by communities. The existence of a number of plaints could constitute grounds also. By the 1340s *clamour* had come to denote the grounds for an action that was other than the individual plaint; the term implied several plaints or widespread complaint, and covered plaint in all of these admissible varieties. If interpreted in the extreme, clamour procedure potentially brought a whole new range of acts of complaint and complaint texts within the definition of legal plaint, according them a status recognized by the law. Over the fourteenth century we can see the implications of clamour being worked out, exploited, developed, and contested. This chapter will illustrate the textual and legal history of clamour from its emergence to the first clear vernacular examples. Dividing the material into

---

[3] MS Harley 913 is usually dated first quarter of the fourteenth century, although if a rubric 'Prouerbie comitis Desmonie' does refer to Maurice Fitz Thomas, created Earl of Desmond in 1329, it could have been copied a decade or so later. For the Earl of Desmond and the manuscript more generally, see Cartlidge, 'Festivity, Order, and Community' (for Desmond, see 44); Cartlidge does not discuss the date of the manuscript in any detail. The text in MS Royal 12. C. xii is written in the hand of the main scribe of MS Harley 2253, dated *c.*1340 (see Ch. 1, 33, n. 112). *Trailbaston*, only witnessed in this manuscript, could have been composed rather earlier than the time it was copied here, since it opens by attacking the 'articles de Trayllebastoun' (1305), and names four justices commissioned in 1305 (Aspin (ed.), *Anglo-Norman Political Songs*, 67–8).

[4] Kaeuper characterizes the period as one of 'marked change and experimentation', ('Law and Order in Fourteenth-century England', 737); while Musson sees the period 1294–1350 as 'the final and most important phase in the judicial revolution that had been occurring since the twelfth century, encompassing developments which transformed criminal justice and in effect the whole governance of England' (*Public Order and Law Enforcement*, 2).

four sections, I shall deal first with the early explorations of plaint justice (and injustice) by satirists such as the *Song on the Venality of the Judges* and *Trailbaston* poets and their positioning of their writings in relation to criminal bills. The following section will describe the contestation of clamour associated with some high-profile cases of mid-century, and sections three and four will identify and analyse evidence for the production and manipulation of vernacular clamour texts in late fourteenth-century England.

In the thirteenth century, the *appeal* was the main way of starting a prosecution for felony (a *felony* was a very serious offence; in continental feudal law the word meant 'treason' or 'disloyalty' (in other words, the betrayal of the trust of one's lord); in the reign of Henry II its meaning was extended, possibly under the influence of continental usage, to include serious crimes such as theft, possibly because these were regarded as breaches of an oath of loyalty to the king.)[5] The appeal was a private complaint accusing a defendant of a crime. Under appeal procedure in the thirteenth century an appellant made a complaint to a coroner, who recorded it and took sureties or pledges with the purpose of trying to ensure that he would appear at the county court and prosecute his case. The appellant then recited the appeal again at the county court. He had to follow a strict form, as variations from the previous account he had made to the coroner would invalidate it. In the fourteenth century the appeal was allowed to be read from a written schedule. It was largely superseded by indictments in reign of Richard II.[6]

The *bill*, or written plaint, emerged as an alternative to the appeal. As we saw in Chapter 1, written bills date from late in the thirteenth century, when the crown attempted to protect its fiscal interests by inquiring into the conduct of its officials. A bill initiated an action for damages to be paid to the victim of the crime, and for the defendant to be convicted and punished. The itinerant court of royal justice known as the eyre (from Old French *eire*, 'a journey', from Latin *ire*, 'to go', and *iter*, 'journey') heard oral complaints at least from the early thirteenth century. As we saw in Chapter 1, a big change was the development of the bill (written plaint). Justices in eyre were obliged to receive bills and have them considered by jurors. If they found a bill to be true they had it endorsed 'ista billa est vera', and included the complaint in their *veredictum*.[7] The earliest surviving written bill in eyre dates from 1286.[8] When bills impeded the progress of the eyre, leading to its suspension, commissions of oyer and terminer were set up to clear the backlog. *Oyer et terminer*, 'to hear and determine', meant to hear

---

[5] On felony, see Bellamy, *Criminal Trial*, 8, and for the (little understood) accusatory process in criminal trials see 15–16, 19–56. See also Prescott, 'The Accusations against Thomas Austin', 164–5; and Hudson, *The Formation of the English Common Law*, 161–2. Defining a crime as felony meant that the judge could confiscate the defendant's property if he was convicted.

[6] Prescott, 'The Accusations against Thomas Austin', 165.

[7] Bellamy, *Criminal Trial*, 19–24; Harding, 'Plaints and Bills', 76. Little is known about the processes by which juries assessed bills; for discussion see Bellamy, *Criminal Trial*, 24–6.

[8] Harding, 'Plaints and Bills', 75.

and give judgement on bills.[9] The king issued commissions to invite and hear complaints throughout the realm.[10] There were general commissions and special commissions; both heard complaints against king's officers.

Bill procedure also seems to lie behind the use of the *indictment*. In late fourteenth-century proceedings before a Justice of the Peace, an *indictment* is a bill found to be true by a jury, while a *presentment* is a declaration of jurors or officers without a bill being offered first.[11] However, very little is known about how presenting juries got their information. Possibly they were relying on individual complaints and so 'presentment may have represented a sort of attenuated bill procedure'.[12] Indictments often arose from allegations made by a private individual to an appropriate official who then submitted the complaint to a presenting jury. Probably the clerks of the court recast informal accusations into the proper form of an indictment first, because bills presented to juries often begin 'Let it be inquired for the king whether…' Indictments had to include basic information: the names of the jurors, the year, date, and place of the alleged offences, a description of any chattels involved and their value, and a statement of the nature of the alleged offence, using the adverbs *felonice* where felony was imputed and *proditorie* where treason was alleged. Indictments would sometimes stress the seriousness or enormity of the crime, but generally they were formal and laconic. They were mainly written in Latin but some survive in French and English, following the Latin form.[13] The wording of indictments was tightened up during the reign of Edward II and the early part of the reign of Edward III.[14] If the jury believed that there was a case to answer, they endorsed the bill 'billa vera'. If they considered it false, they endorsed it 'ignoramus'. The 'true bill' (a bill that had been endorsed because it was accepted that there was a case to answer) became the most common method of making an indictment in the fifteenth century.[15] Making an indictment was a risky procedure because jurors could be prosecuted for defamation or conspiracy, and fined or imprisoned.[16]

Alongside bills, appeals, and indictments, notoriety could be used to initiate proceedings. The 1166 Assize of Clarendon authorized proceedings against those found by a jury to be *either* 'accused' *or* 'notoriously suspect'.[17] Notoriety could also be a crime in itself—the crime of being a 'common thief'. It has been

---

[9] Harding (ed.), 'Early Trailbaston Proceedings', 149–50: 'commissions of oyer and terminer were defined by their concern with plaints and bills … the hearing of bills was precisely what made it an oyer and terminer'.

[10] Harding, 'Plaints and Bills', 66–8.

[11] Harding (ed.), 'Early Trailbaston Proceedings', 150.

[12] Musson, *Public Order and Law Enforcement*, 179; cf. Bellamy, *Criminal Trial*, 24–5.

[13] e.g. Chambers and Daunt (ed.), *Book of London English*, 233–5. For the transformation of bills into indictments, see Bellamy, *Criminal Trial*, 28–9.

[14] Musson, *Public Order and Law Enforcement*, 176.

[15] Prescott, 'The Accusations against Thomas Austin', 169.

[16] Bellamy, *Criminal Trial*, 34–5; Plucknett, 'The Origin of Impeachment', 67.

[17] Bellamy, *Criminal Trial*, 29, 34–5; Hudson, *The Formation of the English Common Law*, 130.

suggested that the inclusion of words and phrases indicating that the accused was a notorious or common criminal protected those making the accusation against a counter-action of conspiracy, should the accused be acquitted.[18] The principle of accusation on the basis of notoriety became important later in connection with the development of clamour as a means of initiating criminal proceedings.

Song on the Venality of the Judges and *Trailbaston* are among several poems (and other texts) from the first quarter of the fourteenth century which can be linked with disquiet at changes in criminal justice. The new procedures were held to profit corrupt plaintiffs, judges, and law officers. Complaint by bill was open to many abuses. It provided weapons that could be used in local conflicts and feuds. Feuding gentry, some of whom were justices, could exert influence on juries to get bills endorsed. In 1306 chapter 2 of the Second Statute of Westminster was suspended; this forbad the arrest of anyone not indicted on the oath of twelve jurors, and its suspension probably offered more opportunities for abuse.[19] If they were not justices themselves, aggressive gentry could procure commissions of oyer and terminer and name the justices whom they wished to hear their cases, seeking to secure a justice who would be favourable to their cause.[20] From the late thirteenth century, conspiracy, the organized abuse of legal procedure, was defined as an 'enormous trespass'. A parliamentary ordinance of 1293, 'De Conspiratoribus', provided for people who wished to complain about corrupt juries, sheriffs, bailiffs, maintenance, and related abuses.[21] The class of special and general commissions included the trailbaston commissions. Trailbaston justices were particularly concerned with abuses of justice; they were mandated to try cases of organized violence, protection rackets, and also, importantly, conspiracy. Four commissions of trailbaston were issued in 1305 to cover all of England except for Cheshire, Durham, and the home counties.[22] But these commissions too were accused of injustice. The chronicler Murimuth writes of the trailbaston justices:

… tam rigide et voluntarie processerunt quod nullus impunitus evasit, sive bene gesserit regis negotia sive male, ita quod sine delectu omnes, etiam non indictati nec accusati, eccessive se redemerunt, qui voluerunt carcerem evitare.[23]

[… so severely and wilfully did they proceed that none could escape punishment, whether they carried out the king's business well or evilly, so that all, even those not indicted or appealed, had to pay large bribes, if they wished to avoid imprisonment.]

Besides *Trailbaston* and *Song on the Venality of the Judges*, texts from this period which position themselves in relation to the new criminal bill and its procedures

---

18   Plucknett, 'The Origin of Impeachment', 60–1.
19   Aspin (ed.), *Anglo-Norman Political Songs*, 68.
20   Harding (ed.), 'Early Trailbaston Proceedings', 150–1.   21   Ibid., 148.
22   Aspin (ed.), *Anglo-Norman Political Songs*, 76, citing Edward Foss, *The Judges of England …
1066–1864*.
23   Cited by Lapsley, 'Archbishop Stratford', 238.

include *A Song on the Times* (also from London, British Library, MS Harley 913), and *Versus compositi de Roger Beler*.

The *Trailbaston* speaker's claim (with which this chapter began) that he can be imprisoned on the strength of a servant's 'bille', and not released until he pays a ransom, highlights the abuses of the private bill as a means of initiating a criminal case. *Trailbaston* opens by attacking the 'articles de Trayllebastoun', and specifically names four of the five justices commissioned in 1305.[24] Moreover, the speaker is the victim of false and wicked jurors ('mavois jurours', l. 29) who have indicted him with their false speech ('parmi lur fauce bouches me ount enditee', l. 22), and have made menaces (l. 32). Trailbaston is presented as a means of extortion and private feuding: the speaker is not guilty but has been indicted out of malice ('Car je ne fu coupable, endité su par envye', l. 82), and monks and merchants alike are threatened by its provisions (ll. 49–52). Even knowledge of the law is a liability rather than a protection: if he invokes his knowledge of the law, his enemies will accuse him of being a false conspirator:

> Si je sache plus de ley qe ne sevent eux,
> Yl dirrount: 'Cesti conspyratour comence de estre faus.'
>
> (ll. 89–90)

[If I know the law better than they do, they will say: 'That conspirator begins to be untrustworthy.']

As we have seen, *conspiracy* was the term used from the late thirteenth century to define various kinds of corruption of legal proceedings such as those imputed to juries, lords, and royal officials. Therefore, the speaker has fled to the forest and, lacking safe means to complain in any other way, has written down his poem on parchment and thrown it on the road so that it might be found and remembered:

> Cest rym fet al bois, desouz un lorer,
> La chaunte merle, russinole e eyre l'esprever;
> Escrit estoit en perchemyn pur mout remembrer
> E gitté en haut chemyn qe um le dust trover.
>
> (ll. 97–100)

[This rhyme was made in the wood, beneath a laurel tree, there sing blackbird and nightingale and hovers the sparrow hawk; it was written on a parchment to keep it the more in remembrance, and thrown on the highroad that people should find it.]

The poet's complaint has been committed to parchment and has been 'cast' ('gitté') on the road for people to read. The speaker claims that poem itself ('cest rym') is the text of the speaker's complaint. It has been published in this manner because the speaker fears being accused of conspiracy.

---

[24] Aspin (ed.), *Anglo-Norman Political Songs*, 76, n. to ll. 5, 77, nn. to ll. 33–4.

The poem's awareness of legal vocabulary has long been recognized—as Aspin points out, legal terms appear 'in almost every stanza'—but what has not been noticed is that the poem engages with the language and forms of contemporary practices of bill and indictment.[25] The poem is positioned in relation to criminal complaint. Recent analysis has seen the relationship between the poem and the law as oppositional, and in line with this it is tempting to read this gesture of bill-casting, and the poem itself, as standing in parodic, oppositional, relation to the textualities provided by common law.[26] Not only is the poem written, as Green notes, in the greenwood, a place readable as an idealized, marginal, space, far from courtly corruption ('La n'y a faucecé ne nulle male lay, En le bois de Belregard', ll. 18–19, 'there is no deceit there nor any bad law, in the forest of Belregard') but, we might also note, it is composed and presented in the presence of a 'parliament of birds' (ll. 19–20, 98). It does not, however, follow that, as Green proposes, 'presumably … a plaint … will fare better in the court of common opinion than under the common law'.[27] There is an alternative to reading the poem as standing in parodic, oppositional relation to legal bills. In line with the complaint doctrines of criminal justice, the speaker's appeal to public opinion gives his poem the status of a variety of bill. Accusing his accusers in turn of corruption, the poet claims for his poem the force of legal complaint.

If the poem stages itself as a variety of legitimate bill, it also offers the opportunity to explore and reflect on the problems associated with the criminal bill. In the absence of a reliable judge and jury, the reader is called upon to evaluate the veracity of the speaker's claim, to test whether the bills against him are more likely to be true than his own bill against his accusers. In the light of the poem's ironic tone, and the long list of accusations against the speaker, it is difficult for the reader to know whether to trust the speaker, to decide whether the reader is being invited to join a conspiracy, or to oppose conspiracy. *Trailbaston* does not simply oppose the common law and glorify another system, and nor does it simply embrace the criminal bill.[28] When the poem is considered in relation to the developing and controversial means of initiating criminal trials, it may be seen as dramatizing the instabilities and manipulations attendant on the bill of complaint.

Song on the Venality of the Judges reworks satirical commonplaces in ways that link the poem's themes and practice with developments in criminal justice. As we have seen, the poet offers a benediction on those who 'faciunt justitiam' without

---

[25] Aspin (ed.), *Anglo-Norman Political Songs*; cf. Green, 'Medieval Literature and Law', 422–3.

[26] Green, *Crisis of Truth*, 186–7, sees in the poem's fantasy of outlaw life in the forest of Belregard the promotion of a 'rival system of justice'; and Scattergood, 'Authority and Resistance', 188, sees it as evoking 'the spirit of provincial resistance, possibly ironized, to a centralized legal system which it sees as intrusive'.

[27] Green, *Crisis of Truth*, 172.

[28] A reading of the poem as in straight opposition to common law culture is also hard to square with the fact that, while justices Henry Spigurnel and Roger de Belafago are 'gent de cruelté' (ll. 33–5), the other two mentioned, William Martyn and William de Knovill, are mentioned favourably as 'gent de pieté' (l. 33).

allowing bribery to turn them from rigorous justice and the complaint of the poor. Like *Trailbaston*, this poem represents the manipulation of juries through threats and menaces:

> De vicecomitibus,
> Quam duri sunt pauperibus,
>> quis potest enarrare?
>> Qui nichil potest dare,
> Huc et illuc trahitur,
> Et in assisis ponitur,
>> et cogitur jurare,
>> non ausus murmurare.
> Quod si murmuravit,
> Ni statim satisfecerit,
>> est totum salsum mare.[29]

[On the subject of sheriffs, who can narrate how hard they are to the poor? He who can give nothing is dragged hither and thither, and is placed in the assizes, and is forced to take his oath, without daring to protest. But if he should murmur, unless he makes satisfaction straight away, all is salt sea.]

Those who cannot bribe the sheriff are obliged to serve on (corrupt) juries without complaint; those who complain—unless they can make 'amends' (pay a bribe)—are reduced to the ineffective lament of tears ('salt sea'—'salsum mare'). The rhetorical profession of modesty ('quis potest enarrare?') aligns the legal complaint with satirical complaint poem. *Narracio* was equivalent to *querela*, 'complaint', and a *narrator* was a professional lawyer who spoke in court on behalf of a litigant, delivering the 'count' or formal statement of a case.[30] Hence, this injustice exceeds anyone's ability to make full complaint about it, either in court or in a poem.

Also found in London, British Library, MS Harley 913 is a Middle English legal fable about the lion's court which was edited by Thomas Wright as *A Song on the Times*. The poem begins with a complaint about the domination of law by covetousness, pride, and envy. The speaker calls on the Church not to withhold judgement and punishment of all who rob lawful men, despite any intimidation by lords:

> Holy cherch schold hold is riȝt
> For no eie no for no love;
> That hi ne schold schow har miȝt
> For lordingen boste that beth above.
> To entredite and amonsi
> Al thai, whate hi evir be,

---

[29] Wright (ed.), *Political Songs of England*, 228.
[30] Richardson and Sayles (eds.), *Procedure without Writ*, p. xxii, n.; Brand, *Origins*, 94.

That lafful men doth robbi,
Whate in lond what in see;
And thos hoblurs, namelich,
That husbond benimeth eri of grund;
Men ne schold ham biri in non chirch,
Bot cast ham ute as a hund.

Thos kingis ministris beth i-schend,
To riȝt and law that ssold tak hede,
And al the lond for t'amend,
Of thos thevis hi taketh mede.[31]

Of course, the corruption of justice through bribery was a long-standing and widespread satirical topos. This is only one of countless representations of the impact of 'mede' on the law, one of the most famous examples of which is *Piers Plowman*.[32] Yet features of the poem enable us to detect here an engagement with the culture of the criminal bill as it was developing in the early fourteenth century. The speaker identifies 'hoblurs' who steal the fruits of the soil from husbandmen as particularly worthy of excommunication, and asserts that these thieves are able to bribe the king's ministers who should uphold the law. *Hobelarii* are included in a list of royal officials and agents accused of extortion and other crimes in the commission of inquiry into abuses of purveyance and tax collecting issued in Hertfordshire in 1341.[33] The poet also uses the precise legal terms 'feloni' and 'trespas' (197): both are condoned, says the speaker, where there is meed.

The speaker then proceeds to relate an exemplum ('vorbisen', 197) that he has heard on this subject, in the form of a fable. The lion, king of the beasts, proclaims that the fox, the wolf, and the ass shall come to trial for alleged misdeeds. The fox and the wolf send presents garnered from their loot (presumably to the court); the ass, who only eats grass and has not stolen anything, sends no gifts. At court, the fox and the wolf are acquitted, and the ass is condemned to death. The speaker points out the meaning of the fable: 'Also hit fareth nou in lond' (201), concluding with a disquisition on the evils and deceptions of this life. Although again much is commonplace, features of the fable demonstrate an engagement with early fourteenth-century developments in criminal justice, and in particular the ways in which complaints were used. The trials of the animals are initiated as a result of frequent complaints to the king:

The Lyon lete cri, as hit was do,
For he hird lome to telle;
And eke him was i-told also

---

[31] Wright (ed.), *Political Songs of England*, 195–205, quotation from 196–7.
[32] For the tradition, see Yunck, *The Lineage of Lady Meed*.
[33] TNA (PRO), JUST 1/337/1. *MED* defines *hobeler* (n) as 'a light-armed horseman' and gives examples from chronicles.

That the wolf didde noȝte welle.
And the fox, that lither grome,
With the wolf, i-wreiid was;

…

And so menne didde that seli asse,
That trespasid noȝt, no did no gilte,
With ham bothe i-wreiid was,
And in the ditement was i-pilt.[34]

The use of legal terms here creates a focus on the procedures of criminal justice. Alongside the native word 'i-wreiid', from Old English *wregan/wregian*, 'accuse', the poet uses 'ditement'—an *indictment*, meaning a complaint endorsed by a jury. He also uses the more problematic word 'i-pilt', which Wright translates as 'put'. *MED pilen* (v.(1)) and (v.(3)) are not very likely, the first meaning 'rob, steal' and 'remove the hair from' (i.e. 'fleece'), and the second 'to heap up'. One (rather remote) possibility is that we have here an early anglicization of Old French *apeler*. As mentioned above, the *appeal*, the private complaint made to a coroner or other official, was the primary method of initiating criminal proceedings for felony in the thirteenth century.[35] The line would mean then that the ass was appealed in the indictment. However, in *MED*, the earliest example of *a(p)pelen* (v.) in this sense (1(a)) is dated 1393. One could argue that the word in the poem is an earlier example only on the basis of a fluidity of terminology at this date. Although the appeal and the indictment were later distinguished, in this period, when procedure was fluid and evolving, there was some interchangeability between the two terms.[36] But much more likely is the possibility that 'i-pilt' refers to the posting up of the indictment with nails. *MED pilen* (v.(2)) means 'to fasten' or 'establish … firmly in position', using piles (or nails). We shall see below that there is physical evidence that appeal texts may have been displayed in this way.[37] If so, the poet transfers the pinning up of the indictment metaphorically to the 'nailing' of the ass.

The choice of protagonists is another way in which the poet engages with the evolving and controversial procedures of criminal complaint. The fox has been caught carrying geese and hens on his back. The wolf has killed some sheep. These images are of course thoroughly familiar and widespread in medieval art and literature for those who thieve and deceive. By using these animals as his defendants, the poet has chosen a scenario analogous to that of the trial based on notoriety. These animals are *notorious* thieves. The poem relies on the audience's ready knowledge of the criminal associations of the fox and the wolf, putting readers and listeners in a position analogous to that of those in the community who share common knowledge about criminals.

---

[34] Wright (ed.), *Political Songs of England*, 197–8.
[35] Prescott, 'The Accusations against Thomas Austin',165.
[36] Musson, *Public Order and Law Enforcement*, 177–8.   [37] See below, 72.

The fable represents the dangers attendant on indictment of criminals by showing that the plaintiffs and juries risk unjust counter-accusations. When the fox and the wolf are each acquitted, the king is persuaded that complaints have been brought against them maliciously. The king accepts the fox's defence that 'Thos men me wreiith of the tune, And wold me gladlich for to spille', invoking God's wrath on those who brought the indictment: 'Godis grame most hi have, That in curte the so pilt!' (198). Likewise, accepting the wolf's defence, the lion pronounces 'Hi nadde no gode munde, Thai that wreiid the to mei' (200). The poem therefore represents criminal complaint procedures by means of a fable, showing that complaint can bring notorious criminals to trial, but because the system is open to corruption, innocents can be indicted and wrongly convicted, and the guilty can escape justice and exact revenge on those who complained against them. The poet lays the blame at the feet of ministers of the crown, who, he says, are profiting from judicial corruption:

> Thos kingis ministris beth i-schend,
> To riȝt and law that ssold tak hede,
> An al the lond for t'amend,
> Of thos thevis hi taketh mede.

(197)

His use of a 'vorbisen' means that he can avoid directly naming any offenders himself in the poem, and so, by distancing his complaint from legal complaint, he can evade the fate that lay in store for those who complained against the wolf and the fox.

Another poem from this period combines the theme of corrupt judges with particular interest in the procedures and textualities of the criminal indictment, but in this case a malefactor is named. This is a ten-line macaronic (Latin and English) poem about Roger Beler. The poem against Beler has been written on a flyleaf in London, British Library, MS Royal 12. C. xiv, a book containing Lanfranc's *Surgery*, where the scribe has supplied a subscription 'versus compositi de Roger Belers':

> Miles Rogerus by ten mile wons he to neer vs.
> Omnibus austerus fuerat, quod scit bene clerus.
> Ut rosa pulcher heri marcet terrore seueri
> Simplicis armigeri. Of falsnes was he neuer weri.
> Si modicus natus, tamen asper ad alta leuatus;
> Sic sublimatus, dicebat: 'Who dar arat us?'
> Blandilocus, cupidus, patrie radians quasi sidus;
> Ut lupus hic rapidus dixit: 'Dar no man abid us?'
> Tum cum vi regis tum cum velamine legis,
> Pauperis ipse gregis, in il tyme flithe hys segis.

Versus compositi de Roger Belers.[38]

---

[38] Ed., trans., and discussed by Bowers, 'Versus compositi de Roger Belers'. For translation, see the discussion below.

Roger Beler was a baron of the exchequer, that is, a judge who specialized in taxation cases. He was a royal justice from 1318, mainly carrying out commissions of oyer and terminer.[39] He was murdered on a road in Leicestershire in 1326. Eustace, Robert, and Walter de Folville were among those indicted for the crime.[40] Beler was one of several royal judges who were the targets of crime and murder.[41] He was a supporter of the Despensers and was involved with a commission to investigate attacks on the Despensers' properties in the Midlands which allegedly had been carried out by the la Zouche brothers, his own murderers.[42]

The naming of Beler is an unusual and marked feature of this poem, and this unusual feature suggests the relation of the poem with complaint.[43] As we have seen, of the examples of poems on legal corruption discussed above, only *Trailbaston* names individuals, and arguably it does so in a very different way from the poem against Beler—it names judges in passing, not as its main target. *A Song on the Times* gives very sound reasons for not naming individuals. But here Roger Beler is named explicitly in the subscription to the poem. Moreover, there are several plays on his name within the poem: 'Miles Rogerus', Sir Roger, lives ten *miles* too near 'vs' the speakers (l. 1). Like a beautiful rose—'Ut rosa pulcher'—he has wilted in fear of the knight. This image, evoking comparison of the judge with a shrinking maiden, is at first sight bizarrely inappropriate; however, possibly it is to be explained by another wordplay: Beler (*bele* (French) = *pulcher* (Latin)) has cowered in fear.[44] These wordplays foreground the naming procedure. Just as complaints were invited by commissions of oyer and terminer and trailbaston against named royal officials, so this poem accuses a named individual.

Another link with indictment procedures is that the poem invokes notoriety as a ground of complaint: he has been harsh ('austerus') to all 'as the clergy well know' ('quod scit bene clerus'). It also hints at widespread knowledge of Beler's crimes: the poem is written in the first-person plural, indicating a communal point of view. The deployment of the vernacular and the witty 'mis-translation' of 'Miles' increase the impression of widespread, popular, complaint. The judge regally suggests that he is above complaint. Raised up ('sublimatus'), he defies anyone to complain against him; speaking with the force of the king and the protection of the law ('Tum cum vi regis tum cum velamine legis'), he proclaims

---

[39] Röhrkasten, 'Beler, Sir Roger (*d.* 1326)'.

[40] Stones, 'The Folvilles', 119. It seems that the Folvilles were probably accessories.

[41] Insurgency against justices is familiar from the rising of 1381, but had its origins in the early part of the century; see Harding, 'Revolt'.

[42] Musson, *Public Order and Law Enforcement*, 267. The local and particular affair was possibly part of the wider rebellion against Edward II and the Despensers.

[43] Bowers, 'Versus compositi de Roger Belers', notes that the poem is important because it is a rare example of an attack on a named political person in Middle English verse.

[44] However, possibly 'clerus' is the subject of 'marcet'—the clergy cower at the knight (despite Bowers's translation in 'Versus compositi de Roger Belers').

in the vernacular (by implication, to intimidate monolingual plaintiffs and jurors) 'Who dar arat us?', and 'Dar no man abid us'.[45] Possibly 'patrie radians quasi sidus' is a figure for the way that Beler oppresses a jury in a threatening manner. Bowers translates 'beaming as if he were a patriotic luminary', but *patria* can mean 'jury'—hence (possibly) 'high up like a star bearing down over the jury'. The image of Beler as a wolf recalls the use of this image of rapacity in *A Song on the Times*. Beler is also associated with 'falsnes'; the line is ambiguous, suggesting both that he pursues falseness (punishes it as a judge) but also possibly that he practises it. The poem mixes tenses oddly: sometimes the verbs are past tense ('dicebat', 'dixit'), but sometimes they are in the present, suggesting that Beler lives still, even though the reference at the end may be to the attack on Beler ('in il tyme flithe his segis'—possibly 'falls from his throne'). The poem seems to call for justice to be exacted on the judge, but the past tenses suggest that he is already dead. It is perhaps the complaint that the author and audience would have made before his death, had they not been intimidated by the judge. Or perhaps it represents complaint against Beler that has been partially emended after the event of his death.

The texts we have been discussing so far in this chapter demonstrate that from early in the fourteenth century plaint procedure was perceived to have both positive and negative effects on the administration of criminal justice. The poem against Beler and the other poems we have examined explore the impact of complaint on justice by positioning satirical complaint in relation to the written plaints used to initiate criminal trials. The poems are shown to be subject to similar kinds of pressures and even corruptions as criminal plaints, but are also shown to be able to evade them.

COMPLAINT AND CLAMOUR OF THE PEOPLE

The Beler affair has many similarities with that of Sir Richard Willoughby. Like Beler, Willoughby was a royal justice. He was subject both to criminal attack in the way that Beler was—indeed, he was a victim of the very gang that attacked Beler—and to written complaint against him. In 1332, Willoughby, then puisne justice of the king's bench, was judge on a general commission of oyer and terminer in Nottinghamshire, Derbyshire, Warwickshire, and Leicestershire. It was alleged that he was captured on the road in Leicestershire and taken to

---

[45] I read 'Dar no man abid us' as a statement (not a question, unlike Bowers) seeing 'abid' as *MED* abiden (v.) 12 (b) 'to face (judgement, punishment), stand one's ground before (sth)', hence, 'no one dare stand their ground before me'. Compare Stanley (ed.), *Owl and the Nightingale*, 'For þu ne darst domes abide' (1695)—'you dare not face judgement'.

hiding-places ('from wood to wood' according to one indictment) and held to ransom for 1,300 marks. People indicted for this crime were associated with the Folville family, three of whom had been indicted (and pardoned) for the murder of Beler.[46] He was besieged once more by a gang in Leicestershire in 1340, again while on judicial business (now as chief justice) in the county. In the summer of that same year he was deprived of the rank of chief justice and imprisoned. The following year he was tried before a commission of oyer and terminer on charges of corruption that were based on written complaints against him.[47] These complaints were described by a term we now meet for the first time in the texts: as *clamour of the people*. The *Year Book* record of his trial says that when the king was overseas, Willoughby accepted bribes, and on account of 'clamour de poeple', the matter was 'shown' (complained about) to the king:

... il avoit bestourne et vendi les leys com boefe ou vache, dount par *clamour de poeple* pardecea et de la chose est moustre a Roi.

[... he had then perverted and sold the laws as if they had been oxen or cows, whereof, by *clamour of the people* about the same, matter was shown to the King.][48]

The *clamour of the people* was a crucial element in Willoughby's trial. The adoption of the phrase signals a development in the status and uses of bills of complaint in criminal proceedings.

It was a development that Willoughby contested. Willoughby objected that his arraignment was improper because there was no indictment, and no private appeal by a party. The Justice Parning replied that 'clamour de poeple' was sufficient to put him on trial:

Wilby. Le Roi ne voet estre resceu sans ⟨estre⟩ apris par enditement ou par suyte de partie atache par plegge.—PARN. Il est apris par clamour de poeple.

[*Willoughby.* The King will not be admitted without having been informed by indictment or by suit of the party with pledges to prosecute.—PARNING. He is informed by clamour of the people.][49]

The *Year Book* record gives some examples of complaints that fell into the category of 'clamour':

---

[46] Stones, 'The Folvilles', 122–9.

[47] Payling, 'Willoughby, Sir Richard (*c*.1290–1362)'.

[48] Pike (ed. and trans.), *Year Books of the Reign of King Edward the Third Years XIV and XV*, 258–9 (my italics). It was alleged that Willoughby had arranged for people to be indicted and then took bribes to acquit them. In his defence, Willoughby replied 'Il est manere de Justice daler a les enditours de les conforter et enformer' ('It is the custom for Justice to go to the indictors, to encourage and inform them'); Pike (ed. and trans.), *Year Books of the Reign of King Edward the Third Years XIV and XV*, 260–1, and see also pp. xxvi–xxviii.

[49] Pike (ed. and trans.), *Year Books of the Reign of King Edward the Third Years XIV and XV*, 258–9.

Et plusours billes furent lieux qe ne furent pas affermes par plegges, a quex nul suyte. Et entre autres la commune del counte de Notingham se pleindrent, et la ou plusours furent endites illoeqes pur la foreste, dount ascuns firent fine au Roi par demi marc, et ascuns pur x.*s.*, et Wilby prist dascuns x. marcz, dascuns x. *li.* pur abreger la fine.

[And several bills were read which were not affirmed by pledges, to which there was no suit. And amongst others the commonalty of the county of Nottingham complained that, whereas many were indicted there for breach of the forest laws, of whom some were fined to the King half a mark and some 10*s.*, Willoughby took of some 10 marks and of some 10*l.* to lessen the fine.][50]

Bills of complaint had not, it seems, previously been used to initiate a criminal trial in this way. As we saw at the beginning of this chapter, a trial was usually initiated by private appeal brought by a plaintiff (what the *Year Book* calls 'suit of the party with pledges to prosecute'), or by an indictment sworn by a jury to be a 'true bill'. In some circumstances a trial could be initiated on the basis of the notoriety of the defendant. But Willoughby was brought to trial on the basis of the 'clamour of the people'. Willoughby called the legitimacy of this procedure into question but his defence was not accepted by the judge.[51]

The expression *clamour of the people* has been traced back to use in the reign of Edward II. *Clamour of the people* was then used to establish that a person's treason was *notorious*, in other words, widely known. In such a case the king might record the fact of treason, and judgement be passed against the person without trial. *Clamour of the people* was given its new and extended significance as part of the development by the crown of complaint procedure. Willoughby was one of the first of a number of royal ministers and officials to be removed from office and brought to trial during the royal inquiries into corruption and abuses committed by officials and ministers. The key role of clamour of the people in the process is underlined by the commission issued to the judges who were to try Willoughby and the other defendants. It directed them to hear the cases of those said to be corrupt 'by the common report and clamour of the people and divers petitions shown before him [the king] and the council'.[52] These procedures were therefore explicitly designed to elicit and manipulate clamour of the people. As well as eliciting the bills from the county communities read at Willoughby's trial, this invitation also seems to have elicited bills of complaint against him in the localities. After his trial, Willoughby appeared at various courts in the localities to

---

[50] Pike (ed. and trans.), *Year Books of the Reign of King Edward the Third Years XIV and XV*, 258–60.

[51] Plucknett, 'The Origin of Impeachment', 65–6. Use of private bills—*informations*—to initiate proceedings also excited protest (ibid., 66, n. 2).

[52] Lapsley, 'Archbishop Stratford', 239, citing *Calendar of Patent Rolls, 1340–3*, 110–11.

answer further charges.[53] The case established that clamour of the people could be used to establish notoriety of the facts and provide grounds for putting a royal official or minister on trial.[54]

The mid fourteenth-century *Croniques de London* narrates the trial in language which suggests that Willoughby was subject, metaphorically, to a 'storm' of complaint:

... sire Richard de Willeby, un des chief justice le roy, estut à la barre à Weimouster par deus jours devant sys persones pur respoundre à divers articles dount il fust areint par sire Robert Perninke, sire Robert de Sadingstone, sire William Scot, sire Thomas le Wake, le baroun de Stafford, and [*sic*] sire Johan Darcy, qe luy acouperent de divers pointz q'il avoit fait encountre son lige seignour le roy. Et le dit Richard respondi à touz lour demaundez, taunt q'il devint si laas q'il ne poeit plus parler, mès pria eyde come de grace aver un homme de ley à luy assocyé de luy eyder en parlaunce pur luy ayser, et à graunt peyne luy vodreient graunter cele suete. Et quaunt il ne poeit plus endurer à eux respondre, le dit sire Richard se mist en la grace le roy, et fust recomaundé à le tour de Loundres pur attendre le grace le roy. Et mesme la nuit vint si horrible tempest de vent et de pluvie, de foudre et de toneyre, qe treboucha à tere et debrusa la tresbele oevere del esglise des frere menours à Loundres.[55]

[... Sir Richard Willoughby, a chief justice of the king, appeared for two days in court at Westminster before six persons to reply to various articles of which he stood arraigned by Sir Robert Parning, Sir Robert de Sadingstone, Sir William Scot, Sir Thomas le Wake, the baron of Stafford, and Sir John Darcy, who accused him of various things which he had done against his liege lord the king. And the said Richard replied to all of their questions, until he became so weary that he could speak no more, but requested leave to have the help of a lawyer colleague to help him reply to relieve him, and they begrudgingly granted him this request. And when he could not manage to reply to them any further, the said Sir Richard put himself at the mercy of the king, and was committed to the Tower of London to await the king's pleasure. And the same night came such a terrible tempest of wind and rain, of lightning and thunder, that it razed to the ground and destroyed the very beautiful building of the church of the Friars Minor in London.]

This account shows Willoughby facing a barrage of complaints in court, and when he is finally so exhausted by the attempt to reply to them he first has to ask for someone to speak on his behalf, and at last, completely spent, he is forced to give up. Silenced in the face of innumerable complaints, he is committed to

---

[53] Fryde, 'Removal', 157.

[54] Cf. Plucknett, who sees clamour as a precursor to impeachment: 'His case therefore constitutes an important illustration of the right of the crown to put a subject on trial when (a) named persons present bills against him, or when (b) there are bills from local communities which can be construed as showing "the clamour of the people" against notorious misconduct'; 'the notoriety of the facts in this case consisted in the clamour of the people expressed in bills proffered by the commons of various counties' ('The Origin of Impeachment', 68, 71).

[55] Aungier (ed.), *Croniques de London*, 87–8; for evidence for the date of the chronicle, see p. i.

prison. The barrage of complaint is symbolized by the fierce storm that rages that night. The noise, wind, and rain that destroy the fabric of the friars' church parallel the clamour that has finally silenced Willoughby.

Perhaps the most high-profile minister of those arraigned at this time was John Stratford, Archbishop of Canterbury, and chief minister to Edward III. Like Willoughby, Stratford attempted to resist arraignment, though using rather different legal arguments. As we have seen, Willoughby argued that his arraignment was illegal because it was initiated on the basis of clamour of the people. Stratford, by contrast, claimed that the clamour against him was *defamatory*. Stratford extended clamour to include *various* kinds of public accusation, and he tried to reverse the legal force of that clamour by showing that, rather than constituting a basis for judicial process against him, it was in itself actionable.

Stratford was chief of the ministers whom Edward III entrusted with home affairs while he was abroad on campaigns against the French.[56] A fortnight before his return Edward sent a letter to the pope, Benedict XII, charging the archbishop with treason. He blamed Stratford for encouraging him to go on campaign, and for failing to provide promised money and horses, thereby, he imputed, trying to have the king killed.[57] According to Murimuth, Stratford was publicly accused in the London Guildhall by the royal courtier William Kilsby.[58] Summoned in Canterbury to appear before the king, on 29 December 1340 Stratford countered by preaching in English on Ecclesiasticus 48: 13, 'In his time he did not fear the prince'. He denounced those who had arrested clerks, justices, and knights in violation of Magna Carta (clause 29 of the 1225 Charter), and those who defamed him of treason, in contravention of the controversial bull 'Clericis laicos', pronouncing sentences of excommunication against the offenders.[59] He avoided being accused of defamation in return by not actually naming individuals.[60] He circulated these sentences of excommunication to bishops in the province, pointing out that ecclesiastical liberties were at stake.[61] On 1 January 1341 Stratford wrote to the king, repeating the points he had made in his sermon. He again cited Magna Carta and 'Clericis laicos' as authorities for his claim that the judicial process that Edward had invoked against his ministers was illegal:

… par malveis consail … vous comences de prendre devers clers, peeres, et aultres gentz de la terre, et faire proces nient covenable, countre la ley de la terre, a le quele garder et maintenir vous estez tenuz par serement fait a vostre coronement, et encontre la graunt chartre, dount toutz sount excomengez par toutz lez prelatz Dengleterre qe vienent al encontre et la sentence conferme par bulle de pape, la quele nous avomps devers nous …

---

[56] Haines, *Archbishop John Stratford*, 278–327; cf. Haines, 'Stratford, John (*c*.1275–1348)'.
[57] Fryde, 'Removal', 153–4.   [58] Haines, *Archbishop John Stratford*, 284.
[59] Lapsley, 'Archbishop Stratford', 241 and n. 2; Haines, *Archbishop John Stratford*, 284–6.
[60] 'Quibus neminem diffamavimus cum nullum nominaverimus in eisdem' ('in which we defame no-one since we name nobody in them'); text cited by Haines, *Archbishop John Stratford*, 287, n. 60.
[61] Haines, *Archbishop John Stratford*, 288.

[... by evil counsel ... you begin to seize divers clerks, peers, and other folk of the land, and to make suit nothing fitting, against the law of the land, the which to keep and maintain you are bound by the oath taken at your coronation, and contrary to the great charter, against which all who come counter are excommunicate by all the prelates of England, and the sentence confirmed by the pope's bull, which we have by us ...][62]

Claiming again that the charges against himself of treason and falsehood were false, and reiterating that the people making the charges were therefore excommunicate, he proposed a process by which all those accused might be properly tried:

Et purceo qe ascuns qe sount pres de vous nous sourmetient faucement tresoun et faucine, par quei ils sount excomengetz ... et auxi dient dascuns aultres qils vous ount malement et faucement servi ... voilletz, sire, si vous plest, faire venir lez prelatz, grauntz, et peeres de la tierre en lieu covenable, od nous et aultres gentz purrons seurement venir, et faites, si vous plest, veer et enquere en qi mains, puis le comencement de vostre guerre, laynes, deniers, et aultres choses ... sount devenuz et vient dependuz ... Et en qaunt qe a nous appent, nous enterroms en toutz pointz a juggement de noz peres, sauve toutes voies lestat de seint eglise ... Et pur Dieu, sire, ne voilletz crere de nous ne de voz bones gentz si bien noun, avaunt qe vous sachetz la verite; car, si gentz serrount puniz saunz respounse, tout serra un juggement dez bones et dez malveis.

[And, forasmuch as certain who are near to you do falsely charge us with treason and falsehood, therefore they are excommunicate ... and also they say of some others that they have evilly and falsely served you ... be willing, sire, if it please you, to make come the prelates, great men, and peers of the land, in fitting place, where we and others may securely come, and cause, if it please you, to see and enquire in whose hands, since the beginning of your war, wools, moneys, and other things ... have come and have been expended ... And in whatsoever concerneth us, we will stand in all points at the judgment of our peers, saving always the estate of holy church ... And for God's sake, sire, be unwilling to believe of us and of your good people aught but good, before that you know the truth; for, if folk shall be punished without answer, judgment of the good and of the evil shall be all one.][63]

Stratford was arrested on 26 January 1341, and two days later wrote to the king and council complaining that his arrest infringed his legal rights and privileges. Angry writings were publicly circulated on both sides, until parliament was summoned to gather on 23 April and Stratford attempted to get his hearing. Stratford was careful not to recognize the legitimacy of any charges of treason or perjury against him, claiming that no secular judge could give judgement on an ecclesiastic on these matters. Insisting that he had been defamed, he claimed the right to defend himself in full parliament.

Stratford's assertion that the judicial process being used by the crown against its ministers was illegal, and his proposal that those accused of abuse in office should be allowed to answer before parliament, were taken up in petitions of the

---

[62] Thompson (ed.), *Robertus de Avesbury*, 326–7, 328 (translation).
[63] Ibid., 325–6, 329 (translation).

lords and commons in the 1341 parliament. A commons' petition complained that clerks, peers of the realm, and other free persons of high estate were being arrested and imprisoned without indictment or appeal being lodged against them 'queux ne furent appellez n'enditez, ne suite de partie vers eux affermez' ('that they were neither appealed nor indicted, nor had suit of a party been pledged against them').[64] It is noteworthy that this petition makes precisely the point that Willoughby made in his defence—suggesting that the Stratford case was perceived to raise issues shared with the other cases being pursued by this process of invoking clamour of the people.

A petition from the lords requested that peers of the realm should be required to answer allegations of trespass only in parliament.[65] Stratford appeared before the king and presented a petition which is reported in similar terms to that of the lords:

Et puis pria l'ercevesqe au roi q'il pleust a sa seignurie, qe desicome il est diffamez notoirement par tut le roialme et aillours, q'il puisse estre aresnez en pleyn parlement devant les pieres, & illoeqes respoundre …[66]

[And then the archbishop petitioned the king, that if it pleased his lordship, that he could be arraigned in full parliament before his peers, and reply there, on account of being notoriously defamed throughout the realm and beyond …]

Stratford invokes parliament as the only fitting opportunity for him to defend himself against clamour, to show that clamour to be in fact defamation, and asserting that he has been 'defamez notoirement'.

In Stratford's case, clamour of the people was not confined to bills elicited by the royal inquiry. It included a range of literary and other textual modes to which the process of eliciting complaint now gave potential legal force. On 10/12 February a letter patent was issued from government circles to Stratford. It describes Stratford unflatteringly as a mouse gnawing at the wallet, a serpent, venom in the lap, a fire in the king's breast. He is timorous in the face of adversity; he is a mercenary rather than a good shepherd; he is cunning as a fox. His sentences of excommunication of ministers are defamatory—he has contravened convention by publishing unsigned letters in public places ('per suas literas in pluribus locis insignibus publicari').[67] The letter accuses Stratford of corrupt practices amounting to treason: he has abused his office by accepting bribes, promoting favourites, and diverting the king's goods for his own purposes. It was sent to bishops of the southern province with instructions that it should be published, and within a few weeks it had circulated widely. At Canterbury, William Kilsby read out the letter before a crowd at the cross outside the gate of the priory. Presumably, given the venue, he used English.

---

[64] *PROME*, parliament of Edward III, 1341 April, item 9; my translation.
[65] Ibid., items 6, 7, and 9. For the assents, see items 35 and 51.
[66] Ibid., item 8; my translation.   [67] Haines, *Archbishop John Stratford*, 295 and n. 104.

Stratford countered the government's attempt to create clamour of the people in several ways. A few days after Kilsby read out the letter, when Stratford was preaching at the cathedral, the king's letter patent was read out in English, and Stratford replied article by article.[68] Stratford also issued a lengthy written reply known as his *excusaciones*.[69] Here, he characterized the letter patent as more properly termed a *libellus famosus*. In Roman law, a *libellus* is 'the original declaration of any action in civil law'—one civilist defines it thus: 'Libellus est scriptura in qua continetur res quae petitur et causa petendi et nomen actoris et rei' ('A *libellus* is a writing in which are contained the suit which is sued, the case for the suit, and the name of the disputant and the action').[70] It is, therefore, equivalent to the bill or complaint (*billa* or *querela*). The related term *libellus famosus* was used by classical and medieval Latin writers for a *defamatory* document.[71] By characterizing it thus, Stratford meant to show that authoring and publishing this document were both illegal and subject to heavy penalties under canon and civil law. In a letter dated 10 March 1341 which he had circulated to the bishops of his province, Stratford replied to the charges of the king and characterized the letter as a *libellus famosus*, saying that all involved in its production and dissemination had offended against the law: 'Non solum dictatores et scriptores libellorum huiusmodi famosorum sed eciam recitantes et publicantes eosdem contra patres spirituales loca apostolorum tenentes' ('not only the composers and scribes of these libels, but even those who recite and publish them against spiritual fathers who hold apostolic office').[72] A riposte issued by the government on 31 March 1341, *Cicatrix cordium superbia*, denounces Stratford for describing royal letters as *libelli famosi* ('Detestabiles & Libellos Famosos intitulat'), and for issuing defamatory letters of his own, and requires the bishops to publish the royal letter, Stratford's prohibition notwithstanding.[73]

The campaign against Stratford's reputation continued once parliament was in session. Stratford's biographer claims that John d'Arcy, chamberlain of the royal household, and William Kilsby drew up articles against Stratford which they showed to the mayor, aldermen, and commune of London in the Chapter House at Westminster Abbey, in order to excite the city against him ('ut sic contra eum dictam civitatem excitarent').[74] The following day they published the same articles in parliament; in the words of Stratford's biographer, 'communitati Angliae' ('before the community of England'), in order that 'he

---

[68] For a summary, see Haines, *Archbishop John Stratford*, 306, and for circulation 303 and 305–6. Cf. Lapsley, 'Archbishop Stratford', 243–4.

[69] Haines, *Archbishop John Stratford*, 296–305; Lapsley, 'Archbishop Stratford', 245.

[70] Bolland (ed.), *Select Bills*, pp. xiii–xiv.

[71] For discussion of later uses in England, see Scase, ' "Strange and Wonderful Bills" ', 236–8.

[72] Haines, *Archbishop John Stratford*, 310, n. 172.

[73] Rymer (ed.), *Foedera*, ii. I. 96; cf. Haines, *Archbishop John Stratford*, 311–12.

[74] Lapsley, 'Archbishop Stratford', 249 citing Birchington. The articles do not appear to have survived, but their content is indicated from letters patent issued in 1346 confirming that Stratford was 'excused' the charges (Haines, *Archbishop John Stratford*, 323).

should lose the good-will of the whole community of England, wishing him to be estranged from the hearts of the English' ('ut sic ipse archiepiscopus totius communitatis Angliae perderet voluntatem; volentes ipsum archiepiscopum exulem fore a cordibus Anglicorum').[75] From these statements of Stratford's biographer it has been inferred that the 'community of the English' to whom publication was made was the parliamentary commons.[76] But a broader interpretation is possible. The intention may have been that the articles would subsequently be conveyed to county communities by the burgesses and knights of the shire. By the beginning of Edward II's reign the knights of the shire and the burgesses transmitted popular complaints from their constituents to parliament. Reporting back to the constituencies became important at the time of the inquiries.[77]

In this section we have seen that the 1340s inquiries into the conduct of justices and ministers gave new importance and status to bills and complaints as ways of initiating criminal proceedings. The adoption of complaint process against high-profile political persons was associated with the exploration and manipulation of complaint, with the broadening of the category of legitimate complaint, and with the development of new ways of orchestrating and using complaint. We have also seen the use of various modes of publication of complaint—public readings of articles of complaint to a range of audiences, as well as the circulation of letters by the government and ecclesiastics, and a range of ways of reporting parliamentary business—and we have seen how these modes of publication could be exploited both by plaintiffs and defendants. These episodes provided a focus and occasions for exploration, analysis, and debate over the principles involved in the use of bills and the clamour of the people to initiate judicial proceedings. As such they crystallized problems that had already emerged in the early years of the century, and provided a foundation for developments in later decades.

CLAMOUR OF THE PEOPLE IN THE LATER FOURTEENTH CENTURY

For the period up to the middle of the fourteenth century we have had to rely on exiguous sources to build up a picture of the ways in which clamour

---

[75] Lapsley, 'Archbishop Stratford', 249.   [76] Ibid.

[77] Kinds of reporting included the dissemination of draft petitions and oral and written informal reports. In 1327 the commons asked to be allowed to carry back to their counties for publication a written account of their petitions and of the answers of king and council—a statute resulted. In 1339 reporting back grew into consultation with the shires before knights of the shire would agree to taxation. Sometimes reports of grants and conditions were requested in the form of letters patent to the counties. Knights also used proclamations in the counties (the normal way in which the royal government made its will known) to record and explain parliamentary activities. In this way, audiences in county courts, boroughs, and market towns must have been made aware of the doings of parliament. See Maddicott, 'Parliament and the Constituencies', 81–2; and Maddicott, 'County Communities', esp. 33–9.

was orchestrated and resisted. The second half of the century, and in particular the period from the 1370s onwards, provides us with much richer materials for examining the textualities of clamour. As in the cases examined in the last section, many of these materials are associated with opposition to high-profile government ministers. Materials associated with the Good Parliament of 1376 and the Appellant crisis of 1387–8 provide us with particularly good opportunities for studying clamour. The action against unpopular ministers and courtiers in both of these episodes has been related to judicial process founded on notoriety. Plucknett suggested that the process of notoriety underlay the parliamentary proceedings of 1376, and Rogers has argued that it is this process which underlay the Appellants' action in 1388.[78]

During the Good Parliament, complaints presented in parliament were claimed to be 'clamour' which gave proof of notoriety. The parliament roll that records the impeachments of William Latimer, chamberlain to the king, and the London alderman Richard Lyons states 'William sire de Latimer estoit empeschez et accusez par clamour des ditz communes' ('William Lord Latimer was impeached and accused by the clamour of the commons'). As Sir Richard Willoughby had done nearly forty years earlier, Latimer objected that there was no specific accuser to answer ('the commons maintained the said accusations in common'—in other words, no private appeal had been made), but he was made to answer the charges.[79] Likewise, Adam Bury, also a London alderman, was 'empeschez par le clamour des communes en ce parlement ... come pluis au plain appiert en une grant bille baille en parlement de darrain jour de cest parlement a Eltham' ('impeached by the clamour of the commons ... as appears more fully in a large bill delivered in parliament on the last day of this parliament at Eltham').[80] But petitions delivered by the commons in parliament were not the only kind of evidence for clamour. Notoriety was not only based on the fact of bills delivered in parliament. The *Anonimalle Chronicle* says that William Wykeham was charged because the lords 'mistrent sur luy plusours grevouses articles et forfetours queux le roy mesmes avoit certeinment entendu et par plusours evidences notorez et par *comune clamour de soun pople*' ('put before him many grievous articles and forfeitures which the king had certainly heard both by many notorious evidences and by the *common clamour of his people*'.[81] The conviction of Latimer

---

[78] Plucknett, 'The Origin of Impeachment', is a seminal piece that sums up the debate of the earlier twentieth century. Rogers, 'Parliamentary Appeals of Treason', builds on Plucknett's work to analyse the process of 1388. Lambrick, 'The Impeachment of the Abbot of Abingdon', and Harding, 'Plaints and Bills', 80, both show that the processes adopted during these parliaments are related to the broader and more long-standing developments in criminal justice with which we are concerned.

[79] *PROME*, parliament of Edward III, 1376 April, items 20 and 26; my translation. Plucknett, 'The Origin of Impeachment', 70.

[80] *PROME*, parliament of Edward III, 1376 April, item 47; my translation. Cf. Plucknett, 'The Origin of Impeachment', 70.

[81] Galbraith (ed.), *Anonimalle Chronicle*, 96, my italics and translation; cf. Plucknett, 'The Origin of Impeachment', 55.

is associated with 'clamour' in a contemporary chronicle from St Albans. Latimer was accused of betraying and defrauding the crown in connection with a period of military command in Brittany. While action regarding the charges was awaited, he was also accused of trying to suppress dispatches brought to the king from Rochelle by a messenger. Presumably it was supposed that this messenger brought evidence that would help to incriminate Latimer. Through Latimer's influence the messenger was taken into custody, and his message disappeared. This caused uproar among the citizens of London and, 'cum clamore et minis' ('with clamour and threats'), they demanded that the detainee be produced for examination. The sheriffs were forced to comply. The Duke of Lancaster and the judges set a later date for the examination of the messenger. But they were unable finally to prevent the hearing, and Latimer and Lyons were eventually convicted of the charges.[82] Here, by describing the crowd's uproar as 'clamour', and showing that their outburst forced a trial, arguably the chronicler is not just describing mob rule. Rather, he is presenting the citizens' action as an expression of complaint with legal standing and force, one which overrides Lancaster's attempt to wrest powers of arrest and jurisdiction from them.[83] In both cases, the clamour of the people has a legal standing that the king and the duke are forced to recognize. It is this clamour which initiates the judicial process. Here, clamour seems to be a broader category than formal petitions presented in a judicial forum.[84]

There is evidence of conflict over whether the category of legitimate complaint could include libels. One chronicler describes libels posted in London against John of Gaunt as 'clamour'. The commons of the city allegedly fixed up writings at Westminster and St Paul's, while parliament was in session. These writings are described as 'escrowes' in the *Anonimalle Chronicle*, and as 'rhythmos sive schedulas' in the *Chronicon Angliae*.[85] According to the *Anonimalle Chronicle*, in these writings it was claimed that the duke was not an English royal prince at all, but the son of a Flemish butcher who had been substituted for the real new-born prince because the boy was sick; the poorly infant had been killed by his nurse, and the queen and her entourage had substituted a boy child of similar age. They claimed that the case was clearly proved by the fact that the duke loved the

---

[82] Thompson (ed.), *Chronicon Angliae*, 81–7, quoted passage at 81; see pp. xlii–xlvi for discussion of the episode.

[83] John of Gaunt was closely identified with proposals to take the city 'into the king's hand'—to extend the jurisdiction of the marshal (president of the court of the royal household) over the city, giving him power to make arrests in the city, and to appoint a 'captain' in place of the mayor, thereby infringing the city's privileges and jurisdictions (Bird, *The Turbulent London of Richard II*, 25).

[84] I find no evidence or authority to support Steiner's assertion that *clamour* was 'the technical term for vocalized common assent of the Commons', or that it denotes a 'uniform cry' of a deliberately contrasting kind in this passage in the *Chronicon Angliae*, where, Steiner claims, it refers to 'the demands of an unruly and spontaneous urban crowd'; 'the undifferentiated *vox* of a socially inferior or ill-defined *populus*', 'the uniform cry of a social entity temporarily empowered to effect political change' ('Commonalty and Literary Form', 202–4 and n. 14).

[85] Galbraith (ed.), *The Anonimalle Chronicle*, 104; Thompson (ed.), *Chronicon Angliae*, 129.

Flemish people twice as much as he loved the English. By fixing up his arms in reverse fashion, they declared publicly that he was a traitor. These claims about the duke led to 'graunt noys et graunte clamour par tute la cite de Loundres et par tute Engleterre' ('great noise and great clamour throughout the city of London and the whole of England').[86] It seems likely that these attacks implied that the duke had ambitions to take the throne (newly occupied by the boy-king Richard II) himself. They were certainly read by the duke as accusations of treason. He petitioned the king in parliament to be cleared of what the commons had maliciously said about him, calling for recognition that he harboured no treasonous intentions. He announced that he was prepared to defend himself by judicial combat, should anyone make an appeal of treason against him.[87] By 'throwing down the gauntlet', the duke was saying that he would answer to an *appeal of treason*, and, by implication, that he did not recognize the clamour against him as answerable in court.

CLAMOUR AND THE APPELLANTS

As so often, for the libel campaign against John of Gaunt we have only the second-hand evidence of the chroniclers to go on. We do not have the texts of the libels themselves, and, although we know where and in what form they were published, we do not know how the texts were produced; how this clamour was orchestrated. With the Appellants' crisis we have source materials that allow us to study the production of complaint texts that would qualify for recognition, legally, as clamour. Procedure based on notoriety, provable by the evidence of clamour, was the foundation of the Appellants' strategy. In order to understand why this was, it is necessary briefly to consider the constitutional and legal implications of the crown's response to the purge of royal favourites achieved by the 'Wonderful Parliament' of 1386.

In the 'Wonderful Parliament' of 1386 Michael de la Pole, chancellor (minister with overall responsibility to Richard for government), was impeached by the commons on charges of corruption and abuse of office. He was removed from office, convicted of the charges, and imprisoned, and a commission was appointed to reform government. The lords and commons claimed that their authority to act in this way was founded 'ex antiquo statuto' ('under an ancient law'), under which a summons to parliament was a summons 'tanquam ad summam curiam tocius regni' ('as to the highest court in all the land'). They also claimed that ancient law provided that it was lawful to depose a king if he did not rule in accordance with law and good counsel. They asked Richard to be mindful of

---

[86] Galbraith (ed.), *The Anonimalle Chronicle*, 104–5, quotation at 105; Goodman, *John of Gaunt*, 61.

[87] *PROME*, parliament of Richard II, 1377 October, item 13.

this fact and remove incompetent counsellors.[88] The crown had no choice but to comply, but the following year the king convened a panel of judges to consider the legitimacy of the events that had occurred in parliament. In reply to a series of pointed questions designed to confirm the crown's prerogative, the judges gave the opinion that parliament could not pass judgement on a minister of the crown without the king's assent, and that anyone who attempted to take the king's power in such a way should be punished as a traitor.[89] In practice, this meant the reversal of what had been achieved in 1386. Michael de la Pole was released from prison and restored to the king's entourage. There were profound constitutional and legal implications for the future. The judges' replies meant that henceforth ministers could not be brought to trial at the instigation of the parliamentary commons without the consent of the king, and that therefore impeachment was no longer available as a means for bringing members of the government to trial.

The appeal, and procedure based on notoriety, were the procedures to which the reformers now turned. On 14 November 1387 the Duke of Gloucester and the Earls of Arundel and Warwick lodged an appeal accusing Michael de la Pole of high treason, together with Alexander Neville, Archbishop of York, Robert de Vere, Duke of Ireland, Robert Tresilian, chief justice of the King's Bench, and Nicholas Brembre, recently mayor of London. The appeal was repeated before the king and council on 17 November, and again—with the three Appellants now joined by the Earls of Derby and Nottingham—in the parliament that assembled on 3 February 1388.[90] As we have seen, the appeal was a private complaint alleging criminal wrong doing. It provided a way of circumventing the problems caused to opposition lords by the opinions of the judges.[91] Unlike impeachment by the commons, an appeal did not require the king's consent. The appeal was a well-established means of initiating judicial proceedings in a variety of courts, including cases heard by the council. It was unprecedented as a means of initiating a trial in parliament. But the designation of parliament as the venue for hearing the case followed from the fact that it was an appeal of treason. Under the 1352 Statute of Treason, parliament was designated the proper forum for state trials of treason. The submission of an appeal did not in itself determine what procedure should be adopted, however. After some deliberation, the lords determined that the process to be used was 'les leys et cours du parlement' ('the law and procedure of parliament'). In effect, they invoked the process used in earlier state trials. This was the old procedure of conviction based on notoriety,

---

[88] Martin (ed. and trans.), *Knighton's Chronicle*, 356–61. It has been suggested that the authority for this 'ancient statute' was the *Modus Tenendi Parliamentum*; see Martin, n. *ad loc.*

[89] Ibid., 393–9; for discussion, see Chrimes, 'Richard II's Questions to the Judges'; and Saul, *Richard II*, 173–4.

[90] Rogers, 'Parliamentary Appeals of Treason', 106–7.

[91] The following analysis of the use of the appeal by the Appellant lords is indebted to Rogers, 'Parliamentary Appeals of Treason'.

as modified in the trials of the 1340s. Notoriety had to be 'alleged by sufficient people to be claimed to be proved.'[92]

The process of generating proof of notoriety provides a framework for understanding several complaint texts from this period. These examples provide us with evidence of the recognition of the legal status and political importance of complaint texts, evidence of the relation between complaint texts and literary production in the period, and quite remarkable material evidence for how the manipulation of clamour of the people for political purposes worked at material, textual, and literary levels. These texts include ten petitions of the London guilds against Nicholas Brembre, preserved together in the Public Record Office; a further petition which formerly was part of this bundle but is now archived separately; another petition which was probably associated with the group but is also now archived separately and is preserved only in part, and a libel against Alexander Neville.

None of these petitions has previously been analysed in relation to the process of 1388. Of the petitions of the guilds against Brembre, one, the petition of the Mercers, has long been familiar to scholars. It was published by Chambers and Daunt as one of only two petitions to parliament dated before 1400 that are written in English (all of the other petitions are in French), and dated by them 1386.[93] In fact, the assertions made by Chambers and Daunt about the date of the petition and the address to parliament are not quite accurate. We shall come to the matter of the address below. Regarding the date, in the printed Rolls of Parliament the petitions are associated with the parliament of October–December 1386, and presumably on this basis, Chambers and Daunt dated the petitions 1386. However, an unsigned note in a modern archivist's hand in the Public Record Office bundle demonstrates conclusively on the basis of two internal references that this dating must be wrong, and that they must belong to the parliament of February–June 1388.[94] Nigel Saul states (without

---

[92] Rogers, 'Parliamentary Appeals of Treason', 112–13.

[93] TNA (PRO), SC 8/20/997; quotations below are from Chambers and Daunt (eds.), *Book of London English*, 33–7 (and see 273); cf. *RP*, iii. 225–6, 'Petition of the Mercers of London', and Fisher, Richardson, and Fisher (eds.), *An Anthology of Chancery English*, 194–7. The French petitions are TNA (PRO), SC 8/20/998 (Cordwainers, printed *RP*, iii. 226–7); SC 8/20/999 (Saddlers, trans. Sherwell, *A Descriptive and Historical Account of the Guild of Saddlers*, 41–4); SC 8/20/1000 (Embroiderers); SC 8/20/1001B (Leather-sellers and Whittawers); SC 8/20/1002 (Founderers); SC 8/20/1003 (Pinners); SC 8/20/1004 (Painters); SC 8/20/1005 (Armourers); SC 8/20/1006 (Cutlers, Bowyers, Fletchers, Spurriers, and Bladesmiths). The two petitions archived separately are those of the Drapers, TNA (PRO), SC 8/94/4664, printed by Johnson, *Worshipful Company of Drapers*, i. 208–11, and the Tailors, TNA (PRO), C 49/10/3, printed by Leadam and Baldwin (eds.), *Select Cases before the King's Council*, 74–6. That this is clearly the last part only of a larger document is indicated by 'les ditz' in the opening words 'Item les ditz suppliantz soy pleignant versus Nichol Brembre'. None of these petitions appears on the parliament roll; see *PROME*, 'Appendix February 1388'.

[94] TNA (PRO), SC 8/20/997. On the basis of its association with the other petitions against Brembre, Leadam and Baldwin incorrectly date the Tailors' petition to 1386 (*Select Cases before the King's Council*, p. xcvii). The Drapers' petition is dated 1387 by Johnson, *Worshipful Company of*

discussion) that the 1386 date is wrong, suggesting that the petitions 'probably have their origins in the Appellants' search for evidence against Brembre'.[95] Critical analysis, however, has yet to become aware of the re-dating and its interpretative possibilities.[96]

The petitions include grievances specific to the individual crafts, but also overlaps of topics and wording that suggest a concerted effort of some kind. All of them are petitions against Brembre, and all of them—the Mercers' petition excepted—are addressed to the king and council in parliament (the Mercers' bill is addressed to council alone; the address of the fragmentary Tailors' petition is lost). The Cordwainers complain that Brembre and a gang of armed men accroached royal power by cutting off the head of John Constantine, cordwainer, and imprisoning many others, contrary to law and right. This complaint is repeated in briefer form by the Saddlers; in their petition the death of Constantine is followed by detail of threats to and imprisonment of members of the Saddlers' Guild. The Cordwainers, Saddlers, and Drapers all include complaints about how Brembre intimidated citizens, interfering with the process of the mayoral election. The Saddlers preface this complaint with a grievance concerning their charter which, they allege, Brembre removed and detained by force. The Tailors also allege that Brembre has confiscated their charter. The Mercers combine the grievance about the election with a lengthy account of how Brembre suppressed complaint with threats of counter-accusations of treason. They ask for due process should any such allegations be made, asserting that, just as the branches of a bramble or briar reveal 'a ragged subiect or stok' within, so the truth about Brembre ('the forsaid Brere or brembre') is revealed by the wrongs he has committed.

Overlaps in wording may be illustrated by comparing the Mercers' and the Cordwainers' petitions. A common source of some kind is particularly clear where the two documents quote the cries of Brembre's men when they intimidated the citizens at election time (I have italicized passages which appear interdependent at a verbal level):

Lequel Mons' Nicholl', *la noet ensivant, fist carier a la dite Gyhall graunt quantite d'armure, ove quele si bien foreins come autres feurent armeez en la dite Gyhall lendemain,* pur la dite election faire, & *certeins abushementz* des gentz armeez *feurent illoeques myses.* Et *quant les bones gentz de la Citee la venoient pur la dite eleccion faire,* solonc la franchise & l'aunciene custume de dite Citee, les avant ditz gentz *armeez failleront sur eux ove graunt noise, criantz tuwez, tuwez, lour pursuivantz* hydousement; *par ount les ditz bones gentz, pur paiour de mort, se suwyrent & ascondirent en mesons & autres liewes secretz, come en*

Drapers, i. 208, but is incorrectly dated 1384 in the online PRO catalogue and on the document guard (the petition *refers* to 1384). For the address of the Mercers' petition see 68, 77.

⁹⁵ Saul, *Richard II*, 193, n. 69.

⁹⁶ For example, in her recent essay Lindenbaum sees the Mercers' petition in terms of 'factional disputes' in the city (Lindenbaum, 'London Texts and Literate Practice', 290–1).

terre de guerre; & adonques eslirent le dit Mons' Nicholl' pur Mayre. *Et issint la Mairaltee du dite Citee depuis le dit temps tan que en cea ad estee tenuz par conquest & maistrie …*[97]

And *in the nyght next after folwynge he did carye grete quantitee of Armure to the Guyldehalle, with which as wel straungers of the contree as othere of with-jnne were armed on the morwe,* ayeins his owne proclamacion that was such that no man shulde be armed; & *certein busshmentz were laide*, that, *when free men of the Citee come to chese her Mair, breken vp armed cryinge with loude voice 'sle! sle!' folwyng hem*; *wherthourgh the peple for feere fledde to houses & other (hidy)nges as in londe of werre, adradde to be ded* in comune. *And thus yet hiderward hath the Mairaltee ben holden as it were of conquest or maistrye …*[98]

The dependencies among the twelve texts would repay further study.[99] For our purposes here, however, whatever the precise relationships between the documents, the overlaps are significant. In view of the correspondences in content, the parallel passages in French and English between the Mercers' and the Cordwainers' petitions, and the contemporary narrative accounts of the role played by the guilds in Brembre's downfall, which I shall now outline, it seems likely that the twelve petitions were drafted to provide evidence to support the appeal against Brembre, to demonstrate clamour, and provide evidence of notoriety.

Contemporary narrative accounts of the process against the five appellees suggest a context for the production of these petitions. Thomas Favent's account of the Merciless Parliament of 1388 narrates how the craft guilds presented complaints against Brembre. He suggests that it was their complaints, sworn by the guilds with no fear or favour, that brought the process against Brembre to an end:

… crastino tamen pro grauiori comparuerunt plures artes ciuitatis Londonii conquerendi causa se de pluribus iniuriis et extorcionibus per ipsum Nicholaum Brembre alias tortuose commissis et illatis. Et cum artes ipse in animam suam iurassent non fore corruptas odio, metu, vel favore alicuius vel munere, neque maliciose ea proponebant sed super vero ipsum accusabant, tunc stetit Brembre confuse tantum.[100]

[… none the less on the next day, as an even heavier matter, appeared many of the crafts of the city of London complaining about many injuries and extortions torturously committed and carried forward against them elsewhere by that same Nicholas Brembre. And since the crafts themselves swore on their souls that they were not corrupted by hatred, fear, or favor of anyone or any reward, nor were they declaring these things maliciously but rather were accusing him concerning the truth, Brembre then stood undone at last.][101]

---

[97] *RP*, iii. 226 (my italics).

[98] Chambers and Daunt (eds.), *Book of London English*, 34 (my italics).

[99] I discuss the use of English for the composition of this and other petitions in Ch. 5.

[100] McKisack (ed.), *Historia Mirabilis Parliamenti*, 17. For recent analysis of this text, see Oliver, 'A Political Pamphleteer'. Oliver argues that Favent was an independent, non-partisan commentator rather than a propagandist for the Appellants.

[101] Galloway (trans.), *History or Narration Concerning the Manner and Form of the Miraculous Parliament at Westminster in the Year 1386*, 245. 'Crafts' here refers to 'guilds'.

Favent describes how, before proceedings were finally concluded, Tresilian, who had fled into hiding, was discovered and brought before parliament with cries (in the vernacular, tellingly styled 'publica voce') of 'we hauet hym'.[102] The *Westminster Chronicle* also attributes to the crafts a role in Brembre's downfall, but one somewhat more equivocal than that Favent suggests. According to this chronicler, the Appellants held a meeting with the guilds on 18 January 1388, as part of their efforts to collect evidence to support their appeal against the appellees. On 17 January they summoned representatives of the guilds and told them that if anyone had injuries to complain of they should attend the following day at the Guildhall:

'… Nunc autem si que gravamina sive querimonie inter vos versantur producite in medium coram nobis: jam est tempus audiendi. Nam constat omnibus nobis vos nullatenus esse unanimes utrobique quia, ut apparet, una ars istius civitatis aliam delere affectat; quod est absurdum, presertim inter cives tales inter illos discordias sustinere; immo si pacem et concordiam inter vos fovere volueritis nullam adversitatem vobis dominari sperare poteritis.' Pauca vero ad ista erant prolata, quia videbatur eis non equaliter eos stare cum omnibus prout decet: odeo forte noluerunt eos tanquam judices acceptare nec coram illis aliquid allegare.

['… But today, if there are any grievances or complaints which are being bandied about between yourselves, bring them out into the open before us; now is the time for them to be heard. It is evident to us all that the different elements among you are by no means of one mind when, as it seems, one city craft is seeking to destroy another; which is senseless, especially when it is between fellow citizens that quarrels of this sort are kept alive. If, on the contrary, you are prepared to foster peace and harmony among you, you can count on never having to bow to misfortune.' Few matters, however, were raised in response to this invitation, because it seemed to the citizens that the members of the tribunal were not as impartial in their sympathy for all parties as they should have been: it was therefore perhaps for this reason that they declined to accept them as judges and to make any allegations before them.][103]

In this source, the guilds play their part again later in parliament, after the process against Tresilian:

Istis denique sic peractis iterato redierunt domini predicti ad judicium domini Nicholai de Brembre: miseruntque pro duobus de qualibet arte London', quibus vellent informari an esset culpabilis super contentis in articulis supradictis vel non; qui circa verba superflua vacantes demum sine effectu ad propria redierunt.

[This episode concluded, the lords returned once more to considering their judgement on Sir Nicholas Brembre, and sent for two representatives of each of the London crafts, through whom they wished to learn whether or not he was guilty of the matters comprised

---

    102 McKisack (ed.), *Historia Mirabilis Parliamenti*, 17.
    103 Hector and Harvey (eds. and trans.), *The Westminster Chronicle*, 234–5; for discussion of this episode, see Saul, *Richard II*, 190–1.

in the articles mentioned above [the articles of the appeal]; but after spending some time in needless chatter these people at length returned home with nothing accomplished.][104]

In the Westminster chronicler's narrative, it is the testimony of the mayor, aldermen, and recorder that brings about Brembre's conviction.

These accounts offer a broad context for the composition of the twelve petitions. The Westminster chronicler details a process in which the Appellants involve the guilds in their collection of evidence and preparation of support for their appeal. Both Favent and the Westminster chronicler describe a process in which guildsmen appear (summoned by the lords, according to the Westminster monk) in parliament. Some sort of oral examination is suggested: the Westminster chronicler writes of 'verba superflua' between the lords and the guildsmen; Favent refers to the guildsmen taking an oath ('cum artes ipse in animam suam iurassent'). The petitions, of course, must have been written some time before these events in parliament took place—they would have taken some time to produce, and, in any case, it appears that the guildsmen were summoned only shortly before Brembre was executed. When, and in what way, were they delivered to parliament, and how, if at all, did their composition relate to the Appellants' attempt to garner evidence of Brembre's notoriety?

As I have already suggested, the overlaps of wording and grievance suggest some co-ordination of effort. Whether this was in response to the suggestion of the Appellants that they shelve factional disputes and work together in a common cause is impossible to say; clearly the end result would have satisfied the lords, however it had been achieved. Some clues may be offered by the physical and linguistic properties of the petitions. We know that they were not produced communally, for the documents are in different hands and are of different sizes.[105] All of the petitions exhibit the file hole commonly observed in petitions submitted to parliament, which indicates that they have been placed on a spike like other petitions. They also all show damage on the top left side, indicating that they have been bundled together (the Drapers' petition, although now archived separately from the others, exhibits the same pattern of damage as the rest; we have only the lower portion of the Tailors' petition). These properties also suggest that they have been treated in the same way as other private petitions. However, compared with many other petitions to parliament from this date, these petitions share some unusual characteristics. Physically, they are of quite different size and shape from other private petitions of this parliament. The Mercers' petition, for example, measures 36 cm wide (max.) × 53.5 cm long. This is of a similar width, but some four times as long, as other private petitions of this date. All of the rest (with the exception of the fragmentary Tailors' petition) are similarly distinctive in size and shape. For example, the Cordwainers' petition is 34 cm wide × 36 cm

---

[104] Hector and Harvey (eds. and trans.), *The Westminster Chronicle*, 312–13.

[105] It is likely that they were produced by clerks working for the individual guilds—the scribe who wrote the Mercers' petition also copied accounts for the Mercers—see further below.

long, the Leathersellers' petition is 32 cm wide × 48 cm long, and the Cutlers' petition is a massive 44 cm wide × 50.5 cm long. Another distinctive feature shared by each of the petitions, but not by others of similar date, is a hole in the top margin. These holes may distinguished from file holes because they occur as well as obvious file holes, are smaller than the file holes, and whereas the file holes are off-centre, some quarter way down the document, they occur near the top edge, often above, through, or under, the address line, in a central position.[106]

These documents therefore appear to have had a common model, and it was not the model of the private petition to parliament. It is notable that they physically resemble appeals more closely than private petitions. For example, an appeal to the king made by Robert Ryder in 1424 has similar properties to the petitions of the guilds. Ryder's appeal measures 24 cm wide × 45 cm long, has a displayed heading 'Appellum Roberti Ryder', and a hole in the middle just below the heading.[107] These similarities suggest that the guilds' documents may have been modelled on appeals. It is possible that they were produced for display. The presence of a small hole in the centre of the top margin of each petition might be evidence that they were in fact displayed. The fact that none of the holes in the top margins of the documents (with one possible exception) has been ripped, suggests that, if they were displayed, they were taken down carefully for use in a subsequent process.[108] Where might such publication, if it occurred, have taken place? We can only speculate. One possibility is that the completed petitions were posted in the guilds' own halls, before being forwarded to parliament. Another possibility is that they were displayed together in the Guildhall, possibly as part of the process of co-ordinating clamour. A further possibility is that they were posted up in Westminster Hall to provide visual evidence of clamour. This would have served the Appellants' purposes, and provided a basis for summoning the guildsmen to have their complaints heard.

While we can only speculate about the precise means by which these petitions were transmitted, received, and processed, and how this related to the Appellants' strategies and the parliamentary process, we can say a little more about the resources and infrastructure that enabled the production of clamour. The Mercers' petition is particularly suggestive. Although clearly related to the other petitions, the Mercers' petition is distinguished from the others in several ways. Whilst the others are written in the language and hands of the law—in Anglo-Norman, and in chancery hands—the Mercers' petition is written in English, in a large anglicana hand, and contains material that is expressly related to its vernacular medium.

---

[106] See Plates 1–3.

[107] TNA (PRO), KB 9/203/12. The text of the header reappears as a footer. Cf. the appeal of John Wodecok (m. 5).

[108] The Saddlers' petition has a near-vertical rip from the centre top edge to just below the address line; however there is a second hole just below the address line a little to the right.

Plate 1. TNA (PRO), SC 8/20/997. The Mercers' Petition against Nicholas Brembre. Reproduced by kind permission of the Keeper of the National Archives.

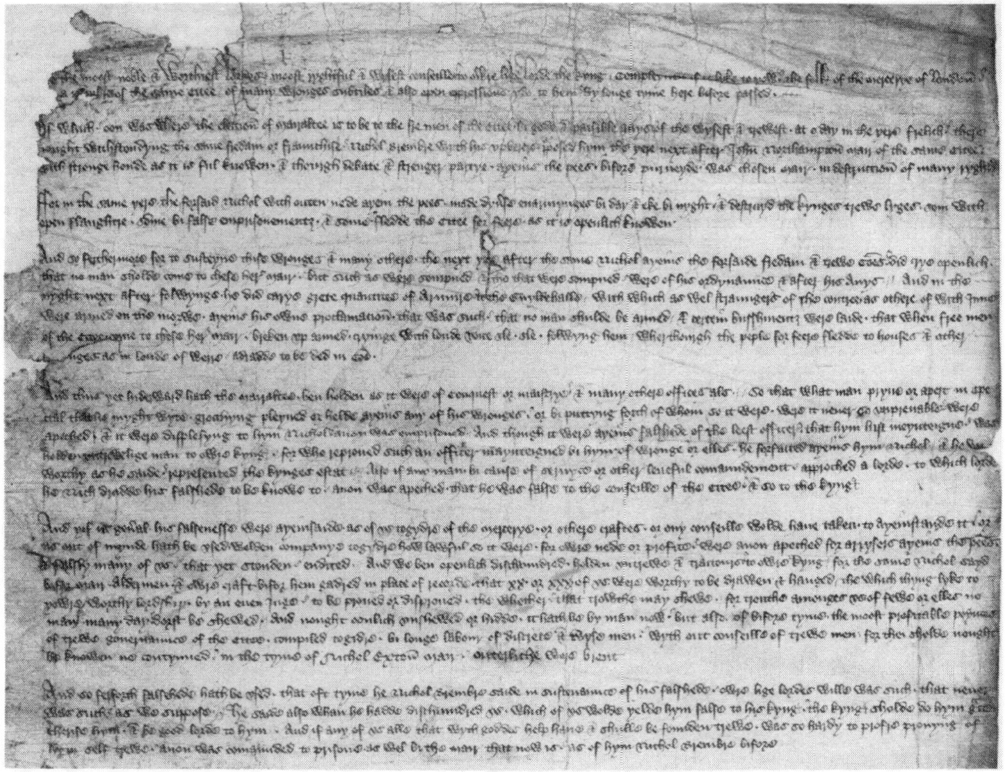

Plate 2. TNA (PRO), SC 8/20/997. (Detail). The Mercers' Petition against Nicholas Brembre. Reproduced by kind permission of the Keeper of the National Archives.

Plate 3. TNA (PRO), SC 8/20/1004. The Painters' Petition against Nicholas Brembre. Reproduced by kind permission of the Keeper of the National Archives.

The Mercers assert that Brembre has impeded complaint to the king by means of issuing threatening and intimidating proclamations in the king's name. Brembre's proclamations were, of course, issued in English, claiming royal authority 'on the kynges bihalf'.[109] The Mercers complain that invoking royal authority 'famulerlich' amounts to an accroachment of the king's power:

Also we haue be comaunded oft tyme vp owre ligeaunce to vnnedeful & vnleueful dyuerse doynges. And also to withdrawe vs, bi the same comaundement, fro thynges nedeful & lefful, as was shewed whan a companye of gode women, there men dorst nought, trauailleden barfote to owre lige lorde to seche grace of hym for trewe men as they supposed, for thanne were such proclamacions made, that no man ne woman sholde approche owre lige lorde for sechyng of grace … And lordes, by yowre leue, owre lyge lordes comaundement to symple & vnkonnyng men is a gret thyng to ben vsed so famulerlich … '[110]

By being written in the vernacular, the Mercers' petition makes self-conscious use of language that could be associated with the plaints of a barefoot 'companye of gode women' or 'symple & vnkonnyng men'. The petition also foregrounds its vernacularity in the way in which it names the defendant and sums up its claims against him:

For thy, graciouse lordes, lyke it to yow to take hede in what manere & where owre lige lordes power hath ben mysused by the forsaid Nichol and his vpberers, for sithen thise wronges bifore saide han ben vsed as accidental or comune braunches outward, it sheweth wel the rote of hem is a ragged subiect or stok inward, that is the forsaid Brere or brembre …[111]

The wrongs rehearsed in the petition manifest a ragged root at their source, this 'briar' or 'Brembre'; the wrongful deeds are 'accidents' of a 'ragged subject'. This play on the name of the accused was available only in English. In Middle English, *brember* is an unusual variant of *brem(b)el* (the bramble or briar), the alternative to *brer/breir* (the briar rose, or the bramble). The petition was not the first to make an unflattering pun on Middle English *brem(b)el*. In Knighton's text of the articles of appeal, Brembre is cited as 'Nichol Brembul(le), faux chiualer de Londres'. This echoes the usage in a letter sent by the Appellants to the citizens of London late in the previous year, where he is 'Nicholl Brambulle, fauce chyualere de Loundrez'.[112] Arguably, the choice of the more usual variant is pointed. The philosophical vocabulary of *accident* and *subject* used in the petition had just come into English in connection with debate over Wycliffite views of the eucharist.[113] The petition uses this language to make an erudite point about what is likely therefore to have been a notorious pun on Brembre's name—or at

---

[109] See Chambers and Daunt (eds.), *Book of London English*, 31–2.
[110] Ibid., 36.   [111] Ibid.
[112] Martin (ed. and trans.), *Knighton's Chronicle*, 480, 410. Knighton evidently drew on pro-Appellant materials (see Martin (ed. and trans.), *Knighton's Chronicle*, p. xlvii).
[113] Hudson, *The Premature Reformation*, 281–90.

least one promoted by the Appellants: this name *Brembre* is the 'accident' of a 'faux chiualer', a treasonous ('ragged') 'subject'. Little wonder, in the light of this notoriety for the name *Brere* or *Brember*, that Chaucer's Prioress preferred the French word for the briar (albeit the French of Stratford atte Bowe), and styled herself Madame Eglentyne.

We can relate the Mercers' petition rather closely to other developments in vernacular literary production. Thanks to the researches of Linne Mooney, we now know that the scribe of the petition was probably Adam Pinkhurst, scribe for the Mercers, and copyist of some of the most important early manuscripts of vernacular poets, including Chaucer, Gower, and Langland.[114] The Mercers, then, even as they drew on their own scribal resources to express their complaint, also drew on the developing language and infrastructure used for vernacular literature. But the really crucial significance of this text for the history of relations between literature and complaint is that someone saw its potential to become complaint of legal standing, to provide evidence of *clamour*. The Mercers themselves addressed their complaint to the lords in council. They were most probably addressing the Appellant lords—who had asked to hear their complaints.[115] This text seems to have been the basis for the French petitions, somehow becoming part of a bundle of petitions with them. It is not quite accurate to say that it was the first vernacular petition presented to parliament. It was not addressed to parliament, and it was never entered on the parliament roll. But the probability that it was the basis for the French petitions addressed to the king and council in parliament, and the fact that it was bundled with them, suggests that the Mercers' petition was recognized as having parallel force to the French petitions addressed to parliament. There was one thing that linked them all: they all counted as clamour.

Alexander Neville was another appellee in connection with whom there is evidence of attempts to manipulate clamour. This evidence is extremely valuable because it includes a Middle English *libellus famosus* directed against Neville. For evidence of such texts in this period, we normally have to rely on second-hand reports in chronicles or legal documents. The Neville libel text is a rare survival. The text is addressed to the commons of England. It asks the commons why they blame the king and his council for evils in the realm, when there was never 'a more rightfull, worthier, a more gentil Kyng'. However, there is *another* king in the kingdom, one 'Alisaundre Nero'. God, the lords, and the commons know well that there was never such a tyrant among the clergy or the commons. He oppresses the country more, causes more extortion, destruction, and discomfort, than the king and all the lords of England—the commons know it well. He extorts goods as a condition of proving wills, he extorts money from rich clergy

---

[114] Mooney, *Late Medieval English Scribes*, and 'Chaucer's Scribe', and for an analysis of the hand, see 123–5. For further discussion, see Ch. 5.
[115] As suggested by Nightingale, *A Medieval Mercantile Community*, 312.

Plate 4. TNA (PRO), C 49/9/22. Libel against Alexander Neville. Reproduced by kind permission of the Keeper of the National Archives.

and deprives them of their benefices—God and the commons know it well. He is a robber, a thief, and a traitor to God and the king. He appears saintly to the king, but the fairer he speaks the falser he is. If 'King Alisaundre' were examined for what he has falsely taken from the king's goods by extortion, maintenance, and tyranny, it would amount to £ 60,000. Only a southern man dare say this; no northern man in King Alisaundre's lordship dare do so; alas that no-one dare tell the king. The author calls God, the World, and the Devil to be his witnesses. Apparently there was formerly a label attached to the parchment (now lost, however there are slits in the document where something could have been attached) which advised the commons to beware 'Alisaundre Nero, Rex in Eboraco'. The Neville libel survives as part of the C 49 classification of documents in the National Archives (Public Record Office).[116] This category comprises documents related to the proceedings of council and parliament, including original texts submitted, as well as copies of texts. The bill is written in a secretary hand and conforms in terms of size and shape with chancery documents.[117] But the probability that it once had a satirical label appended indicates that this document is likely to be an original libel and not a copy made by a chancery clerk.

The libel could, therefore, be viewed as an attempt to stimulate complaint and proof of notoriety. We might associate the production of this libel with the Appellants' attempts to gather evidence for their case. Although the text is not dated, there are sound reasons for associating it with the events of 1387–8. Despite being embroiled in political battles in his archdiocese, Neville only came to prominence on the national political stage as a close ally of the king in August 1385.[118] The libel must post-date that time, because it refers to the king's expedition to Scotland in that year.[119] We know that libels were posted against Neville during the course of a parliament. The evidence for this is a petition addressed to the king and council in parliament:

… per ascunes des enemys de dieu nostre dit seigneur le Roi et le dit Archeuesque … en cest present parlement en la mesone du chapitre de Westminstre ou lasemble est des seignurs et comunes du Reaume pur les busoignes du Roi et de Reaume faucement et maliciousement firent fair trois billes—dont deux billes feurent fichez sur le pylar du dit mesone et la tierce sur le huyse de lesglise seint Paule de Londres—queux sont adioyntez et annexez a ycest bille en apert desclaundre si bien du Roi son conseils et autres seigneurs du Reaume come du dit Archeuesque come apiert per les ditz billes quel desclaundre est plus horribles et heynouse quonques ne fu vewe sur ascune seigneur fait en ascune parlement.[120]

---

[116] TNA (PRO), C 49/9/22; ed. Illingworth, 'Copy of a Libel against Archbishop Neville', 82–3.

[117] See Plate 4. The document measures 12.5 cm high × 32 cm wide, with writing on one side only. It has been folded and filed.

[118] Dobson, 'Neville, Alexander (c.1332–1392)'; Davies, 'Alexander Neville', 97.

[119] For the expedition and its implications for the dating of the libel, see Aston, *Thomas Arundel*, 279 n. 2.

[120] TNA (PRO), SC 8/262/13079.

[… by some enemies of God, our lord king, and the said archbishop … in this parliament in the chapter house at Westminster where the assembly is of lords and commons of the realm to discharge the business of king and realm, three bills were falsely and maliciously made—two of which were fastened on the pillar of the said hall and the third on the door of St Paul's church—which are joined and annexed to this bill, in open slander as much of the king, his council, and other lords as of the said archbishop, as appears by the said bills, which slander is more horrible and heinous than ever was seen made against any lord in any parliament.]

The petition is undated, but one reason for associating it with the Appellants' crisis, rather than earlier, is that it was submitted not by Neville himself but by others on his behalf. This would be consistent with the period after November 1387, when Neville fled. No bills are now annexed to this document (nor is there any sign that any ever were; probably the document is a copy.) However, the statement that the three bills were submitted in evidence might explain how our libel could have found its way into the archives of council and parliament.

The libel draws on the language of complaint against Neville that was aired in formal contexts. Some of the claims made in the libel parallel those made against Neville in the articles of appeal. The claim in the libel that he is 'king' in the north parallels the key allegation in the appeal that Neville and the other appellees are guilty of 'accrochantz a eux roial poair' ('accroaching to themselves royal power'), in other words, that their crimes amount to treason.[121] Articles 6 and 13 allege that the appellees have taken bribes in return for giving their support in lawsuits, paralleling the claim in the libel that Neville is guilty of maintenance.[122] The claim that the king has been deluded by the appellees is also found in both texts; Neville 'maketh to his Kyng as he wer a saynt' by means of fair speech; the articles claim that the appellees 'luy firent entendre com pur verite tantz de faux choses … qe entierement eux luy firent de tout a eux doner son amour et ferme foy et credence …' ('caused him to apprehend as truth so many false things … that they entirely engrossed in all things his love and firm faith and belief').[123]

The Neville libel also seems to pick up on the language and topics of commons' complaint at this time, and more broadly those of popular complaint. It is possible that it was targeted at mobilizing and redirecting this discourse in particular. The characteristics distinguishing commons' complaint and more popular complaint at this time are suggested by a petition that survives only in Knighton and has been largely overlooked by historians. The petition is from the commons to the king and lords in parliament and seems to have been composed when parliament had been in session for some time.[124] It warns that there could be popular

---

121 Hector and Harvey (eds. and trans.), *The Westminster Chronicle*, 240–1.
122 Ibid., 244–5, 248–9.   123 Ibid., 240–1.
124 Martin (ed. and trans.), *Knighton's Chronicle*, 442–51; for date and provenance, see p. lxxi, and 442 n. 2. One of the few discussions of this text is Maddicott, 'Law and Lordship', 67–8.

uprisings on account of continued abuses such as corruption of royal officials and the judicial process, especially in view of the fact that the king and lords have been so long in parliament ('pur long tariance'), that the commons' patience is being sorely tried.[125] It claims that the poor are oppressed by royal officials, 'et nomement par. iij. oue par. iiij. en chescune conte appellez seconde royez' ('and especially by the three or four within each county who are known as Second Kings'), and asks the king to uphold justice and withstand the extortions of 'touz ceux qe sont appellez secondes royes' ('all those who are called Second Kings').[126] This provides evidence that the 'other king' accusation directed against Neville in the libel was popular and widespread, and that this popular complaint was pointedly taken up by the commons in their complaint against the king and lords for allowing oppressions to continue. It provides evidence that the libeller was not only 'replying' (satirically) to commons' complaint against the lords but was also attempting to appropriate and redirect the language of popular complaint. We do not know the chronology of the libel and the petition. If the petition was written after the appellees were convicted, none the less it still provides evidence of the popular discourse upon which both documents draw. If the commons' petition was indeed written much earlier in the decade, and only 'recycled' at this point, as Valente suggests, then it is possible that the libeller was aware of this very text.[127]

The Neville libel could also be seen as an attempt to demonstrate that Neville's crimes are notorious, and to explain the absence of clamour. The allusion to 'other' or 'second' kings suggests his notoriety. Furthermore, a recurrent assertion in the document is that Neville's crimes are well known:

… for godde wote, & *þe lordes witen wel*, & *þe comines wyten wel*, þat þer nas never siche a tirraunt in holy chirche, no among þe comines of þis cuntree …

… & *þat ᵹe wyten wel*; bot þe Kyng not þerof a worde …

… *godde & ᵹe & þe world wot it wel*, þat he shuld be a prelat of holy chirche, he is a predo, a þef, a Traytour, bothe to godde & to his Kyng …

… but *al þe world wot it wel*, þe fayrer he speketh þe falsser he is.

In these ways, the document asserts that Neville's crimes are notorious. As we have seen, notoriety was the foundation of the Appellants' case against him. The libel questions and laments the absence of complaint against Neville, asking why there is complaint against the king and his council but not against Neville, who is more richly deserving. It offers to explain the absence of complaint as a function of his power over those whom he oppresses in his northern kingdom. Some of

---

[125] Martin (ed. and trans.), *Knighton's Chronicle*, 446–7.

[126] Ibid., 444–5, 448–9. Martin notes that the expression also occurs in the *Anonimalle Chronicle*, where it is applied to an Essex tax commissioner (444, n. 1).

[127] Valente, *The Theory and Practice of Revolt in Medieval England*, 169, n. 30, 185, n. 67.

the other claims chime with the grievances of the northern clergy with whom Neville had come into conflict. The vicars and clergy of Beverley petitioned parliament in 1388 claiming that Neville had deprived them of their benefices and had used liveried men to resist royal ambassadors whose mission was to secure their re-instatement.[128] Such may be the 'nothern' men whom the libel claims would not have dared to allege treason against Neville, but who would have had reason, like the Appellants, to welcome complaints from others that would prove Neville's notoriety.

Complaints about the corruption of justice and the extortion and tyranny of royal ministers, and about the dangers of complaining were almost as old as the written plaint itself. The claims in the guilds' petitions and the Neville libel echo the early satirical poems that first addressed the perils of criminal complaint. The recognition that informal, even vernacular, acts and discourses of complaint might have legal force built on the recognition of peasant plaint and other extra-legal modes of plaint. But the formalization of the notion of clamour as a flexible category of plaints that required a hearing, and the composition of vernacular texts for the purposes of complaint, were also to have far-reaching implications in the future.

---

[128] Aston, *Thomas Arundel*, 290–1, citing *RP*, iii. 182–3. Aston points out that the petition is wrongly dated in the parliament rolls and that its date can be established by reference to the patent roll entry.

3

The Literature of Clamour

THE BEGINNINGS OF CLAMOUR LITERATURE

The taxe hath tened vs alle,
Probat hoc mors tot validorum; [the death of so many healthy
people proves it]
The Kyng þerof had small,
ffuit in manibus cupidorum. [it was in the hands of the greedy]
…
laddes lowde they lowght,
Clamantes voce sonora, [crying out in a loud voice]
The bischop wan þey slowght

'The Course of the Revolt'[1]

Et adonqes le dit Wat rehersa les poyntes queux furount a demander, et
demanda qe nulle lay deveroit estre fors la lay de Wynchestre, et qe nulle
ughtelarie serroit en nulle processe de laye fait de ore en avaunt, et qe nulle
seignur ne averoit seignurie … fors … la roy; et qe les biens de seint esglise
ne deveroient estre en mayns des gentz de religione … et qe nulle nayf serroit
en Engleterre, nulle servage ne nayfte …

Anonimalle Chronicle[2]

[And then the said Wat [Tyler] rehearsed the points which were to be
demanded, and he requested that there should be no law except the law
of Winchester, and that there should be no outlawry in any process of law
from now on, and that no lord should have any lordship … but … the king
and that the goods of Holy Church should not be in the hands of the
religious … and he demanded that there should be no bondman in England,
no servitude or villeinage …]

We have many representations of peasant plaint and petition from the materials
of the 1381 rising. In some ways the rebels' complaint is traditional—it is

---

[1] Robbins (ed.), *Historical Poems*, no. 19, pp. 55–7, ll. 1–4, 17–19.
[2] Galbraith (ed.), *Anonimalle Chronicle*, 147.

the discourse of peasant plaint, and clamour. 'The Course of the Revolt' appropriates and twists traditional peasant plaint. Recalling the techniques of *Song of the Husbandman*, or *Satire on the Retinues of the Great*, this macaronic lyric appropriates the peasant plaint of the rebels. The tax has indeed harmed 'vs alle'—and the slaughter of Archbishop Sudbury (chancellor and, hence, perpetrator of the tax) by clamorous rebels is just one example of the harm that the tax has brought. The rebels' acts of violence are well known. What has not been recognized is that the rebels also expressed their complaints in written form. We have been asked recently to recognize the six odd little vernacular texts associated with John Ball as 'acts of assertive literacy'.[3] If we concentrate on these sources as evidence for the rebels' literary achievements, we neglect a good deal of evidence for the quantity and nature of the rebels' textual output. The *Anonimalle Chronicle* passage quoted above is just one of several sources from which we can infer a rather different form of expression of rebel plaint—different both from the acts of violence, and the odd-Ball texts. In the passage quoted, Wat Tyler presents a list of demands to the king. This is one of several pieces of evidence, I suggest, that the rebels had a list of grievances and demands for redress. In other words, it suggests that they articulated their oppression in the judicial form of the petition or plaint that listed grievances and requested remedy. Nicholas Brooks compares Tyler's demands with those reported in indictments of the rebels in Essex, noting 'these demands would seem to have been at the root of the revolt almost from its start.'[4] From this coincidence of demands, we may infer that their list of grievances was publicized widely. The *Anonimalle Chronicle* also tells us that when the king would not come to hear the demands of the rebels, they sent him a petition calling for the execution of the Duke of Lancaster and fifteen named ministers.[5] Given that this petition involved a list of sixteen names, and that naming malefactors and calling for their execution reflects the basic form of the written plaint or appeal, it seems highly probable that the rebels' petition was written. How were this petition and the lists of grievances and remedies composed and disseminated? We know that the rebels proclaimed the rising in order to rally support.[6] Presumably they were imitating the methods used by the crown to publicize legislation and other matters, sending out documents whose contents were to be proclaimed in English. According to the *Anonimalle Chonicle*, the rebels rallied support by sending letters to Kent, Norfolk, and Suffolk.[7] Possibly the letters

[3] Justice, *Writing and Rebellion*, 24 *et passim*.
[4] Brooks, 'The Organisation and Achievements of the Peasants of Kent and Essex in 1381', 252.
[5] Galbraith (ed.), *Anonimalle Chronicle*, 139.
[6] Brooks, 'The Organisation and Achievements of the Peasants of Kent and Essex in 1381', 255–6.
[7] Galbraith (ed.), *Anonimalle Chronicle*, 135.

communicated the lists of grievances for proclamation. After the revolt, some lawyers claimed they had been coerced into supporting the rebels.[8] Whether or not they really did come to the support of the rebels under coercion, such persons could have easily provided the skills and expertise needed to write petitions.

In another episode in the *Anonimalle Chronicle*, the king offers the rebels the opportunity to submit their grievances to him and the council in writing, and the rebels respond by ordering the murder of lawyers and officials of chancery and the exchequer:

... et toutz crierent a une voice qils ne vodroient aler avaunt qils avoient les traitours deinz la Toure et chartres destre free de toutz maners de servage et des autres maners des poyntes qils vodroient demander; et le roy les graunta bonement et fist une clerk escriver une bille en lour presence en ceste maner: Le roy Richarde Dengleterre et de Fraunce enmercy moult ses bones comunes de ceo qils ount si graunde desir pur luy vere et tener lour roy, et pardone a eux toutz maners des trespas et mespressiones et felonye faitz avaunt ces houres; et voet et comande desore en avaunt qe chescune soy hast a soun propre hostelle et voet et comande qe chescune ses grevances en escript et les facent envoier a luy et il ordenera par lavyse de ses loials seignurs et de soun bone counseil tiel remedy qe profit serra a luy et as eux *et al* roialme ... [the bill is read aloud so everyone can hear] ... Et quaunt les comunes avoient oie la bille, ils dissoient qil ne fuist forsqe troefles et mokerie; et purceo retournerount a Loundres et fesoient crier parmy la citee qe toutz les gentz de la ley et toutz ceuz de la chauncellerie et del eschequer et toutz qe savoient brief ou lettre escriver, deveroit estre decolles ... [9]

[... and they all cried in unison that they would not go away before they had the traitors from the Tower, and the charters granting freedom from all kinds of servitude and the other points that they wanted to demand; and the king granted these things and had a clerk write a bill in their presence on these lines: 'The king of England and France thanks the good commons that they have such a great desire to see and acknowledge him, and pardons them all trespasses, misprisions, and felonies committed before this time, and wills and commands that everyone hastens home and wills and commands that everyone sends him their grievances in written form, and he will ordain with the advice of his loyal lords and good council such remedy as will profit himself, themselves, and the realm.' ... [the bill is read aloud so everyone can hear] ... And when the commons had heard the bill they said it was nothing but trifles and mockery, and because of this they returned to London and had it proclaimed through the city that all men of law, and all those of chancery or the exchequer who knew how to write a writ or a letter must be beheaded ...]

In other words, Richard invited the submission of plaints against royal officials, in the time-honoured tradition that we have traced from the reign of Edward I. Richard's offer is compelling evidence that the rebels were seen to have grievances

---

[8] Galbraith (ed.), *Anonimalle Chronicle*, 138.   [9] Ibid., 143–4.

that they could get expressed for them in writing. This is added support for the argument that the rebels had formally articulated grievances. Secondly, it shows that the rebels rejected the judicial complaint process. Offered the opportunity to have plaints submitted to king and council, they preferred to prevent any such process by murdering the writers of petitions.[10] Wat Tyler also, we might note, explicitly bypassed the petitionary process (though rather less dramatically). He presented the rebels' grievances in the form of a petition—as a list of grievances and demands—but he bypassed the proper process, presenting these demands directly to the king. That this was seen to represent a disregard of proper process is clear from the response of the lords and commons in the next parliament. They agreed to the repeal of the concessions granted, commenting that they were invalid because given under coercion, and also because assent to the demand for manumission could not be given without the agreement of parliament. Thus the peasants' plaint against servitude failed to get a judicial hearing.[11]

The rebels' petitionary gestures—and their opponents' responses to them— reflect contemporary refinements and developments in the forms and processes of plaint. Late in the reign of Edward III, and in the reign of Richard II, a series of important changes to petitionary practice occurred. At this time, for the first time, petitions appear that indicate that they are presented in the context of parliament. In a related new development, petitions are addressed to the commons in parliament. And two developments concern the language of address. At least from the reign of Richard—there are signs of the change earlier—a new mode of address to the monarch emerges. The rebels seem to have positioned themselves in relation to this tradition. They chose to refer to themselves as 'the trew communes', referring to themselves in the manner of the

---

[10] Justice, *Writing and Rebellion*, 50–64, sees the episode as illustrating the rebels' understanding of, and contempt for, the judicial process, their cynical rejection of petition or bill against royal ministers contrasting with their nostalgia for plaint, from the rebels' point of view, an 'ancient legal privilege' rendered 'meaningless' by 'the recent evisceration of royal justice' (63). Justice does not recognize that process by bill, plaint, and petition are all essentially the same thing. As we saw in Chs. 1 and 2, plaint procedure underlay all of these judicial processes, and plaint was seen from very early in its history as subject to corruption.

[11] 'Estoit autrefoitz effectuelment demandez de toutz esteantz illoeqes en plein parlement … si celle repelle lour pleust … A quoy … respondirent a une voice qe celle repelle fuist bien faite, adjoustant qe tiele manumission ou franchise des neifs ne ne poast estre fait sanz lour assent q'ont le greindre interesse … Enpriantz humblement a nostre seignour le roi, sibien c'estassavoir les prelatz et seignours come les dites communes, qe celles manumissions et franchises issint faitz et grantez par cohercioun … feussent annientz et adnullez par auctoritee de ce parlement, et le dit repelle affermez, come celle qe bien et joustement estoit fait …' ['Those present in full parliament were then directly asked once again … whether that repeal would please them … To which [the lords and commons] answered with one voice, that the repeal was well made, adding that such a manumission or enfranchisement of the villeins could not be made without the assent of those who had the chief interest in the matter … And the prelates and lords and the said commons humbly prayed our lord the king that as those letters of manumission and enfranchisement had been made and granted by coercion … they might be quashed and annulled by authority of this parliament, and the said repeal confirmed, because it had been well and justly done … '] (*PROME*, parliament of Richard II, 1381 November, items 12–13; my translation.)

commons in parliament, and pointedly distinguishing themselves from this, or any other group, claiming to represent the commons.[12]

The rebel literature of complaint whose existence we have inferred from the chronicle and other sources may have been the first body of clamour texts to be drawn up and circulated widely, the first full-scale literary production to have been informed by, and to reject, the forms and processes of judicial complaint. The 1381 rising is the first occasion when we can detect the potential of clamour being exploited in the production of writings that claimed legitimacy and aimed for wide, extra-judicial, distribution. Of course, the texts of the petitions drawn up by the rebels do not survive. But from the last two decades of the fourteenth century to the mid-sixteenth century (and beyond) complaint texts survive that are framed as petitions that invoke—and reject—the forms and processes of plaint, developing the model of the 1381 rebels. This clamour literature displays awareness of, and appropriates and adapts, developing petitionary practices. As petitions for far-reaching political reforms, in their day they provoked extremely hostile reactions. Some are well known to modern scholars under editorial titles, such as the *Twelve Conclusions of the Lollards*, the *Lollard Disendowment Bill*, and Jack Cade's *Bills of Complaint*. These and some of the other better-known texts have attracted some discussion individually. There has, however, been little analysis of any of these texts in relation to contemporary petitionary practices and procedures, or consideration of whether they belong, and contribute to, a tradition. In this chapter I propose to explore these texts in relation to the new petitionary practices, and to one another, tracing the creation of what I propose to call the literature of clamour from the earliest surviving texts to the flood of textual activity associated with the Cade rebellion in the 1450s.

LOLLARD PETITIONS AND LIBELS

Among the earliest surviving contributions to the literature of clamour are several lollard texts. The text known to modern scholars as the *Twelve Conclusions of the Lollards* is framed as a parliamentary petition. It participates in the diplomatic of the parliamentary petition as it had developed by the end of the fourteenth century, cleverly appropriating and adapting the form. For example, it is addressed 'to þe lordis and þe comunys of þe parlement'.[13] It was only in the 1370s that petitions came to identify themselves explicitly as submitted in the specific context of parliament. Before this, petitions almost never state the context for their submission. From the 1370s new modes of address developed which specify

---

[12] Galbraith (ed.), *The Anonimalle Chronicle*, 139. Watts reads the epithet rather differently, as implying that the rebels saw themselves as 'part of the ruling community of the realm' (Watts, 'The Pressure of the Public', 160).

[13] Hudson (ed.), *Selections*, 24–9.

not merely the addressees but the context of address. The new *Parliament Rolls of Medieval England* edition states that many petitions use address formulas such as 'to the king and council in parliament', or 'to the lords in parliament'.[14] The French petitions against Nicholas Brembre that we looked at in Chapter 2 illustrate this mode of address. For example, the petition of the Painters is addressed 'A tresexcellent et trespuissant seignur nostre tresredoute seignur le Roy et as tresnobles et sages seignurs diceste present parlement'.[15] Likewise, the address in the *Twelve Conclusions* explicitly specifies that the context of address is parliament.

The address formula in the *Twelve Conclusions* reflects too another characteristic of petitions from late in the reign of Edward III onwards. At this period petitions began to be addressed to the commons as well as the lords. As we saw in Chapter 1, from mid-century there were two routes for a private petition to reach the council. By one process, a private petition was presented for examination by 'triers' and 'auditors', who might then send the petition to the council. But later, from about 1327, an alternative route was possible if the petitioner could achieve sponsorship of his petition by the commons. His petition might then be incorporated in a commons' petition which would be submitted to the clerk of parliament for presentation to council. The address formula was gradually modified to reflect the new procedures, with the development of a twin address to lords and commons, for example.[16] The earliest example of a petition addressed to the commons alone dates from 1378. Some petitions in this group explicitly ask the commons to mediate, for example the petition of 1389 addressed to the commons on behalf of Thomas Russhok, former bishop of Chichester.[17] The device of addressing a petition to lords and commons is first exemplified by a petition of 1378, which is addressed 'A nostre seigneur le Roy et as seigneurs et communs du parlement'.[18] The form of address in the *Twelve Conclusions* is, therefore, a particular way of requesting sponsorship by the commons and their mediation with the lords in parliament.

The petitioners are identified as 'pore men, tresoreris of Cryst and his apostlis'. Many petitions were submitted to parliament in the name of a particular social grouping, often one described as a *communitas*. Such groupings could be very varied—examples include Jews, clergy of the province of Canterbury, and the seven hundreds of Windsor.[19] The description of the petitioners as 'pore men' is typical of the ways in which petitioners styled themselves as the rhetoric of petitions grew more elaborate from the reign of Richard II. Just as the lollard petitioners style themselves 'pore', so, for example, a petition was submitted at the 1305 parliament by 'pauperes homines terre', *c.*1370 some petitioners from

---

[14] *PROME*, 'General Introduction'.   [15] TNA (PRO), SC 8/20/1004.

[16] Sayles, *Medieval Parliament*, 48–53; Myers, 'Parliamentary Petitions', 398–9.

[17] Rayner, ' "Commune Petition" ', 214.   [18] Myers, 'Parliamentary Petitions', 399.

[19] Sayles, *Medieval Parliament*, 45.

Shropshire styled themselves the king's 'pore liege men', those petitioning on behalf of Thomas Russhok in 1389 styled themselves 'les povre amys de Thomas Russhok', and in 1421 some soldiers of Calais called themselves 'the pore liege men and Soudeours in the Tovn of Caleys'.[20] The terms chosen for recipient and petitioner dramatized the gulf of power between addressee and petitioner. A variety of terms was available. The addressee could be described by terms such as 'noble', 'haut, 'puissant', and the petitioner by such terms as 'humble', 'pover', and 'obeisant'.[21] By choosing the epithet 'pore' from this range, the lollards aligned petitionary diplomatic with their own ideology.

The petition from the poor friends of Thomas Russhok, like the lollard petition, claims to speak on behalf of others. While this petition is in favour of an individual, the lollard text, requesting reform of oppressions that afflict 'puple her in Yngelonde', is like many that ask for remedy on behalf of the realm, as do two of the earliest examples: a petition of 1321 from 'the knights, citizens and burgesses on behalf of the shires, cities and boroughs of the realm'; and one of 1325 for 'the whole community of the whole realm'.[22] The 1305 petition of the 'povre homines terre' may, it has been suggested, represent 'the views of the people at large', but often this device was a rhetorical gesture designed to further the interests of particular groups or individuals.[23] In some cases, those petitioning were identified as having the power of attorneys or procurators, agents legally empowered to act on behalf of others. The lollard petitioners invoke this practice when they claim to be representing God in a suit which seeks that those with cure of souls should not hold temporal office:

… we, procuratouris of God in þis cause, pursue to þis parlement þat alle manere of curatis boþe heye and lowe ben fulli excusid of temperel office, and occupie hem with here cure and nout ellis.[24]

The *procurator* was a representative in an ecclesiastical court, but the term is also found in the context of parliamentary actions, for example, the Roll of Parliament for 1290 records that the 'poor men of Norfolk' have petitioned 'per procuratores juratores'.[25] By calling themselves 'procuratouris', the lollards present a claim to authority; just as the law recognizes the authority of an attorney to act on his client's behalf, so the lollard petitioners are, they claim, empowered

---

[20] Haskins, 'Three Early Petitions', 315; Maddicott, 'County Community', 36; Rayner, '"Commune Petition"', 214; Fisher, Richardson, and Fisher (eds.), *An Anthology of Chancery English*, 208.

[21] Myers, 'Parliamentary Petitions', 387.   [22] Sayles, *Medieval Parliament*, 47–8.

[23] Haskins, 'Petitions of Representatives', 17.

[24] Hudson (ed.), *Selections*, 26; for ecclesiastical usage, see Latham (ed.), *Revised Medieval Latin Word-list*.

[25] Haskins, 'Petitions of Representatives', 15; and see Post, *Studies in Medieval Legal Thought*, 91–108.

to represent God. The conceit is developed in the closing section of the text, which summarizes their position:

Þis is oure ambaciat, þat Cryst has comaundid us for to pursue, at þis time most acceptable for manie causis.[26]

The lollards act on the instruction of Christ, 'pursuing' an 'embassy' on his behalf, at a time appropriate for 'causes', that is, suits. This language repositions the petitioners with regard to their addressees. A *procurator* could act for a litigant or defendant who was suing for justice in a civil case, but the term also referred to an ambassador who was empowered to act in diplomatic embassies between powers. By casting themselves as *procuratores* in a diplomatic scenario, as well as a judicial scenario, they imply that they are delegates rather than simply supplicants.[27]

The lollard text casts some of its conclusions in ways that recall topics regularly broached in parliamentary petitions. The seventh conclusion proposes reform of almshouses as a way of improving the finances of the realm. If fewer almshouses and idle religious were financed, 'þerof schulde falle þe grettest encres possible to temporel part'. Parliament was called to agree subsidies to the king, and the function of the petition was to negotiate what was needful and acceptable. The framework for such discussions was that of parliament as the highest court of justice. Complaints about corruption of justice through the granting of liveries and maintaining of retainers, regularly aired in parliament, are echoed in the language of the second conclusion: bishops give out 'crownis' (tonsures/coins) as signs, the 'leueree of antecryst', instead of 'whyte hartys' (pure hearts/the livery badge given out by Richard II).[28]

The lollards' appropriation of petition diplomatic—and their assumption of an audience that would understand its nuances—was enabled by the spread of knowledge of and access to the petitioning process in the fourteenth century (it was also enabled by the association of lawyers with the movement—see below). Petitioners to parliament comprised a wide range of individuals and groups. Proclamations inviting the submission of petitions were widely publicized, and petitions were drawn up in county communities. Proclamations were also a means by which knowledge of taxation granted and concessions won was transmitted back to petitioners.[29] Petitions also had some degree of transmission in manuscript books. For example, parliamentary petitions from the citizens of London in 1327 on issues of liberties and purveyance occur in London, British Library, MS Cotton

---

[26] Hudson (ed.), *Selections*, 28–9.

[27] For the development of procurations in diplomacy that were modelled on powers of attorney in law, see Chaplais, *English Diplomatic Practice*, 59–63. The word 'comaundid' is also diplomatic terminology; *mandare* signified the act of empowerment to represent whereas *commendere* simply meant to 'recommend' (65). On both points, see also Queller, *The Office of Ambassador*, 26–59.

[28] Hudson (eds.), *Selections*, 26, 25. For parliamentary complaints on livery and maintenance, see Maddicott, 'Law and Lordship', 61; and Saul, 'The Commons and the Abolition of Badges'.

[29] Maddicott, 'Parliament and the Constituencies', 66–9.

Faustina B. i (ff. 206–22).[30] The petition from the commons to the king and lords in parliament, probably composed at the time of the Appellants' crisis, seems to survive only in Knighton's chronicle.[31] In other instances, chroniclers narrate the circumstances even if they do not provide the text of petitions.[32] Manuals of parliamentary process such as the *Modus Tenendi Parliamentum* achieved wide distribution.[33] Imaginative literature provided another source of accounts of parliamentary process, such as the famous description of the commons in *Mum and the Sothsegger*, and the sequence in *Piers Plowman* in which Pees 'puts up a bill' in parliament, only to be bought off.[34] By means such as this, knowledge of the content, process, and diplomatic of parliamentary petitioning would have spread to audiences not immediately connected with political elites. It would have provided the lollards with a form and process to appropriate, and also an audience that would recognize this gesture.

The *Twelve Conclusions* survives in both Latin and English versions. There has been some debate as to which came first, but the balance of the evidence seems to support composition in English followed by translation (possibly by hostile opponents) into Latin.[35] The lollards' opponent Roger Dymmok replied to an English version, using the adverb 'vulgariter' to describe the way the lollards spread the text, both gestures indicating vernacular dissemination, while the lollard authors highlight the vernacular language of the text by referring to a more extended exposition of the matters covered in 'another book ... al in oure langage'.[36] Composing a petition in English was a notable departure from the norm of petitions to parliament at this date. Petitions to parliament followed the conventions and forms of bills in eyre, and like them were usually in French.[37] Petitions were very varied in form at first, but gradually a canon of form developed, becoming more elaborate towards the second half of the fourteenth century.[38] In its language, the *Twelve Conclusions* is not only aligned with new developments in parliamentary petitioning of the later fourteenth century, it is in the vanguard. It is often said, following the lead of Chambers and Daunt, that two English language petitions to parliament pre-date 1400: the petition of the Mercers against Nicholas Brembre of 1388; and a petition of 1344 to Edward III

---

[30] The petitions relate to those in TNA (PRO), Parliament and Council Proceedings, Chancery, roll no. 1; see Richardson and Sayles (eds.), *Rotuli ... Inediti*, 103–4.

[31] Martin (ed. and trans.), *Knighton's Chronicle*, 442–51. Cf. discussion of this text in Ch. 2, 80–1 and n. 124.

[32] For example, the accounts of Wat Tyler's petition (above, 83–6).

[33] See the list of manuscripts of the *Modus* in Pronay and Taylor (eds.), *Parliamentary Texts*, 202–9, and for circulation in late fourteenth-century England and early fifteenth-century Ireland, see Kerby-Fulton and Justice, 'Reformist Intellectual Culture'.

[34] See further below, 103–4.

[35] See discussion and references in Scase, 'The Audience and Framers of the *Twelve Conclusions of the Lollards*', 284–5, 299–300.

[36] Cronin (ed.), *Rogeri Dymmok, Liber*, 24; Hudson (ed.), *Selections*, 29.

[37] Harding, 'Plaints and Bills', 80; Richardson and Sayles (eds.), *Rotuli ... Inediti*, p. ix.

[38] Myers, 'Parliamentary Petitions', 386–7.

from John Drayton and his wife, Margery King.[39] But, as I argued in Chapter 2, this is rather inaccurate with regard to the 1388 petition. The Mercers' petition is pointedly vernacular, but it seems to have been addressed to the Appellant lords and only later bundled with petitions submitted to parliament. The supposed example of 1344 is questionable also, for this petition was, in fact, heard in chancery. Presumably many complainants first expressed their complaints in English, but their advisers cast their complaints in the legal French of the petition. Alternatively, as Fisher has suggested, petitions to parliament may have been written by chancery clerks, an even more highly professionalized body of men.[40] But whether French petitions were written by chancery clerks, or by 'country lawyers' or scriveners, in any case the complainant's English was almost certainly transformed by professionals into petitionary language and form.[41]

The lollard petition does not conform with parliamentary procedure in several other ways. A petition to parliament conventionally began with the address, followed by a verb signalling that the text is a petition, followed by the identification of the petitioner. For example, the commons' petition of 1388 preserved in Knighton's chronicle begins 'A nostre tresdoute seignur le roy, et a touz noz altres seignurs du roialme, monstrent lez humblez comines de uostre dit roialme lez causez et damagez aduenez en displesaunce du Dieu et de seynt esglise … ' ('To oure very redoubtable lord the king, and to all our other lords of the realm, the humble commons of your said realm show the matter and the harm that have come about, to the displeasure of God and Holy Church … '), while a petition of 1414 from Thomas Paunfield of Cambridgeshire begins 'To the worshipful and wyse syres and wyse Communes that to this present parlement ben assembled, Besecheth mekely ʒoure pore Bedeman Thomas Paunfield oon of the fre tenentȝ of oure liege lord the kyng of his maner and touneship of Chestreton in the Shyre of Cambrigg: that ʒe wole considere … '.[42] The lollard text, however, reverses the order, beginning with the identification of the

---

[39] Chambers and Daunt (eds.), *Book of London English*, 272–3.

[40] Fisher, *Emergence of Standard English*, 42, 159, n. 19. Fisher bases this claim on the observation of similarities in style, form, and physical appearance of the Ancient Petitions (class SC 8 in the Public Record Office). This is somewhat called into question by the evidence for the employment of scriveners and lawyers to write petitions. At least by the reign of Richard II, petitioners engaged professionals conversant with Anglo-Norman legal formulas to help them draw up petitions. In some cases they appear to have gone to scriveners; in other cases perhaps they went to provincial lawyers (Myers, 'Parliamentary Petitions', 387–8; Musson and Ormrod, *Evolution*, 147). Fisher's position is implicitly challenged by Haskett's work on petitions to chancery. Haskett, 'Country Lawyers?', 11–18, has used Fisher's evidence to argue that bills in chancery were not written by chancery clerks, as has been suggested, but by 'country' lawyers under the influence of chancery standards. It is also important to note that both Fisher and Haskett use the evidence of English-language documents. They do not provide a methodology for determining the provenance of French petitions.

[41] For further discussion of these matters, see Ch. 5.

[42] Martin (ed. and trans.), *Knighton's Chronicle*, 442; Fisher, Richardson, and Fisher (eds.), *An Anthology of Chancery English*, 198.

petitioner:

We pore men, tresoureris of Cryst and his apostlis, denuncyn to þe lordis and þe comunys of þe parlement certeyn conclusionis and treuthis ... [43]

In place of the usual petitionary verb *moustre*, *se pleyn*, or *besechen*, the lollard text has the uncompromising 'denuncyn', the grievances being listed as 'certeyn con-clusionis and treuthis', rather than simply oppressions suffered.[44] The authors dis-tance themselves from the position of the petitioner who is seeking a remedy in law, instead announcing the justice of the matter and seeking reformation from God.

The lollard appropriation and transformation of the petition to parliament conforms with the lollards' own conflicted relations with secular law. Their adap-tation of petitionary form and procedure betrays knowledge and understanding of judicial process. It is not difficult to see where they could have obtained this knowledge. Maureen Jurkowski has discovered several common lawyers among supporters of the lollards. Thomas Lucas is a prominent example; an Oxford lollard at the end of the fourteenth century, by 1410 Lucas was practising as a lawyer.[45] Yet lollard ideology promoted suspicion of secular law and its practitioners. Wyclif's view of the importance of the secular ruler led him to cite Magna Carta and English law, but lollards also held that the clergy should not hold secular offices or be involved in secular affairs.[46]

The lollard text uses process, as well as language and form, as a way to position itself in relation to parliamentary petitions. From the reign of Edward III private petitions were handed to receivers on certain appointed days, for scrutiny by 'tri-ers'. Commons' petitions were handed in to the clerk of the parliament, usually on different days from those appointed for the receipt of private petitions.[47] As we have seen, petitions were addressed to the commons in order to gain a hearing and sponsorship in parliament. If, having discussed a petition, the commons decided to sponsor it, they might have the original petition redrafted—possibly by the clerk of the commons—to conform with the commons' petition. Alternatively, a group might already have presented a petition with the opening 'prcount les Communes qe ... '. Once approved by the commons, such petitions would have been forwarded to the lords. The petition and response were then entered on the roll of parliament.[48] Addressed to the lords and commons in parliament, and treating oppressions of 'puple her in Yngelonde', the lollard text signals that it

---

[43] Hudson (ed.), *Selections*, 24.

[44] MED *denouncen* (v.) 1 (a): 'To communicate, announce, declare, or state (sth.), esp., officially or publicly; (b) to reveal (the truth); (c) to pronounce (a curse).' 2(a) 'To inform (sb.); (b) to direct or order (sb. to do sth.); (c) to declare or proclaim (sb. cursed, excommunicated, forgiven, removed from office, etc.)'

[45] Jurkowski, 'Lawyers and Lollardy'; for Lucas, see 165.

[46] Hudson, *The Premature Reformation*, 342, 380–1.

[47] Myers, 'Parliamentary Petitions', 396–9.

[48] Ibid., 597–9, 606, 611; for the clerk, see 594. The petitions in the rolls lack the original addresses; once enrolled the original openings were replaced with standard formulas. Some originals which match with enrolled petitions survive in the TNA (PRO), SC 8 (Ancient

is addressed to the commons and therefore would have been subject to the latter procedure.

However, there is no evidence—no revised or enrolled text—to show that the lollard petition was ever forwarded for consideration by the lords. We do know, rather, that the text was presented to the commons in the most provocative and unconventional manner—by being posted up on the doors of Westminster Hall while parliament was in session. The fullest and most explicit source is the narrative in the *Annales Ricardi Secundi*, a St Albans chronicle thought to have been compiled contemporaneously with events.[49] The *Annales* states that the text was fixed up publicly on the doors of Westminster [Hall] and St Paul's:

Lollardi in hoc Parliamento … figentes publice super ostia Sancti Pauli et Westmonasterii abominabiles cleri accusationes, et hactenus inauditas Conclusiones … Conclusiones … quas fixerunt super ostia … [50]

[In this parliament, the lollards … fixing publicly horrendous accusations of the clergy on the doors of St Paul's and Westminster … and previously unheard of conclusions … conclusions … which they fixed on the doors …]

There is some evidence that the *Twelve Conclusions* had one or more precedents. According to Walsingham, John Wyclif, having declaimed his preaching 'in vulgari' to the people, wrote to the lords and magnates assembled in the parliament of May 1382, sending them seven propositions which evidently circulated in a 'sedula', in which form Walsingham had it.[51] A text edited by Arnold in its English version as *A Petition to the King and Parliament*, and by Stein in a Latin version as Wyclif's *Complaint*, which is framed as a petition to King Richard, the Duke of Lancaster, and others 'þat ben gaderid in þe Parlement', sets out four articles for assent.[52] The propositions here are similar but not the same as those attributed to Wyclif by Walsingham. The *Petition* defends the removal of temporalities from erring clerics, and the confiscation of misused tithes, and brands as heretical the preaching of certain friars against these propositions at Coventry. The date of this text is unclear. Margaret Aston dates it 'some time after 1382', because in that year Wycliffite assertions about

Petitions) classification; in *PROME* these are calendared (though unfortunately not edited) in the Appendices to each parliament. The 'Medieval Petitions' project (University of York and The National Archives) is currently surveying all 17,629 documents in the SC 8 classification and should shed much new light on these materials.

[49] See Scase, 'The Audience and Framers of the *Twelve Conclusions of the Lollards*', 291 and references there.

[50] Riley (ed.), *Chronica Monasterii S. Albani, Johannis de Trokelowe*, 174. Cf. 'fixerunt publice super ostia Ecclesiae Sancti Pauli Londoniis, et Westmonasterii, abominabiles cleri accusationes, et hactenus inauditas Conclusiones' ('they fixed up in public on the doors of St Paul's and Westminster, abhorent accusations of the clergy, and previously unheard-of conclusions', Riley (ed.), *Walsingham … Historia Anglicana*, ii. 216).

[51] Riley (ed.), *Walsingham … Historia Anglicana*, ii. 51–2.

[52] Arnold (ed.), *Select English Works of John Wyclif*, iii. 507–23, 508; Stein, 'The Latin Text of Wyclif's *Complaint*'. Somerset, *Clerical Discourse*, 3–9, discusses the problems raised by this text and links it with the *Twelve Conclusions* (9).

disendowment and tithes were declared heretical by the Blackfriars Council. She notes that issues associated with disendowment were given airings in several parliaments—or at times of parliament—from 1385 to 1400, not least in the *Twelve Conclusions* of 1395.[53] The death of John of Gaunt, Duke of Lancaster, on 3 February 1399, gives us the absolute *terminus ad quem* for this text, but an earlier rather than later date seems likely. The authors evidently chose to suggest a parliamentary context for their text because their arguments had special relevance for parliament. They make the point that, if the friars are correct, then the king, and all of his counsellors—lords and prelates—who have removed temporalities have erred, and so have 'alle men of þe Parlement counceilinge þerto'.[54] This could have had resonance for any parliament. But the address to John of Gaunt suggests a period when the duke was interested in disendowment issues—that is, according to Goodman, not after about 1382.[55] The friars and the Wycliffites are known to have made appeals to Gaunt for his support in 1382, appeals which gained some publicity.[56]

Like the *Twelve Conclusions*, the *Petition* both invokes and distances itself from the forms required for a petition to parliament. In specifying a parliamentary context, the *Petition* aligns itself with the forms of the later fourteenth-century petition, and this sense of context is strengthened by the reference to the authority of this institution (which is imperilled by the friars). However, the authoritative rather than supplicatory tone of the text, its scholastic structure and language—it is a series of articles 'proved boþe by auctorite and resoun'—and its failure to identify the senders of the document, distance the text from the parliamentary petition.[57]

Whether or not the *Petition* was presented to parliament, both English and Latin versions achieved some circulation. A second manuscript of the Latin text has recently been discovered by James Carley, and the text was known to John Bale. Survival in English and Latin indicates translation for different audiences—though translation in which direction is not clear. One of the two English copies survives in garbled form, which, Ralph Hanna has suggested, may indicate that the text circulated in a quire meant for copying.[58] Both the *Petition* and the *Twelve Conclusions*, then, are associated with written publication in English in the form of a short, independent, text.

This mode of publication was one already associated with lollards. Some copies of lollard texts survive on single sheets, such as the copy of the Wycliffite poem

[53] Aston, 'Caim's Castles', 108–9.

[54] Arnold (ed.), *Select English Works of John Wyclif*, iii. 514.

[55] Goodman, *John of Gaunt*, 244.   [56] Shirley (ed.), *Fasciculi Zizaniorum*, 292–5, 300.

[57] Arnold (ed.), *Select English Works of John Wyclif*, iii. 508. For analysis of the dictaminal forms in this text and for similarities between it and the letters to Gaunt, see further below, Ch. 5.

[58] Hanna, 'Two Lollard Codices', 56–9; Carley, ' "Cum excuterem puluerem et blattis" ', 185, n. 88. I am grateful to James Carley for drawing to my attention this second manuscript, London, British Library, MS Cotton Vitellius E. xii, ff. 79ʳ–81ʳ.

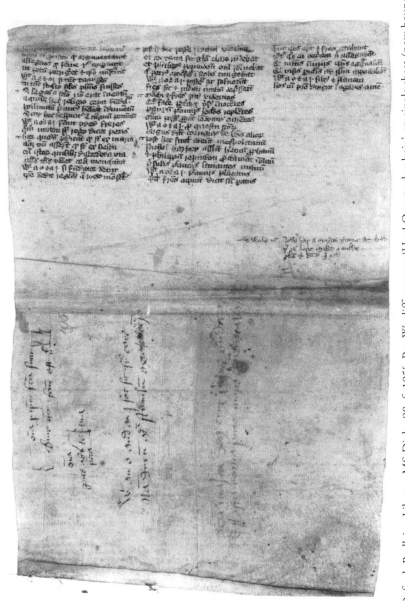

Plate 5. Oxford, Bodleian Library, MS Digby 98, f. 195ᵛ. Pro-Wycliffite poem 'Heu! Quanta desolatio' on single sheet (now bound with codex). Reproduced by kind permission of the Bodleian Library, University of Oxford.

'Heu! Quanta desolatio' (composed *c.*1382) now bound in Oxford, Bodleian Library, MS Digby 98.[59] There are also reports of the circulation of libels in this manner by lollards. According to Walsingham, Peter Pateshull, formerly a friar—or so it was claimed—copied out charges against the friars and nailed them up at St Paul's in London, and sympathetic knights had further copies of the text made and circulated.[60] A satirical pro-lollard stanza 'Plangant Anglorum gentes' is associated with the *Twelve Conclusions* in the *Annales Ricardi Secundi*, where the annalist records that verses were fixed to the doors of St Paul's.[61] A petition to chancery from the mid-1390s provides further possible evidence of lollard libels circulating in forms meant for public display. John Elvet, Archdeacon of Leicester, claimed that John Belgrave had fixed 'priuement et maliciousement vn bille escript de mayn de texte' ('secretly and maliciously, a bill written in text-hand') to the doors of St Martin's church in Leicester in which he defamed Elvet's official, Walter Barnak. He fixed up the libel the night before Barnak was to hold the archdeacon's court at the church, likening him to the evil judges who unjustly condemned Susanna; just so he oppressed the innocent and condoned the wicked, and he was 'jugge de deable de iniquitee' ('judge of the devil of iniquity').[62] The language and charge imputed to Belgrave suggest that he may have held lollard beliefs. Perhaps he was the John Belgrave of Leicester who was charged with lollard beliefs in 1413.[63]

The pro-Wycliffite poem 'Heu! Quanta desolatio Angliae praestatur' appropriates the language of biblical complaint typical of the clerical polemics that circulated in the Schools—indeed, as I have argued elsewhere, this poem should probably be associated with texts and controversies in Oxford, 1382. For example, the antifraternal poem 'Sedens super flumina' casts the poet as disillusioned former friar, lamenting like those who wept by the waters of Babylon, while 'Quis dabit meo capiti' replies for the pro-mendicant cause, opening with a reference to Jeremiah 9: 1, as does the vernacular poem *Friar Daw's Reply*.[64] The opening of 'Plangant Anglorum gentes' also invokes this discourse of lament. But some of the other lollard libels gesture towards the forms and processes of the judicial petition—and at the same time assert their corruption. Pateshull allegedly

[59] Plate 5. The poem is written on both sides of the sheet. For a fuller description and discussion, see Scase, ' "Heu! Quanta desolatio Angliae praestatur', 34–5, and n. 66.

[60] Riley (ed.), *Walsingham … Historia Anglicana*, ii. 157–9. See further Scase, ' "Heu! Quanta desolatio Angliae praestatur', 31.

[61] Riley (ed.), *Chronica Monasterii S. Albani, Johannis de Trokelowe*, 182–3. Cf. Shirley (ed.), *Fasciculi Zizaniorum*, 360–9. For discussion of these verses, see Scase, 'The Audience and Framers of the *Twelve Conclusions of the Lollards*', 291–9.

[62] TNA (PRO), C 1/68/63. The case is noticed by Storey, 'Ecclesiastical Causes in Chancery', 239–40.

[63] For some of the beliefs attributed to a John Belgrave of Leicester in 1413, see Hudson, *The Premature Reformation*, 148, 152, 342.

[64] Scase, ' "Heu! Quanta desolatio Angliae praestatur" ', and for the other Latin poems see 29–30 and references there, and for *Friar Daw's Reply* and its relations with other Oxford polemical texts, see Scase, ' "Let him be kept in most strait prison" ' and references there.

claimed in his bill that certain friars were guilty of specific crimes—murder, sodomy, and high treason—and he named the malefactors. According to Walsingham, he wrote down and published his charges after a riot in which lollards had cried for justice upon the friars as they drove them violently out of their convent, 'cum furore clamantes, et dicentes;—"Disperdamus homicidas, incendamus sodomitas, suspendamus Regis et Angliae proditores"' ('crying out with fury, calling, "Let us destroy the murderers, set light to the sodomites, and hang the traitors of the king and England"').[65] Pateshull's bill expressed the lollards' 'clamour' (note the chronicler's word 'clamantes'). John Belgrave too seems to have used public clamour to legitimate his libel against Barnak. Elvet claimed that when censured for posting the bill, Belgrave defended himself by saying that Barnak's corrupt handling of cases was publicly recognized. Both the *Twelve Conclusions* and the *Petition* take the lollard libel a stage further, invoking the parliamentary petition as their model. Although 'Plangant Anglorum gentes' invokes the language of biblical lament, the St Alban's chronicler's association of the poem with the parliamentary protest of the *Twelve Conclusions* suggests recognition of the parliamentary petition as a new frame of reference for the old clerical libel.

The *Twelve Conclusions* and the *Petition* were among several texts that used petitionary form to promulgate disendowment. Petitions presented in parliament put forward various schemes. According to Walsingham, during the parliament of 1385 the commons and some lords advocated the removal of temporalities from the clergy, clamouring such things ('clamabant') and putting them before the king in brief writings, but, their 'inordinatis clamoribus' having been heard, the king ordered them to erase their writings and cease petitioning.[66] In the Coventry parliament of 1404 a group of parliamentary knights suggested that lands should be taken back into the king's control from that of royal retainers (for whom they funded rewards and annuities). This was one of several calls for the resumption of lands as a response to chaos in royal finances. The main subject of the *Twelve Conclusions* is in fact the endowment of the Church and its consequences. The text opens with the general claim that the endowment of the Church with sources of revenue has led to disaster, while the seventh conclusion complains about the endowment of almshouses and all similar instances in which payments are made for prayers for named deceased persons. Mendicants, possessioners, and other soul-priests, this conclusion claims, 'ben a puple of gret charge to al þe reme mayntenid in ydilnesse'. A hundred almshouses in total would suffice to meet the needs of the realm, and a reduction from the present excessive number would result in hugely improved prosperity for laypeople ('þe grettest encres possible to temporel part').[67]

The *Twelve Conclusions* appears to be closely related, both in content and in form, to the equally famous *Lollard Disendowment Bill*. Like both the *Twelve*

---

[65] Riley (ed.), *Walsingham … Historia Anglicana*, ii. 158.   [66] Ibid., ii. 140.
[67] Hudson (ed.), *Selections*, 26.

Conclusions and the *Petition*, this text survives in English and Latin versions.[68] The *Disendowment Bill* puts forward an alternative to the resumption proposals, an alternative which might have been calculated to appeal to royal retainers rather better. The *Bill* presents detailed calculations to back and develop the suggestions made in the *Twelve Conclusions*.[69] The temporalities enjoyed—'yoccupied and wasted provdely'—by bishops, abbots, and priors could provide the funds for an additional fifteen earls, 1500 knights, and 6,200 squires, £20,000 or more for the defence of the realm, fifteen additional universities, and 15,000 priests and clerks, while a hundred almshouses could be funded to the tune of 100 marks—under the supervision of 'goode and trewe sekulers'—with temporalities removed that were 'morteysed and wasted amonge provde worldely clerkes', which would provide for the needy without cost to townspeople.

Like the *Twelve Conclusions* and *A Petition*, the *Lollard Disendowment Bill* is framed as a petition to parliament. It adopts the convention of specifying parliament as the context for presentation of the bill. The opening lines, 'To the moste excellent redoubte lorde the Kyng, and to alle the noble lordes of this present parlement, shewen mekely alle the trewe comvnes seyynge this sothely ... ', echo the formulas used in contemporary petitions. It differs in its selection of other formulas, however. The bill uses the formulaic petitionary verb 'shewen' to indicate that it is a petition (with 'mekely' as a conventionally humbling adverb). It addresses the king and lords using a conventionally florid mode of address for the king (the Latin text has 'Excellentissimo domino nostro regi et omnibus proceribus in presenti parliamento constitutis').[70] Its identification of the petitioners as 'alle the trewe comvnes' inflects a formula in a way that both appears conventional and signals the true allegiances of the authors. This echoes the formulaic 'monstrent lez humblez comines' of the commons' petition of 1388 preserved by Knighton, but the phrase 'alle the trewe comvnes' (repeated at the end, as 'alle the trewe comeners') could be understood to imply that the petition derives from a group *other* than the parliamentary commons; it may suggest that it comes not from the commons, but from the 'true' commons. The 1381 rebels, who also styled themselves 'true commons', offered a model, while the epithet *true* became one characteristically applied by lollards to themselves.[71] This gesture in the *Bill* neatly allies lollard language and clamour tradition.

It is not clear whether the *Lollard Disendowment Bill* was actually presented and processed as a parliamentary petition. The accounts of the chroniclers suggest that it was, but their accounts are manifestly not free from factual errors. Trying

[68] Hudson (ed.), *Selections* 135–7, 203–7, edits the English text and discusses the manuscripts.

[69] Ibid., 135–7.

[70] Galbraith (ed.), *The St Albans Chronicle 1406–1420*, 52–5, 52–3; cf. the briefer text in Riley (ed.), *Walsingham ... Historia Anglicana*, ii. 282–3. For the convention see below, 175.

[71] Galbraith (ed.), *The Anonimalle Chronicle*, 139; for lollard use of the epithet *true*, see Hudson, 'A Lollard Sect Vocabulary?', 166–7.

to resolve the chroniclers' contradictions and inconsistencies, Anne Hudson suggests that the *Bill* may have been presented at the Gloucester parliament of 1407, or, more likely, at the parliament of 1410 (which was held at Westminster). A request from the commons for the return of a petition concerning lollardy, entered in the parliamentary roll for that year, is however the only possible trace of parliamentary process concerning the *Disendowment Bill*—but it is not certain that this is what it refers to.[72] The language of the text is another factor that should be weighed when considering this problem. As we have seen, like the *Twelve Conclusions* and the *Petition*, the *Disendowment Bill* survives in Latin and English. It is a fair surmise that the text was issued by the lollards in English, and that the Latin version is a translation made by the St Albans chronicler. Anne Hudson notes one place where the Latin version betrays misunderstanding of the syntax.[73] This, I suggest, implies that the Latin is a non-lollard translation. Undoubtedly the choice of English was intended to be provocative—as we have seen, it enabled the authors to inflect petitionary language in their own characteristically lollard vocabulary (the Latin translation renders the loaded phrase 'alle the trewe comvnes' by the less provocative 'omnes communes fideles'). But it would also have been highly precocious, unprecedented in the record (unless one counts the Mercers' petition of 1388), and not followed until 1414 when Thomas Paunfield of Cambridgeshire petitioned the lords and commons of parliament.[74]

Whatever the extent and success of its passage (if any) through parliamentary process, it is clear that the *Disendowment Bill*, and the policies and arguments it promoted, enjoyed considerable informal circulation. The authors of the *Twelve Conclusions* refer to a proof of the seventh conclusion (on almshouses) 'in a bok þat þe kyng herde', 'in uno libro quem rex habuit' in the Latin.[75] Although the *Twelve Conclusions* refers to a book, many of the vehicles for textual dissemination of the disendowment policy were informal bills. The evidence for this includes the preservation of the text by chroniclers, who, it has been suggested, must have

---

[72] Hudson (ed.), *Selections*, 204; the commons asked on 8 February 1410 'q'ils purroient reavoir une peticione par eux liverez en parlement touchant l'estatut nadgairs fait des Lollardes, et que riens ensoit enactez'—a reference too vague to be considered a definite mention of the *Bill* (*PROME*, parliament of Henry IV, 1410 January, item 12). Kingsford argues that the text was 'officially suppressed' (Kingsford (ed.), *Chronicles of London*, p. xxv.)

[73] Hudson (ed.), *Selections*, 205, n. to l. 13. See below, 109–10 and Ch. 5 for further discussion of the Latin and English texts of the *Disendowment Bill*.

[74] Fisher, Richardson, and Fisher (eds.), *An Anthology of Chancery English*, 198–204. This interesting petition complains on behalf of the oppressed tenants of the Prior and Canons of Bernewelle, who claim that the petitioner and his fellows are bondmen, not tenants of ancient demesne as they claim, and have imprisoned him; he observes that 'there is litel charite of priestes' (200) and points out that the actions of the religious are motivated by the desire that the king and his heirs shall never wish to resume their lands, nor have them farmed to the increase of the royal treasury.

[75] Hudson (ed.), *Selections*, 26; Shirley (ed.), *Fasciculi Zizaniorum*, 364.

got their texts from 'copies circulated in the city [of London]'.[76] Walsingham quotes from a Latin poem which—he says—lollards fixed up on the walls of churches in London exhorting people to gather to support Oldcastle's rebellion:

> Jam princeps presbyterorum [i.e. Henry V] abiit,
> Jam hostis noster abcessit,
> Jam nobis arrisit tempus accommodum
> Quo nostras impune licebit injurias vindicare.[77]

> [Now the prince of priests is away,
> Now our enemy has withdrawn,
> Now it is a suitable time for us
> In which it will be lawful to avenge our injuries with impunity.]

Other evidence that bills in favour of disendowment circulated is provided by legal records associated with the Oldcastle rising. An inquiry into the revolt recorded the names of people who wrote and distributed bills in support of Oldcastle with the aim, allegedly, of taking goods from churches, and in 1417 lollards allegedly leafleted all large houses in St Albans, Reading, and Northampton.[78] Even Margery Kempe was accused of distributing letters on behalf of Oldcastle.[79] A return from the post-Oldcastle inquest at Leicester on 5 February 1414 offers a detailed picture of how lollard bills were transmitted. The jury stated on oath that Thomas Ile of Braybrooke was both composer and carrier of bills in support of Oldcastle ('componitor ac asportator billarum'). William Smith of Leicester had received one of these bills from the hands of Thomas Ile, and had delivered it to Roger Barbour of Leicester.[80]

LOLLARD BILLS AND THE LITERATURE OF CLAMOUR

Discussing the lollard petitions in isolation gives a somewhat misleading and incomplete picture. There is substantial evidence that these petitions were part

---

[76] Gransden, *Historical Writing in England*, ii. 238. For further discussion of dissemination, see Ch. 4, 144, 148, 152–3.

[77] Riley (ed.), *Walsingham … Historia Anglicana*, ii. 306 (my lineation). For lollard use of the epithet 'prince of priests' for the king, see Allmand, *Henry V*, 304–5. Allmand stresses the loading of the epithet (a king of priests would have control over their wealth). Note too that Henry V appears to have encouraged the use of epithets to emphasize his defence of the Church against heresy. A praise of the king written in 1414 by a monk of Westminster describes Henry as 'pugil ecclesie' ('champion of the Church') in his suppression of Oldcastle (Cole (ed.), *Memorials of Henry the Fifth*, 63–75).

[78] See Aston, 'Lollardy and Sedition', 25; and Aston, 'Devotional Literacy', 108 and references there.

[79] Windeatt (ed.), *Book of Margery Kempe*, 262.

[80] 'Willielmus Smyth de Leycestre receptauit vnam billarum predictarum per manibus predicti Thome Ile quamquidem billam idem Willielmus liberauit Rogero Barbour de Leycestre' (TNA (PRO), KB 9/204/1, item 141).

of a larger literature of clamour. I have already suggested that lollard bills relate to a culture of libels prevalent among clerics in London and Oxford. But we can also link the lollard petitions with wider vernacular campaigns, with a developing literature of clamour. Sometimes we can infer that lollard campaigns incited, or responded to, opposing campaigns. We can also detect the recycling of old lollard bills as part of new campaigns. And we can find plenty of examples of the association of, and failure to distinguish between, lollard and non-lollard campaigns, at least in the judicial imagination, if not more widely. The English poem 'Defend us all from Lollardy'—which attacks Oldcastle in the manner of a libel—was perhaps composed to counter the perceived threat of lollard bills and libels.[81] As we have seen, the Oldcastle rebellion was closely associated with bill campaigns. It would not have been the first time that one petitionary campaign was answered with another. From the beginning of the reign of Henry IV, knights of the shire pursued a campaign in parliament that the king should 'live of his own'. This demand for 'resumption' of the crown's resources was to be a recurrent call in petitions inside and outside of parliament.[82] The petitioners claimed that the crown's lands and revenues from them were being squandered by royal favourites, corrupt councillors, and others to whom the king had granted them as rewards. If the king were to resume control over these resources, then he could finance the royal household more effectively and would not have to exact such high taxation from parliament. During the parliament held at Coventry in 1404 some parliamentary knights proposed that the king should take back all lands that the crown had held since 1366. Both temporal and spiritual lords opposed the plan, naturally. Walsingham describes the proposals as a plan for disendowment of the Church ('scilicet, ut Ecclesia generaliter de bonis temporalibus privaretur.')[83] In 1405 Archbishop Richard Scrope launched a bill campaign in defence of the Church. Scrope protested against the usurpation of the throne by Henry IV, and challenged the authority of the actions that he had taken since, including exacting money from the clergy, despite promises not to do so.

Scrope replied to the 1404 proposals by issuing popular bills. He seems to have issued at least two sets of articles (almost certainly in English) which were displayed in York and sent to curates in neighbouring places. These texts are not cast as petitions to parliament, but they position themselves tellingly in relation to parliamentary procedure and institutions. His *Articles against Henry IV* are presented as an appeal to Christ as the 'high celestial Judge' (in Foxe's translation) rather than parliament. Scrope impugns the authority of the king and complains of his abuse of parliament in proclaiming himself king and instituting

---

[81] Robbins (ed.), *Historical Poems*, no. 64, pp. 152–7.
[82] For impacts on Chaucer and Hoccleve, see Ch. 5.
[83] Riley (ed.), *Walsingham … Historia Anglicana*, ii. 265. For the policy and its history, see Wolffe, 'Acts of Resumption'.

the Statute of Winchester, against the Church and the authority of St Peter and his successors. In the tenth article he appears to imagine presenting these articles as a petition to the lords and commons at a parliamentary assembly:

… we have here brought before you certain articles concerning the destruction of the same [prelates, lords, and commons], to be circumspectly considered by the whole assembly, as well by the lords spiritual as temporal, and the faithful commons of England: beseeching you all … that ye will be favourable to us, and to our causes which are three in number … [84]

While he takes care to distinguish royal abuse of parliament from the behaviour of parliamentarians here, in another set or sets of articles, Scrope apparently offered specific criticisms of the corruption of parliament and its institutions in favour of the crown. According to Capgrave's *Chronicle of England*, Scrope's complaints against extortion and disinheritance were allied with the demand that 'the puple of the reme schuld have fre elleccion of knytes of the Parlement, aftir the eld forme', while, according to the *Eulogium Historiarum*, Scrope criticized the king's nomination of knights and burgesses, rather than nomination by the citizens and county communities, and he argued that parliament should be held in London, because it was the most public place in the kingdom. [85]

The topics addressed by Scrope are also treated in two closely contemporary vernacular texts in the *Piers Plowman* tradition: *Richard the Redeless* and *Mum and the Sothsegger*. Both texts reprise and engage with Langland's representation of parliamentary petitionary process. A sequence in Passus IV of the B-text of *Piers* (a passage also paralleled in the A and C versions) relates how Peace presents a bill to the king and council in parliament:

> And thanne com Pees into parlement and putte up a bille—
> How Wrong ayeins his wille hadde his wif taken,
> And how he ravysshede Rose, Reignaldes loove,
> And Margrete of hir maydenhede maugree hire chekes.
> 'Bothe my gees and my grys hise gadelynges feccheth;
> I dar noght for fere of hem fighte ne chide.
> He borwed of me bayard and broughte hym hom nevere
> Ne no ferthyng therfore, for nought I koude plede.
> He maynteneth hise men to murthere myne hewen,
> Forstalleth my feires and fighteth in my chepyng,
> And breketh up my berne dores and bereth awey my whete,
> And taketh me but a taille for ten quarters otes.
> And yet he beteth me therto and lyth by my mayde;
> I am noght hardy for hym unnethe to loke!'[86]

---

[84] Pratt (ed.), *The Acts and Monuments of John Foxe*, iii. 231–4, 233.

[85] Hingeston (ed.), *The Chronicle of England by John Capgrave*, 289; Haydon (ed.), *Eulogium Historiarum*, iii. 406.

[86] Schmidt (ed.), *William Langland, The Vision of Piers Plowman*, iv. 47–60.

Peace complains of sufferings caused by royal agents, and tells how his plaints have not been redressed in the courts. Wisdom and others intervene and, as a result of Lady Mede's bribery, Peace withdraws his case.[87] Here Langland represents the classic complaint against purveyance, and indicates that justice is not obtained because the judicial system for processing complaint by bill is corrupt. Peace's complaint is settled privately, and the royal officers go unpunished. The reprise of *Piers* in *Richard* echoes many of the points made by Scrope. Now the focus is on the role of the members of parliament as plaintiffs who should protect those whom they represent against the greed and profligacy of the crown and its ministers and officers. The poet describes how Richard II and his courtiers, their funds exhausted, contrived to raise more funds through parliament:

> And cast it be colis with her conceill at euene,
> To haue preuy parlement for ⟨proffitt⟩ of hem-self,
> And lete write writtis all in wex closid,
> For peeris and prelatis that thei apere shuld,
> And sente side sondis to schreuys aboughte,
> To chese swiche cheualleris as the charge wold,
> To shewe for the schire in company with the grete.[88]

The direct result of this corrupt election and the choice of a secret venue for parliament is that the knights of the shire and the burgesses are incompetent at complaining. When they are supposed to commune and agree how to present their plaints, many keep silent and take bribes, or are fearful, and fail to restrain the squandering of royal funds. Helen Barr identifies the reference here to the 1398 parliament held by Richard at Shrewsbury, but although ostensibly criticizing Richard, the poet was clearly writing after his deposition and death, and therefore, like Scrope, must have been addressing these issues early in the reign of the usurping king.[89] In the summons for the Coventry parliament of 1404 lawyers were specifically excluded from election, ostensibly because of their propensity for furthering private rather than public interests. Some, such as the St Alban's chronicler, saw this move in a sinister light, claiming that it excluded anyone who knew anything about the law from being elected. In 1406 a statute was passed that prescribed free and fair elections.[90]

Richard breaks off at the end of a scathing passage of satire against this corrupt and incompetent group of parliamentary knights and burgesses. However, analysis of the problem is developed in *Mum and the Sothsegger*.[91] *Mum* takes up the theme of resumption of the king's lands ('of his owen were the beste').[92]

---

[87] Schmidt (ed.), *William Langland, The Vision of Piers Plowman*, iv. 47–103.
[88] *Richard the Redeless*, iv. 24–30; Barr (ed.), *The Piers Plowman Tradition*.
[89] Barr (ed.), *The Piers Plowman Tradition*, 17.
[90] *PROME*, 'October 1404, Introduction'.
[91] Barr (ed.), *The Piers Plowman Tradition*, 23 dates *Mum* after 1406 and perhaps after 1409.
[92] Cf. Wolffe, 'Acts of Resumption', 587; *Mum and the Sothsegger*, l. 1667, Barr (ed.), *The Piers Plowman Tradition*.

Here the essence of the problem is personified by Mum, a figure who represents the practice of keeping silent and failing to complain. Mum is shown to be especially active in parliament, which is the 'place that is proprid to parle for the royaulme', and to do most harm there 'principally by parlement to proue hit I thenke'. Lords and knights of the shire fail to speak out about grievances and to get amends on account of fear, so grievances are allowed to fester, leading to the threat of rebellion ('Thenne rise agayne regalie and the royaulme trouble')—such as that fomented by Scrope.[93] Both *Mum* and *Richard* develop the *Piers Plowman* scenario, *Mum* in particular showing a sense that parliament is a distinctive context for complaint, and identifying failure of the institution of complaint as engendering the threat of unrest. In this the poem parallels Scrope's articles, but it establishes a major difference from Scrope's position by claiming that the *only* safe and proper place for complaint is parliament.

The conflict between the parliamentary petitioners and Scrope in which the Langlandian poems engage provides a possible context for the *Lollard Disendowment Bill*. The lollard bill offered an alternative way of addressing the problem of royal finance to that proposed in the 1404 parliament. Instead of proposing the resumption of the crown's lands, it proposed meeting fiscal deficits by disendowing the clergy. Presumably the lollards calculated that this policy would have much greater appeal to the secular lords than would the policy of resumption which threatened to impoverish them.

Scrope's campaign belongs with the earliest rebellions against the Lancastrian monarchy. It stands at the beginning of a tradition of bill campaigns perceived to oppose the royal government that invoke the forms and process of the parliamentary petition. Only some eight years after Scrope's campaign, in 1413, the genre was appropriated by John Whitelock, formerly a groom and yeoman to Richard II. Whitelock was associated with a movement that claimed that Richard was still alive. According to an indictment, he was accused of fixing up bills during Henry IV's final parliament and the first parliament of the reign of Henry V, in May 1413.[94] He promulgated his seditious message by announcing it in bills which were posted on church doors in London, Westminster, and Bermondsey. One of his bills survives, preserved with the records of his trial in July 1413.[95] In his bill, Whitelock claims he has served Richard for thirty years, some 'IX зere and moore' of them in Scotland, where Richard 'is in warde and

---

[93] *Mum and the Sothsegger*, ll. 1117–40, quotations from ll. 1132, 1118, 1128, Barr (ed.), *The Piers Plowman Tradition*.

[94] Sayles (ed.), *Select Cases*, 213.

[95] TNA (PRO), KB 9/203/1. Powell, *Kingship, Law and Society*, 137–8, n. 102 points out that the documents relating to Whitelock's trial here (following on mm. 2–4; m. 1 is attached to m. 2) have been wrongly placed in the file for 1424. See also Allmand, *Henry V*, 309; and for a Lacanian analysis of the revenant Richard, see Strohm, 'The Trouble with Richard'. Cf. TNA (PRO), KB 27/609/14 (crown, Trinity 1413), printed by Sayles (ed.), *Select Cases*, 213–14. This document, also related to the case, refers to a bill as being attached; however, a different document is in fact attached.

kepyng of the Duk of Albanie'. He petitions for an opportunity to defend his claims under oath and, if he is still not believed, by producing Richard from Scotland as proof. He asks to be kept safe from harm until his case is concluded. He petitions for release from prison if he proves his case, and offers to undergo the 'vilest deth þat may be ordeined for me' if he is found guilty.

On the face of it there are some problems with this text that might impugn its authenticity. Whitelock writes as if from prison, where he fears for his life. It is hard to see how he could have had a petition like this written under these conditions. Furthermore, he grants that 'the kyng herry and his sones' may put him to death if he loses his case. This must be a reference to Henry IV because, of course, Henry V did not have even one son in 1413. It therefore dates the composition of the bill to earlier than 20 March 1413, the date of Henry IV's death. But Whitelock was not imprisoned until early June 1413.[96] A solution to these problems may be that Whitelock wrote the bill—or had it written—and arranged for its distribution in *anticipation* of his imprisonment. He was in sanctuary at Westminster (clearly therefore fearing and anticipating imprisonment) 14 March–7 June, that is, from the closing days of the reign of Henry IV until his imprisonment.[97] Perhaps, when he first went into sanctuary, while Henry IV was still alive, he took the initiative to prepare for his imprisonment, composing this bill and having copies made for distribution in the city.[98] It may be that the outdated reference to the former king remained because he had no means of calling back the text for revision. The surviving bill may provide some clues about how it was produced. It is of the characteristic size and shape of petitions at this date, being written on vellum, 29 cm wide × 14.5 cm high, with the text running across the wider dimension. However, the hand is not typical of legal documents of this date. Although neat and professional, it is a clear, squarish, anglicana hand with a slight forward slant. This is the kind of hand one might expect to see in manuscripts of English literature. Perhaps this suggests that the scribe—and perhaps drafter—of the bill was also engaged in the production of English literary texts. A telling comparison is provided by a copy of the bill included in the indictment. Here the bill is copied in precise, faithful detail down to minute particulars of orthography, punctuation, marks of suspension and contraction, even word division—but the hand is the court hand of the roll.[99]

---

[96] The mandate for his arrest is dated 14 April 1413 (*Calendar of Patent Rolls, AD 1413–1416*, part 1, 35).

[97] The dates are given in the indictment, Sayles (ed.), *Select Cases*, 213; cf. Powell, *Kingship, Law and Society*, 137.

[98] Perhaps Whitelock's bill is not the only possible case of anticipatory composition. A similar scenario would explain lollard William Thorpe's assured account of his imprisonment and interrogations by Archbishop Arundel, for example.

[99] The original (from which the court scribe probably copied) is reproduced in Plate 6. Compare the hand of Adam Pinkhurst, Plates 1-2. Further analysis of the hand could perhaps indicate the provenance of the original. The court copy is TNA (PRO), KB 27/609/14.

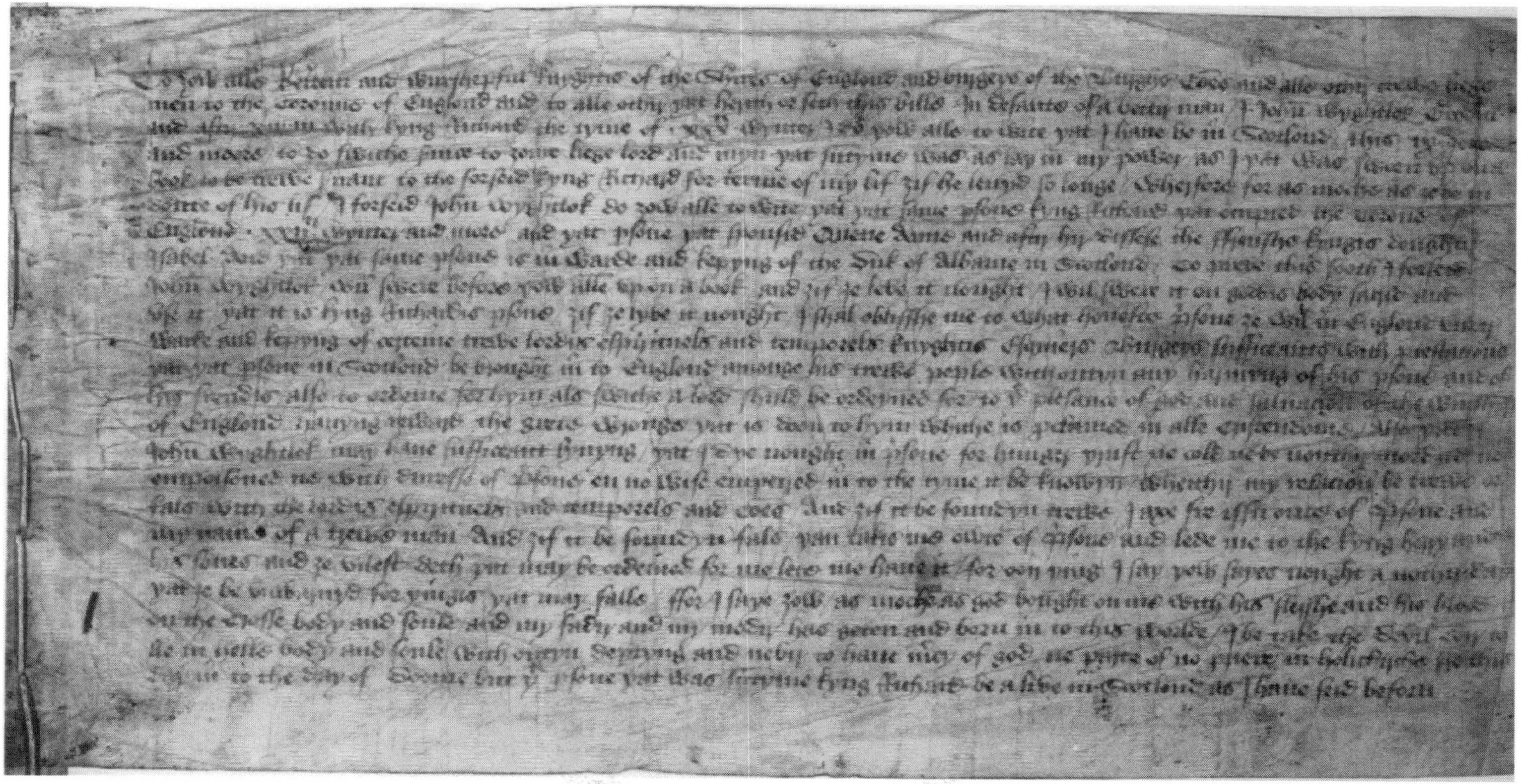

Plate 6. TNA (PRO), KB 9/203/1. John Whitelock's Petition. Reproduced by kind permission of the Keeper of the National Archives.

Whitelock's bill clearly invokes the forms and processes of the petition to parliament. It opens with an address 'To ʒow alle Reuerent and wurshepful knyghtis of the Shires of Englond and burgeys of the Burghs Comunes alle othir trewe liege men to the coroune of Englond and to alle othir þat herith or seth this bille.' This address to the knights of the shires and the burgesses clearly implies a parliamentary audience. This address is reinforced later by a reference to the lords and commons ('the lordis espirituels and temporels and comunes'), who, at a future date, will know whether his account is true or false. In sanctuary in the closing days of the reign of Henry IV, Whitelock would have expected a parliamentary opportunity for the promulgation of his bill. A parliament was summoned for 3 February 1413, and members of parliament gathered at Westminster. As it happened, owing to the king's illness, they never met, dispersing after the king's death.[100] From 3 February, therefore, members of parliament would have been present at Westminster, presenting an opportunity to publish a bill, in the event that he was imprisoned.

Whitelock attempted to adapt the parliamentary bill to his own novel situation, in so far as he could. His use of English, and the inclusion in his address of 'alle othir þat herith or seth this bille' suggest that he anticipated, and provided for, a wide and unpredictable audience beyond that of the members of parliament. His own distance from the parliamentary process is represented graphically by his imprisonment, as he petitions for access to the judicial process offered by parliament, offering to take an oath and produce evidence in person before the members of parliament ('To preve this sooth I forseid John Wyghtlok wil swere before ʒow alle vp on a book and ʒif ʒe leve it nought I wil swere it on goddis body sacrid ... ').

Seditious campaigns like Whitelock's quickly interfaced with the lollard campaigns in the judicial and popular imaginations. Having escaped from the Tower after his arrest in 1413, in 1417 Whitelock was accused of having campaigned against Henry V at the suggestion of the lollard bill-producer Thomas Lucas, who was himself allegedly a confederate of Oldcastle's. It is notable that Lucas had been arrested in 1395 in connection with reprisals after the posting of the *Twelve Conclusions*. The crimes of which Lucas stood accused on this later occasion included asserting that religious orders should not possess or enjoy temporal possessions, and announcing that Richard II was alive and living in Edinburgh. He allegedly promulgated these messages in bills scattered in many streets in Canterbury and London ('dictas billas in diuersis locis regni Anglie videlicet Cantuar' in com' Kant' ac London' in diuersis stratis dictarum villarum proiecctas').[101]

---

    [100] *PROME*, 'Henry IV, 1399–1413, Introduction'.
    [101] TNA (PRO), KB 27/624/9 (crown). For discussion of the 1417 indictment, see Aston, 'Lollardy and Sedition', 27–8; and for Lucas's arrest in 1395, see 22.

In a second example of the association of lollard bill campaigns for disendowment with treasonous rebellion against the crown, the *Lollard Disendowment Bill* surfaced again in connection with a 1431 rising in the south of England. It was alleged that lollards drew up bills on disendowment at secret meetings and distributed them for public display.[102] Towns associated with this campaign include Oxford, Coventry, Northampton, Salisbury, London, Marlborough, and Abingdon. Nicholas Bishop of Oxford recorded the affair as follows:

… falsliche traytourliche as common traytures and felouns of our kyng lete dude wryte divers fals bulles and fals scriptures and gilful and many contraris the doctrine of christyn feyth and conteynyng, and thenne [?them] to the puple of our kyng to be publich and to be comunyd follysch dampnablysch in divers places that is to wytyng in citees of London of Salebur' and of townys Coventre Marleburgh wikkydliche have set styked cast to ground, and every day so to wryte procureth to styke to draw to ground cessit nat ne dredith in grete offens the high maieste of god and of dignite of corowne regal and derision of christian feith in disturbaunce of the kynges pese and wrong and contempt of al chistian [*sic*] pepele … [103]

In the absence of the king in France, Duke Humphrey took charge of prosecuting the rebels, and the ring-leader, Jack Sharp, was charged with treason and hanged, drawn, and quartered. The second surviving fifteenth-century English copy of the *Disendowment Bill* is preserved in association with this year in a chronicle in London, British Library, MS Harley 3775, where it is clearly associated with Sharp, leader of the rising, in a rubric: 'Supplicatio pessima, porrecta per Johannem Scharpe Domino Humfredo, Duci Gloverniae, regni protectori, in subversionem ecclesiae' ('A most evil supplication, presented by John Sharp to Lord Humphrey, Duke of Gloucester, protector of the kingdom, in subversion of the Church').[104] Of course, this is not conclusive proof that the text was circulated by Sharp, but differences between this copy and the other surviving English copy do suggest some circulation and possibly adaptation. Crucially, the Sharp text addresses the commons, and suggests that they, not the king, may be the beneficiaries of confiscation of the Church's temporalities. It also misses out the reference to the foundation of fifteen new universities, and a passage giving details of financial arrangements. These variants could derive from dissemination or adaptation of the English text of 1407/10. But other variants in the Sharp text suggest an alternative scenario. For example, where the London chronicle text opens 'To the moste excellent redoubte lorde the Kyng, and to alle the noble lordes of this present parlement', the Sharp text opens 'The most excellent and dow₃ty lord, oure lege Lord the Kyng, and to alle the Lordys of the reme of this present Parlement'. It is not easy to see how the two English texts can be variants of the same text at this point,

---

[102] For an account of the 1431 rising, see Harvey, *Jack Cade's Rebellion*, 25–8.

[103] Ed. Aston, 'Lollardy and Sedition', 45–6.

[104] Riley (ed.), *Chronica Monasterii S. Albani. Annales Monasterii S. Albani, a Johanne Amundesham*, i. 453–6. For the manuscript, see Hudson (ed.), *Selections*, 203.

or to view either variant as a stylistic improvement. An alternative explanation for this kind of variation might be that this text has been translated from a Latin source, and is thus independent of the other English text. This would suggest, not continued circulation of the English text, but use of a Latin source and renewal of the text as a popular bill by means of a translation back into English.

THE CLAMOUR LITERATURE OF THE 1450s

The bill campaign associated with Jack Cade and the Kentish rebels in the 1450s provides us with a rich and varied corpus of clamour literature. Jack Cade's rebellion is associated with discontent at the crown's financial and military governance. Petitions in parliament for impeachment of royal favourites who were perceived to be corrupt, and once again for the resumption of crown lands to alleviate the royal household's financial crisis, were accompanied by popular bills in prose and verse that appropriated parliamentary forms and took them to the country. The sources are plentiful enough for us to examine the production of complaints, the links between complaints and verse libels, the dissemination of clamour texts, and the relations between judicial complaints and clamorous texts. We have, in other words, for the first time, a full literature of clamour.

Cade and his followers issued at least four bills in which they itemized their grievances and called for remedy. A bill copied by John Stow into MS Lambeth 306 states 'Thes ben the poyntys, causes, and myscheves of gaderynge and assemblinge of us the Kynges lege men of Kent, on the iiij day of June, the yere of owr Lorde M.iiijc.l'.[105] The gathering of rebels, which started by the second half of May, occurred in various places across Kent, among them Blackheath in the north-west of Kent, across the Thames from London.[106] Two shorter documents are closely related to this Lambeth 306 bill. The first, preserved in Oxford, Magdalen College, Magdalen Misc. 306, is a bill that itemizes 'the poyntes, mischeves and causes of the gederynge and assemblynge of us z[ʒ]youre trew legemen of Kent', and ends with seven lines of verse:

> God be oure gyde
> And then schull we spede,
>   Who so evur say nay.
>
> Ffalse, for ther money reulethe
> Trewth for his tales spellethe.
>   God seende vs a ffayre day!
>   Awey, traytours, away![107]

---

[105] Gairdner (ed.), *Three Fifteenth-Century Chronicles*, 94–9, quotation at 94.
[106] Harvey, *Jack Cade's Rebellion*, 74–8.
[107] I cite the edition of Oxford, Magdalen College, Magdalen Misc. 306, printed in Harvey, *Jack Cade's Rebellion*, 188–90, which is from that in Great Britain, Royal Commission on Historical

The second bill which is closely related to the Lambeth 306 petition is a brief list of specific demands addressed to the king found in London, British Library, Cotton Roll II. 23. This text names individuals as traitors, defends the Duke of Gloucester against the charge of treason, and calls for action against purveyance and other extortions. It begins 'These ben the desires of the trewe comyns of your soueraign lord the Kyng'.[108] Finally, there is a bill in Cotton Roll IV. 50 which specifies that it summarizes the complaints of the rebels gathered at Blackheath, beginning: 'The compleyntys & causes of the assemble on blake hethe'.[109]

The relations among all of these texts are very problematic. Harvey and others suggest the Blackheath bill in Cotton Roll IV. 50 was written first; as the 'bill with the most strongly Kentish concerns', it may have circulated during May or early June.[110] However, the rebels were only certainly at Blackheath by 11 June, therefore the Lambeth 306 bill, unlocalized but dated 4 June, could be earlier.[111] Yet we should, I suggest, be sceptical about whether the date on the Lambeth 306 bill refers to the whole text. Historians have not previously questioned the integrity of the Lambeth bill. On its relation to the two shorter texts, Harvey states 'it is clear that this manifesto [i.e. that in Lambeth 306] must have been transformed shortly afterwards into two separate bills [i.e. those in Magdalen Misc. 306 and Cotton Roll II. 23]'.[112] Harvey's assumptions about the chronology of the composition of the texts seem to be related to her inferences about how the different bills might have played different parts in the unfolding drama (a matter I shall discuss further below). However, it is possible that Lambeth 306 conflates material that previously had circulated separately, welding a bill dated 4 June to one or more other texts.

The significance of this dating of the various petitions for our present purposes is that the first bills were drafted and circulated while parliament was in session at Leicester (the third session of the November 1449 parliament ran from 29 April to (probably) 7 June 1450).[113] Timing of publication was one of the ways in which the rebels indicated the relation of their texts with parliamentary petitions.

Manuscripts, *Eighth Report*, Appendix, ii. ff. 266ᵛ–267ᵛ (no pagination). I have re-lineated the verse; cf. Robbins (ed.), *Historical Poems*, no. 24, p. 63. A later version of these verses in John Vale's book reads 'fals for the mene pillith' and omits the final phrase (Kekewich *et al.*, (eds.), *John Vale's Book*, 212.) For discussion of this version, see below.

[108] Ed. Harvey, *Jack Cade's Rebellion*, 191. Cf. also the edition in Kingsford, *English Historical Literature*, 360–2. Another fifteenth-century copy (unknown to Harvey) occurs in London, British Library, Additional MS 48031A, f. 136ʳ, ed. in Kekewich *et al.* (eds.), *John Vale's Book*, 205–6. This petition was also copied by Stow.

[109] Ed. Harvey, *Jack Cade's Rebellion*, 186–8, from London, British Library, Cotton Roll IV. 50. Other copies survive in London, British Library, Additional MS 48031A, f. 135ʳ⁻ᵛ (not known to Harvey), ed. in Kekewich *et al.* (eds.), *John Vale's Book*, 204–5, and London, British Library, MS Harley 543, ff. 165ʳ–166ᵛ, a copy made by Stow from Vale's book.

[110] Harvey, *Jack Cade's Rebellion*, 80, 186; cf. John Watts in Kekewich *et al.* (eds.), *John Vale's Book*, 205.

[111] Griffiths, *The Reign of King Henry VI*, 610–17, provides a chronology of the rising.

[112] Harvey, *Jack Cade's Rebellion*, 188.

[113] For the dates of this parliament, see *PROME*, 'Introduction 1449'.

Thomas Gascoigne (d.1456) observes this significance in his jeremiad on the rebellion:

… et durante Parliamento Laycestriae insurrexit comitas Kanciae, et vocabant seipsos puplicos petitores puplicae justiciae fiendae, et propriae suae injuriae et regni ostensores, et ipsis insurgentibus parliamentum illud finitum fuit … [114]

[… and while parliament was in session at Leicester the county of Kent arose, and they called themselves 'public petitioners for public justice to be done', complaining of their own injuries and those of the kingdom, and in the face of these insurgents, parliament was ended …]

A little later he makes the same point: before answer had been given to many petitions before parliament, the county of Kent arose, headed by Cade.[115] Gascoigne alleges that the rebels represented themselves as ' "public petitioners for public justice to be done", complaining of their own injuries and those of the kingdom'. Besides aligning themselves with parliamentary petitioners through the timing of their petitions, the Cade rebels achieved this self-representation by their choice of the language and structure of their bills, and by the grievances and demands they expressed.

In all of the bills except the brief list of demands in Cotton Roll II. 23, the rebels describe themselves as an 'assemble' (Cotton Roll IV. 50), or a 'gaderynge and assemblynge' (Magdalen College, Magdalen Misc. 306 and Lambeth 306). Petitions and other materials enrolled in the Rolls of Parliament regularly describe parliament as 'assembled', often in the formula 'in this present parlement assembled'.[116] The use of French *assemble* and its English synonym *gather* in the bills therefore parallels the mustering of the rebels on Blackheath and in other places with the coming together of members of parliament. The comparison is further emphasized by the rebels' description of themselves as 'the trewe comyns' in Lambeth 306 and Cotton Roll II. 23. As we have seen, the 1381 rebels also adopted this form of self-styling. The Cade rebels may have followed suit—perhaps consciously imitating their predecessors—in order to reject their labelling as traitors. This is suggested by an item in Magdalen College, Magdalen Misc. 306: 'they … calle us risers and treyturs and the kynges enymys, but we schalle be ffounde his trew lege mene'.[117]

The bills list grievances that fell within the judicial remit of parliament. They call for the crown's resumption of alienated lands—recalling the grievances of the beginning of the century—and complain of the oppressions of purveyance,

---

[114] Rogers (ed.), *Loci e Libro Veritatum*, 189.   [115] Ibid., 190.

[116] The quotation is from from *PROME*, parliament of Henry VI, 1449 February, item 9. A proximity search of the *MED* for *parlement* and *assembled* brings up seventeen examples from the Rolls of Parliament, and a search for 'parlement assembled' in *PROME*, parliaments April 1425–October 1460, finds 140 examples.

[117] For further evidence that the 1450 rebels invoked the example of their 1381 and other predecessors, see below, 118, 135–6.

which was, as we have seen, an even older topic of complaint. They complain of treasonous crimes, providing evidence for them in clamour and notoriety, for example, Cotton Roll IV. 50 says it is 'notyd be the comyne voyse' that the king's lands in France have been alienated treasonously, and Magdalen College, Magdalen Misc. 306 asserts that the Duke of Suffolk was 'enpechid by all the comynealte of Ynglond, wyche nombur passyd a quest of xxiii mill.' This bill calls for 'a just and a trew enquere by the lawe' to investigate corruption and treason, while both this bill and that in Cotton Roll II. 23 name royal officers and ministers who are guilty of treason and corruption, including Stephen Slegge, William Crowmer, William Isle, and Robert Est, who are charged with being extortioners in Kent, and they call for action against notorious traitors: 'all the false progeny and afynyte of the Duke of Southefolke, the whiche ben opynly knowyn traitours' (Cotton Roll II. 23).

The bills carefully set out the reasons why these complaints cannot be presented through the normal judicial channels. Magdalen College, Magdalen Misc. 306 complains that there is no other route, for law is corrupt and 'no remedye is hadde in the Court of Consyens [i.e. chancery] nor otherwyse'. They assert that access to the king's justice has been impeded by corruption. The appointment of improper persons as councillors to the king has prevented complaints from reaching him for these persons 'stoppyth materys of wronge done in his realme from his excellent audiens & may not be redressyd as lawe wull but yf brybys & gyftys be messager to the handys of the seide counsell' (Cotton Roll IV. 50). A similar point is made in Magdalen College, Magdalen Misc. 306: 'thees false traytours wulle suffer no mane to coome to the Kynges presense for noe cause withoutune brybe'. Parliament itself has been corrupted by royal interference in the elections of knights of the shire, and knights are taking bribes for appointments to the office of tax collector. Yet the existence of parliament proves that the power of the crown has constitutional limits: 'they [evil councillors to the king] sey the Kynge schuld lyve upon his Comyns [i.e. upon taxation], and that her bodyes and goodes ern his; the contrarie is trew, ffor than nedid hym nevur to set parlement and to aske goode of hem' (Magdalen College, Magdalen Misc. 306). The fact that the king has to summon parliament to negotiate grants of taxation proves that the crown may not simply take at will from the commons. The Cade rebels' issuing of petitions asserts this constitutional truth, and how it has been suppressed. These claims legitimize the petitions as a literature of clamour and assert that they are the only available means of making complaint.

The Cade petitions establish varying relations with the parliamentary petition by adapting the formulas of address and by choice of content. It seems that these variations reflect the issuing of petitions aimed at different audiences. We know that a petition was presented to a delegation sent by the king to the rebels on 16 June. It has been suggested that the short petition in Cotton Roll II. 23 is a copy of the text that was drawn up for this purpose, since at one point this text shifts from its customary third person into the second person: 'and take to yow the myghty prince the Duke of Excetter ... '.[118] The second surviving fifteenth-century copy of this bill, in John Vale's book (which was compiled in the 1470s), was almost certainly made from a copy of the petition obtained directly from the rebels. John Vale's source was the archive of the Cook family of London. Thomas Cook and his father (also Thomas) were both in London at the time of the rebellion. The younger Thomas Cook, a member of the Common Council, was sent to Cade as a representative of the city. He most likely obtained a copy of the petition on this occasion, and by such means the text could have been transmitted widely among anxious Londoners. Tellingly, this text of the petition omits the stray second-person address to the king. It also omits the phrase 'trewe commons', instead identifying the petitioner as 'the capitaigne of the seid commones', and in a rubric as 'the capitayne of the grete assemble in Kente'.[119] Of course, we cannot know for sure whether these modifications were made by the rebels for the citizenry, or by Cook and others as they transmitted the text.

We know that the audience for the petitions also included landed gentry—who were, we may hazard, concerned at the possible implications for themselves of proposals for resumption of the crown's lands. Sir John Fastolf instructed a servant called John Payn to go to the commons and acquire a copy of their petition. Fastolf himself had fled to the Tower leaving Payn to guard his property in Southwark. John Payn provides a vivid account of his encounters with the rebels—albeit in a letter written some fifteen years later to John Paston which has recently been suspected of some fabrication and embellishment.[120] Harvey has suggested that Fastolf's copy may be that preserved in Magdalen College, Magdalen Misc. 306. Again, it is possible that Payn received a version adapted for a particular audience, perhaps, Harvey suggests, one aimed at 'the whole of the south-east, perhaps particularly ... its upper strata', because the Magdalen College, Magdalen Misc. 306 text emphasizes broader issues over Kent-specific matters and is 'couched in the language of petitioners'.[121] This provenance for the Magdalen document is credible, but, it should be noted, not conclusive. Magdalen College received many of the papers from Fastolf's estate. However, this document is part of the Magdalen miscellaneous papers, rather than being part of the Fastolf papers proper.[122]

Yet a further audience was the rebels themselves, or people whose support the rebels hoped to enlist. The petition that may be the earliest, that in Cotton Roll IV. 50, is thought to have been used for recruiting supporters

---

[118] Harvey, *Jack Cade's Rebellion*, 83.
[119] Kekewich *et al.* (eds.), *John Vale's Book*, 205–6.
[120] Davis (ed.), *Paston Letters*, ii. 313–15. For discussion of the account, see Maurer, *Margaret of Anjou*, 72–4.
[121] Harvey, *Jack Cade's Rebellion*, 87–9; quotations from 88.
[122] I am grateful to Dr Robin Darwall-Smith, archivist at Magdalen College, for discussion of these points and for giving me an opportunity to view the document.

in Kent because of its emphasis on Kentish matters. (Yet it cannot have been confined to such an audience. This version also survives in John Vale's book, and the only substantial difference between this text and that in the roll is in the order of the grievances.) Cotton Roll IV. 50 offers us some material evidence for the way in which bills may have been compiled and adapted for different audiences. Misdescribed by Harvey as written on 'a single sheet of paper', this bill is in fact a roll made of two sheets glued together.[123] The top sheet has been written on both front and dorse, but the bottom sheet bears writing only on the dorse.[124] The text from the article which begins 'Item thereas knyghtys of the Shyre' to the end all appears on this appended sheet. The two sheets seem fairly clearly to have been written in the same (rather variable) hand. One possible explanation for this use of a second sheet is that the scribe misjudged the length of the text to be copied, and finding (or being given) some three further articles to copy when he had filled his first sheet on the dorse, he appended an additional sheet. However, the scribe has not written up to the end of the first sheet; there is a space of 2 cm minimum between the end of the last item on that sheet and the first line on the appended sheet. Furthermore, the left-hand margin of the top sheet is 3.5 cm wide, while that of the bottom sheet is 2.5 cm. Both features suggest that the text on the second sheet was written separately from the text of the first sheet. It is also notable that there is almost no top margin above the first line of the second sheet. This suggests that the second sheet may have been the lower portion of another roll which has been cut off and appended here. Possibly, therefore, these physical features of the roll provide us with material traces of processes of copying, redaction, and accretion that underlay the production of the Cade petitions.

All of these traces of the production and dissemination of bills, fine-tuned for different audiences, provide evidence for the production of a literature of clamour. How were the rebels able to achieve this literary production? The judicial sources provide some clues. Some of the persons indicted for supporting the rebellion are identified as scriveners and notaries, professional writers of legal documents. For example, Henry Wilkhous, a notary from Dartford, Kent, is cited as 'le capteyns [i.e. Cade's] secretary'.[125] An associate of Wilkhous's, William Petur, a notary from Strood, sued for pardon for his involvement. Another record shows that the rebel leader Thomas Cheyne had a scrivener in his service, one William Bell of Sandwich.[126] Harvey has cited such records as evidence for how the rebels communicated among themselves and recruited support, but clearly having access to the services of scriveners and notaries would also have made it possible for the rebels to commission the drafting of petitions and to have copies made and circulated.[127] Indeed, the drafting and circulation of petitions may

---

[123] Harvey, *Jack Cade's Rebellion*, 186. For proposals about the audience for this bill see references at n. 110, above.
[124] Plates 7–8.   [125] TNA (PRO), KB 39/47/1/36.   [126] TNA (PRO), KB 27/81/19.
[127] Harvey, *Jack Cade's Rebellion*, 75.

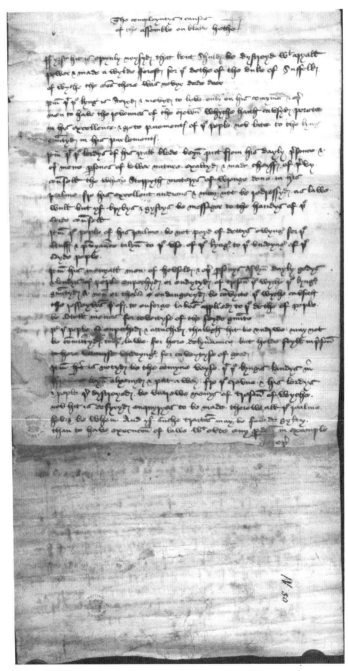

Plate 7. London, British Library, Cotton Roll IV. 50. Petition of the Cade rebels at Blackheath. Permission British Library, Cotton Roll IV. 50.

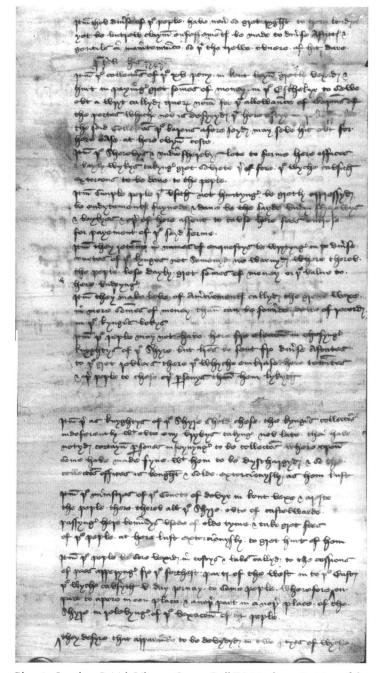

Plate 8. London, British Library, Cotton Roll IV. 50, dorse. Petition of the Cade rebels at Blackheath. Permission British Library, Cotton Roll IV. 50.

have been one of the ways in which the rebels mustered support, just as (as we have seen) the 1381 rebels probably did. We can certainly assume that behind the marshalling and organizing of the rebels was a use of written messages that conveyed both practical arrangements and ideology, and that this had been going on at least since mid-May.[128] The bill in Cotton Roll IV. 50 is written on a roll—an inexpensive and portable format associated with the legal record. This format would be consistent with a bill campaign facilitated by the employment of professional scriveners. The use of professionals might also explain how a copy of a bill aimed at recruitment found its way into the Cook archive in the city of London. The bill in Magdalen College, Magdalen Misc. 306 is copied on a bifolium, in a loose, cursive hand.[129] The fourth page of the bifolium is blank (apart from some practice letter-forms), and the document has clearly been folded three times across its width with this blank page as its outer surface.[130] Folded, it could easily have been transported without damage to the text. Possibly it was made by secretaries acting for the rebels. Payn writes ruefully of the cost of obtaining a text from the rebels: 'and so I gete th'articles and brought hem to my maister, and þat cost me more emonges þe comens þat day þan xxvij s', going on to itemize his expenses. Did Payn purchase a copy of the petition from the rebels? Possibly he did, though we must be cautious. Clearly Payn is referring ironically to the cost to himself of the entire enterprise (including theft of his goods and fine clothing, and his experience of personal danger), and in any case the veracity of his testimony is open to doubt.[131] We cannot entirely rule out the possibility that his copy was made by himself or someone else from an exemplar provided by the rebels.[132]

The bill campaign was not confined to these petitions. Many other bills, many of them accusing named individuals of corruption and treason, circulated also. They are closely related to the circulation of the petitions. Many can be shown to have circulated at the same time, to have attacked individuals targeted by the rebels, and even to have circulated in the same manuscripts. Many of them represent the complaint against individual ministers mentioned in the Cade petitions. Some, judging by the events to which they refer, were very likely issued around the time of the Cade petitions, during the April–June parliament. Others were issued in response to the following parliament which opened on 6 November 1450 at Westminster and for which summonses were issued on 5 September. The chronicle of William Gregory of London, which includes an

---

[128] Cf. Harvey, *Jack Cade's Rebellion*, 75: 'there can be some certainty that a good deal of reading and riding went on in the county [Kent] that May'.

[129] Plate 9.   [130] Plate 10.

[131] Davis (ed.), *Paston Letters*, ii. 314. For doubts about the veracity of the account, see Maurer, *Margaret of Anjou*, 72–4.

[132] Further research on the paper and hands in the Fastolf archive might help to resolve whether Payn or an associate was responsible.

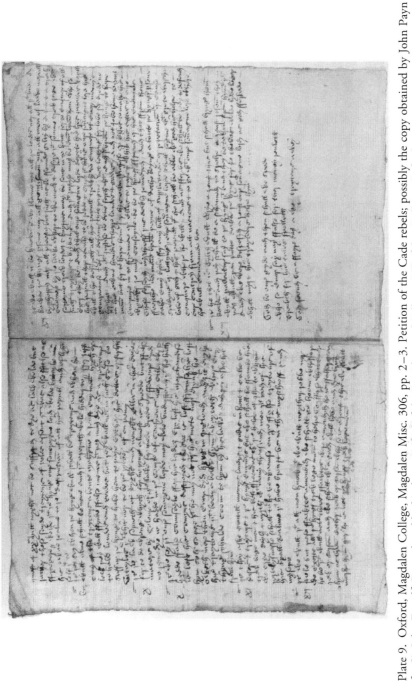

Plate 9. Oxford, Magdalen College, Magdalen Misc. 306, pp. 2–3. Petition of the Cade rebels; possibly the copy obtained by John Payn for Sir John Fastolf. Reproduced by kind permission of the President and Fellows, Magdalen College, Oxford.

Plate 10. Oxford, Magdalen College, Magdalen Misc. 306, p. 4. Petition of the Cade rebels, outer leaf showing folds; possibly the copy obtained by John Payn for Sir John Fastolf. Reproduced by kind permission of the President and Fellows, Magdalen College, Oxford.

extensive account of the rising, observes this association of informal bills and the announcement of a parliament:

And by the kynge and hys counselle a Parlyment was ordaynyde to begyn on Syn Leonarde ys day nexte folowynge. In the mene tyme many strange and woundyrfulle bylle were sete in dyvers placys, sum at the kyngys owne chambyr doore at Westemyster, in hys palysse, and sum at the halle dore at Westemyster, ande sum at Poulys chyrche dore, and in many othyr dyvers placys of London.[133]

Another formal opportunity for complaint was offered by a commission of oyer and terminer set up in response to the allegations of corruption and extortion voiced by the rebels (for example, in Magdalen College, Magdalen Misc. 306). Jury presentments were recorded at hearings at Rochester, on 20–2 August; at Maidstone, on 16–19 September; at Canterbury, on 22–4 September; and at Dartford, on 22 October.[134]

Much of this literature of clamour relates to William de la Pole, Duke of Suffolk. Suffolk, a prominent councillor close to the king, was accused of treasonous complicity in the recent loss of Normandy. Suffolk was forced to reply to clamour against him in the parliamentary session that opened in January 1450. He pointedly asked leave to defend himself against the 'odious and horrible langage that renneth thorough youre lande':

Oure aller moost high and dradde soverayne lord, I suppose welle that it be commen to youre eeres, to my grete hevynes and sorowe, God knoweth, the odious and horrible langage that renneth thorough your lande, almoost in every commons mouth, sowning to my highest charge and moost hevyest disclaundre, ayen your moost noble and roiall persone and youre lande, by a certein confession of the keper of youre prive seall, whome God assoile, shuld have made at his deth, as it is seid; which noise and langage is to me the hevyest charge and birthen, that I coude in any wise receyve or bere as reason is ... [135]

Suffolk's aim was to have the charges considered as 'disclaundre' rather than as clamour, and therefore as not providing grounds for a trial. None the less, the commons presented charges against him of treason on 7 February and of lesser offences on 9 March. However, parliamentary action against him resulted only in his exile, not in his judicial execution.[136] If anything, this only intensified the popular clamour against Suffolk. In petitions composed after his murder the

---

[133] Gairdner (ed.), *The Historical Collections of a Citizen of London*, 195.

[134] The record of the inquests is in TNA (PRO), KB 9/46. The documents are calendared and discussed by Virgoe, 'Some Ancient Indictments'.

[135] *PROME*, parliament of Henry VI, 1449 November, item 15. Suffolk was husband of Alice Chaucer, and formerly keeper of Charles d'Orléans.

[136] For a clear account of the process and its aftermath, see Jacob, *The Fifteenth Century*, 492–5; and, more briefly, John Watts, 'Pole, William de la, First Duke of Suffolk (1396–1450)'. The commons' indictments are in *PROME*, parliament of Henry VI, 1449 November, items 18–27 and 28–47.

rebels cited this event as a travesty of law:

… the ffalse traytour Pole enpechid by all the comynealte of Ynglond, wyche nombur passyd a quest of xxiii mill., myghte not be suffred to dye as lawe wolde, but rather these sayde traytours of Poles assent that was alse ffalse as ffortegere, wolde that the Kynge oure Soveraygne lorde wolde batayle inn his owne realme to the destructione of all his pepulle and of hymself therto.[137]

This 'impeachment' by 'all the comynealte of Ynglond' refers to widespread clamour, including the circulation of charges in a range of formats from formal bill to verse squib.[138] The commons' bill itself achieved some measure of circulation. A copy of the charges of treason against Suffolk, written in a fluent, professional, cursive hand, found its way into the archives of the Paston family of Norfolk, where it is endorsed 'Coumpleyntys ayens the dewke of Suffolk'.[139] Although now bound as two bifolia, it is clear from sewing holes on f. 37 and f. 38 that the bill circulated as a roll.[140] Compared with the text in the parliamentary roll, this text of the bill reverses the order of two articles. Another copy of this text (with the reversed order of the Paston copy) is the first item in British Library, Cotton Roll II. 23. Another bill against Suffolk responds to, and attempts to demolish, his own defence, perhaps attacking the defence summarized in the parliament roll. It answers his articles of defence point by point, providing extensive additional detail to support the charges, with particular stress on the issues of interference in the elections of sheriffs, the accusation that the Duke 'sold' Normandy, and the charge that he has impoverished the crown. As well as providing hard detail (for example, an estimate of the wealth Suffolk holds of the king's gift), it mobilizes an impassioned rhetorical style:

Who but antichrist coude turne the treuthe upse done? who so eville doynge, so inpeitable, who so defyled, so faire withoute soothe? Trowe ye not that Judas kyssed his maister … ?[141]

The document stresses the list of disasters that are attributable to Suffolk by the parallel repetition of 'thereby … ' clauses:

… ther by the kynges obeisaunce was and ys lost … . therby the kynges adversaries … werre releved and sore encresed, therby the kynge's people and soudeours were put from their

---

[137] Harvey, *Jack Cade's Rebellion*, 189. 'ffortegere' is Vortigern, the fifth-century Romano-British king who invited the Anglo-Saxons to invade.

[138] This material has rarely been scrutinized by literary critics; historians have often examined it, though for different purposes from mine, often to illustrate popular feeling. See e.g., McCulloch and Jones, 'Lancastrian Politics'; and Griffiths, *The Reign of King Henry VI*, 639. Scattergood's survey of the verses against Suffolk is also largely focused on public opinion (*Politics and Poetry*, 157–69).

[139] London, British Library, Additional MS 34888, ff. 36ʳ–39ᵛ; Gairdner (ed.), *The Paston Letters*, i. 99–105. Gairdner printed the text from the edition of John Fenn (1787), former owner of the Paston archive, since he could not locate the original. I am grateful to Dr Richard Beadle for the reference to the original. Cf. *PROME*, parliament of Henry VI, 1449 November, items 18–27 (the bill of 7 February).

[140] Plates 11–12.

[141] Oxford, Bodleian Library, MS Eng. hist. b. 119; ed. in Great Britain, Royal Commission on Historical Manuscripts, *Third Report*, 279–80. I have emended slightly. Suffolk's defence is summarized in *PROME*, parliament of Henry VI, 1449 November, item 49.

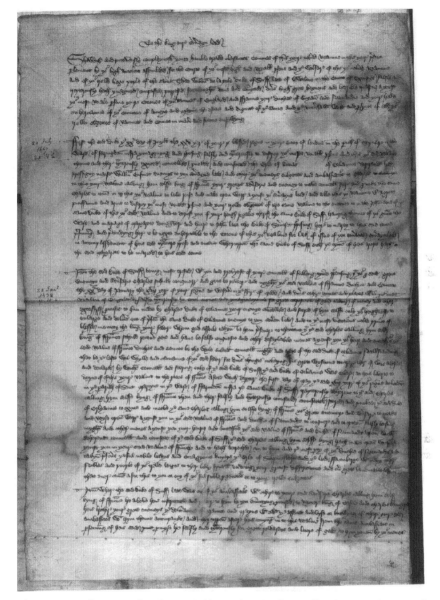

Plate 11. London, British Library, Additional MS 34888, ff. 36ᵛ–37ʳ. Commons' petition against William de la Pole, Duke of Suffolk, top sheet of roll of two sheets, now bound as bifolium with the Paston Letters. Permission British Library, Additional MS 34888.

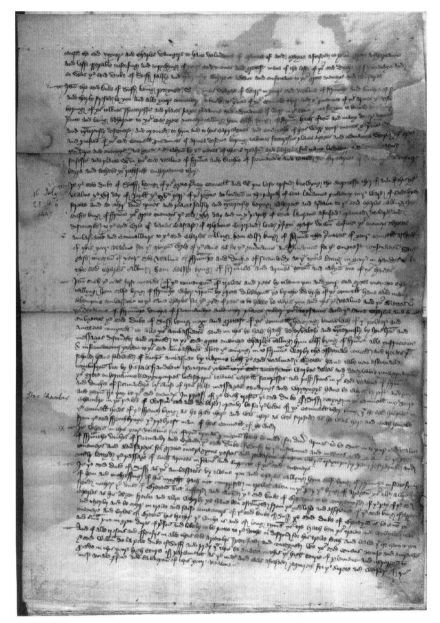

Plate 12. London, British Library, Additional MS 34888, ff. 38ᵛ–39ʳ. Commons' petition against William de la Pole, Duke of Suffolk, bottom sheet of roll of two sheets, now bound as bifolium with the Paston Letters. Permission British Library, Additional MS 34888.

Garisons exiled, poverysshed, and distroied; therby were robbers, pillages, murders, ydelnesse, and cursednesse broghte amonge us, therby our frendes of the kynges amite and of his linage were departed from the leige of oure sovereigne ... [142]

A later passage contrasts the gains of the French and the losses of the English with a series of 'us and them' comparisons:

... therby be the Frensshemenne riched, the Englishmenne povered: they mightly recured of men and peple, we distroied; they to gader, we assundred scarkeled; they well arayed, we exiled and banysshed ... [143]

The text is written in a fluent hand with secretary features on a roll of paper (like the Paston bill but having three folio paper sheets stitched together), the kind of format in which one would expect a popular bill to circulate.[144] The text of another bill against Suffolk (or an extract) was recorded by contemporary Londoner John Piggot. Piggot recorded that in 1448 (perhaps an error for 1450) bills 'were set on the gates of powles writen to this effect':

But Suthfolke, Salesberi [William Ayscough, Bishop of Salisbury], and Say [James Fiennes, Lord Saye] slaine were that England betrayed, on the firste day of Maye we shulde be affrayde and say wele away.

> But Suthfolke, Salesbery and say
> Be don to deathe by May
> England may synge well away.[145]

Say, committed to the Tower, was dragged out by Cade's rebels and beheaded. Suffolk and Say are both indicted again, along with the royal household servant Thomas Danyell, in 'Ye that have the kyng to demene', a verse bill of ten stanzas.[146] This bill reiterates the common charge that 'Suffolk Normandy hath swolde'—also retailed by William Gregory and others[147]—and asserts that Suffolk will become king unless the commons of England help Henry:

> But yef the commyns of Englonde
> Helpe the kynge in his fonde,
> Suffolk wolle bere the crowne.

---

[142] Great Britain, Royal Commission on Historical Manuscripts, *Third Report*, 279.

[143] Ibid., 280.

[144] Plates 13–14. The roll is now preserved as three leaves, following the removal of modern thread, according to a note with the manuscript—presumably earlier sewing had been repaired. Griffiths, *The Reign of King Henry VI*, 682–3, suggests that it may have been composed by a group who had suffered from the losses in France.

[145] Kingsford, *English Historical Literature*, 370. Piggot's memoranda survive in a transcript made by Stow. Kingsford suggests the correction to 1450, though it should be noted that rumours had been circulating against Suffolk for some time. TNA (PRO), KB 9/996/55 contains an indictment for seditious speech in 1446; the accused was alleged to have said that power really lay not with the king but with Suffolk and the Bishop of Salisbury (cited by Harvey, *Jack Cade's Rebellion*, 31).

[146] Wright (ed.), *Political Poems and Songs*, ii. 229–31.

[147] Gairdner (ed.), *The Historical Collections of a Citizen of London*, 189; the rumour was reported in parliament (*PROME*, parliament of Henry VI, 1449 November, item 17); for other instances of the claim, see below.

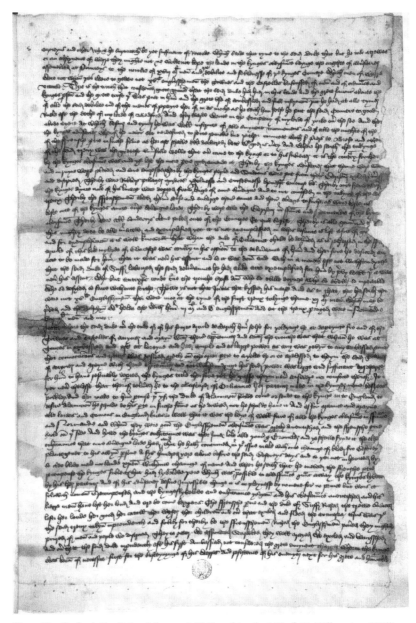

Plate 13. Oxford, Bodleian Library, MS Eng. hist. b. 119, f. 3ʳ. Bill against William de la Pole, Duke of Suffolk, replying to points in his defence. Middle sheet of a roll of three sheets, now bound as leaves. Reproduced by kind permission of the Bodleian Library, University of Oxford.

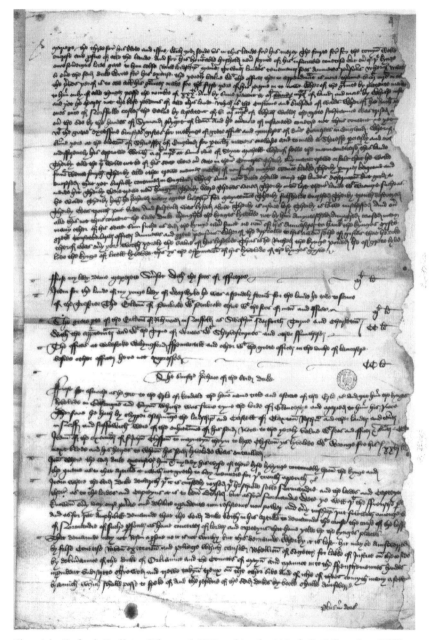

Plate 14. Oxford, Bodleian Library, MS Eng. hist. b. 119, f. 4^r. Bill against William de la Pole, Duke of Suffolk, replying to points in his defence. Bottom sheet of a roll of three sheets, now bound as leaves. Reproduced by kind permission of the Bodleian Library, University of Oxford.

This poem positions itself in relation to parliamentary procedures not only by reiterating charges of treason, but also by identifying itself as a judicial bill:

> This bille is trew; who wille say nay,
> In Smythfelde synge he a day …

'This bille is trew' translates the formula *iste billa est vera* employed to endorse indictments found to be true by a jury, used to initiate criminal trials.[148] The poem is also closely associated with the Cade petitions, since it survives in Cotton Roll II. 23. This roll preserves the briefest of the petitions and much other anti-Suffolk material. A vellum roll *c*.383 cm long × *c*.14.5 cm wide, and written on both sides in a small, neat, clear, secretary hand (apart from the final *c*.30 cm of the dorse, which is blank), this source is of great importance for our understanding of bills of complaint. It preserves many verse and prose texts otherwise unattested, and it includes verse bills and petitionary prose texts copied in sequence.[149] For example, another poem in the Cotton roll, dated 1450 in the manuscript, begins 'Ffor feer or for favour of any fals mane'. This text follows on directly from the copy of the parliamentary bill against Suffolk. It calls more generally for justice to be visited on the king's evil councillors: 'Let ffolke accused excuse theym selff, and they cane; Reseyve no goode, let soche bribry be'.[150] Another, 'Now is the Fox drevin to hole', celebrates the arrest of Suffolk (also called a 'Jack Napys', or monkey).[151] In all, Cotton Roll II. 23 provides a conspectus of the literature of clamour of the 1450s.

A vicious poem that celebrates Suffolk's death may also have circulated with one of the Cade petitions. 'In the moneth of May when gres growes grene', a poem with the refrain 'For Jake Napes sowle *placebo* and *dirige*', was copied by Stow with a Cade petition in Lambeth 306.[152] Parodying the service for the dead, the poem positions itself in relation to complaint against Suffolk and his supporters. As one mourner complains of the duke's death ('For Jake Napis sowle *de profundis clamavi*'), others complain of the failure of their treason and their own impending punishments:

> *In memoria eterna*, seyth Mayster Thomas Kent.
> Now schall owre treson be cornicled for evar.
> *Patar nostar*, seyd Mayster Gerveyse, we be all shent,
> For so fals a company in Englond was nevar.

---

[148] For the phrase, see Harding, 'Plaints and Bills', 76; Bellamy, *Criminal Trial*, 20; and 44–5, above.

[149] Plate 15. Kingsford, *English Historical Literature*, 242; for the contents of the roll, see 358–68. Kingsford believed that this manuscript was compiled by a London citizen in or about 1452.

[150] Wright (ed.), *Political Poems and Songs*, ii. 231.

[151] Ibid., ii. 224–5. In the seventeenth century the fox-hunt conceit was used in libels against Robert Cecil, Earl of Salisbury, which played on the last line of an epitaph for him 'The fox is now earthed in ground'. See Croft, 'The Reputation of Robert Cecil', 57.

[152] Gairdner (ed.), *Three Fifteenth-Century Chronicles*, 99–103. For the murder of Suffolk, on 2 May 1450, see Virgoe, 'The Death of William de la Pole'.

In the closing lines the poet urges the 'trew comyns' to join in and celebrate the end of 'all the fals traytors that Engelond hath sold':

> And all trew comyns ther to be bolde
> To sey *Resquiescant in pace.*
> For all the fals traytors that Engelond hath sold,
> And for Jake Napis sowlle *placebo* and *dirige.*

This parodic liturgical complaint gestures towards the forensic plaint. The longest version of the poem, that which survives in Stow's hand, refers to some forty-six identifiable supporters of Suffolk among the mourners. Many are ecclesiastics, including William Booth, Bishop of Coventry and Lichfield (Chester), and the bishop of Salisbury. It is likely that the bishop of Salisbury to which this refers is William Ayscough (the 'Salisbury' targeted in Piggot's bill). If so, this would establish a date of composition of the poem before 29 June, when Ayscough was murdered by the mob.[153] The poem also names Lord Say ('Rys up, Lord Say, and rede *Parce michi, Domine*'), the third person in the trio cited in Piggott's bill, Thomas Danyell, Thomas Stanley, John Trevelyan, and Stephen Slegge. Danyell and Trevelyan had been among the duke's yeomen and esquires, while Stephen Slegge was sheriff of Kent 1448–9.[154] Many of those indicted in the poem are also named in formal and informal petitions. Slegge is named as a traitor and a 'grete extorcioner' of Kent in the Cade petition in Cotton Roll II. 23. This roll also preserves a list of thirty-three names of those indicted at Rochester ('These ben the namys that were endited at Rowchester afore the Cardinall of York, Bysshop of Canterbury, and the Duke of Bokyngham &c., in the feste of the Assumpcion of oure Lady, and in festo Laurencii anno Regis Henrici xxix.').[155] Sixteen of the names on the Rochester list in Cotton Roll II. 23 are found in the poem.[156] The indictment itself appears not to have survived.[157] However, indictments of some of those named in the poem and on the Rochester list appear among the jury presentments recorded at oyer and terminer hearings at Rochester, Maidstone, Canterbury, and Dartford. For example, John Trevelyan was cited for forcible disseisin of property, Thomas Danyell for seizure of horses, Thomas Stanley for seizure of crops, and Stephen Slegge and James Fiennes deceased (Lord Say), for forcible expulsion from land.[158]

The poem and these indictments would have constituted the 'universall noyse and claymour [that] renneth openly thorough all this your realme' that was cited in a commons' petition to parliament later in the year. The commons' petition

---

[153] Robbins (ed.), *Historical Poems*, 352.   [154] Harvey, *Jack Cade's Rebellion*, 34, 37.
[155] This text is the first item on the dorse of the bill, Kingsford (ed.), *English Historical Literature*, 364–5, 364; cf. Wright (ed.), *Political Poems and Songs*, ii. pp. lvi-lvii; Wright correctly includes a thirty-third name—John Say.
[156] Robbins (ed.), *Historical Poems*, 352.
[157] Virgoe, 'Some Ancient Indictments', 216, n. 2.
[158] Ibid., 215, 221–2, 223, 224–5, 225–6.

asks for the removal of certain persons from the king's presence (in the words of the parliamentary clerk's rubric, it was a bill 'ad removendum certas personas a presentia regia'), accusing twenty-nine persons of annexing royal possessions and corrupting the law:

Prayen the commons: for asmoche as the persones hereafter in this bille named, hath been of mysbehavynge aboute youre roiall persone and in other places, by whos undue meanes youre possessions have been gretely amenused, youre lawes not executed, and the peas of this youre reame not observed nother kept, to youre grete hurt, and trouble of the liege people of this youre reame, and likely subversion of the same, withoute youre good gracious advertisment in all goodely hast in this behalf.[159]

Asking the king to consider the 'noise and clamour' concerning their 'misbe-having', it petitions him to ordain by authority of parliament the removal of these persons from the king's presence and their expulsion from their offices and rewards and fees:

Please youre highnes, the premisses considered, and howe universall noyse and claymour of the seid mysbehavyng renneth openly thorough all this youre reame uppon these sames persones ...

The overlap between persons listed in the petition and the names in the Suffolk poem is even more striking than the overlap between the persons named in the poem and in the Rochester list. Those named by the commons who also feature in the poem are William Booth, Bishop of Chester, Thomas Danyell, John Trevelyan, Thomas Kent, John Say, Reginald Boulers, Abbot of Glouces-ter, Thomas Pulford, John Hampton, William Myners, John Blakeney, John Penycoke, Stephen Slegge, Thomas Stacy, Thomas Hoo, Edmund Hungerford, Thomas Stanley, Bartholomew Halley ('Hanley' in the poem), Ralph Babthorpe ('Thorp' in the poem),[160] John Somerset, and Gervase le Volore, twenty out of the twenty-nine indicted by the commons. There is a close relation among all three texts. Of the names shared by both the poem and the commons' petition, all except Stephen Slegge, Thomas Stacy, Bartholomew Halley, and Ralph Babthorpe appear on the Rochester list.

The textual history of 'In the moneth of May when gres growes grene' suggests a close alignment between the composition of the commons' petition and that of the poem. The poem survives in three manuscripts (an unusually high number for a topical satire, suggesting fairly wide circulation). It occurs in Dublin, Trinity College, MS 516, f. 116[r-v] along with a chronicle of the rising and other events, and other historical documents (among them articles of Archbishop Scrope against Henry IV). The copyist of this manuscript was John

---

[159] *PROME*, parliament of Henry VI, 1450 November, item 16. For discussion of the petition, see Griffiths, *The Reign of King Henry VI*, 308–10.

[160] But 'Thorp' could equally refer to the person named Thomas Thorp, gentleman, in the Rochester list.

Benet (d. by 1474), vicar and later rector in the patronage of John Broughton, a collector of books who is known to have acquired books in London.[161] The poem is also found in an informal mid fifteenth-century booklet now bound with a copy of *Piers Plowman*, London, British Library, MS Cotton Vespasian B. xvi, ff. 1ᵛ–2ʳ.[162] John Stow's copy in Lambeth MS 306, which I have been quoting above, represents a different, longer redaction than that in these manuscripts. There is a particularly close correlation between the commons' petition and this longer version of the poem. The Stow redaction has a different ending from that in the other two manuscripts. Where the other two texts close with two stanzas, the redaction in Lambeth 306 finishes with an alternative sixty lines. Fifteen of the names in the commons' petition occur in these extra stanzas; only Booth, Danyell, Somerset, Say, and Reginald, Abbot of Gloucester are named in both redactions and in the commons' petition. Another difference between the two redactions is that the shorter one refers to 'this pascall tyme', that is Easter, whilst the longer text has 'this joyfull tyme'.[163] The less specific reference would accord with a later redaction perhaps made closer to the time of the indictments and the petition in the second half of the year.

William Booth, listed in both redactions of 'In the moneth of May' and in the commons' petition and the Rochester indictment, was himself the subject of a satirical complaint. Booth benefited from the patronage of the Duke of Suffolk, being appointed as chancellor to Margaret of Anjou in 1445, and bishop of Coventry and Lichfield (Chester) in 1447, as a result of the duke's influence.[164] The satirical verses against him survive in the collection of petitions and satire in Cotton Roll II. 23, where the poem follows directly on from the Cade petition that demands that the king 'voyde all the false progeny and afynyte of the Duke of Southefolke'.[165] Opening 'Boothe, be ware, bissoppe thoughe thou be', the poem is presented as a warning.[166] Booth is presented as a grasping figure who has obtained wealth and position by corrupt means. The poem derives authority and point by being positioned in relation to judicial complaint. The poet plays with the discourse of the indictment by punning on the names of the accused. 'Boothe' puns on *both*, *booth*, and the bishop's name; the bishop has built his position through simony and usury both:

> Thow hast getyne gret goode, thou wost welle how.
> By symoni and usure bilde is thy bothe;
> Alle the worlde wote welle this sawys be sothe.[167]

---

[161] Harriss and Harriss (eds.), *John Benet's Chronicle*, 157–8, 173.

[162] For further description and discussion of this manuscript, see Scase, 'Imagining Alternatives to the Book', 239, 247–8.

[163] Robbins (ed.), *Historical Poems*, no. 76, pp. 187–9, l. 30.

[164] Reeves, 'Booth, William (*d.* 1464)'.   [165] Plate 15.

[166] Wright (ed.), *Political Poems and Songs*, ii. 225–9, 225.   [167] Ibid., ii. 226.

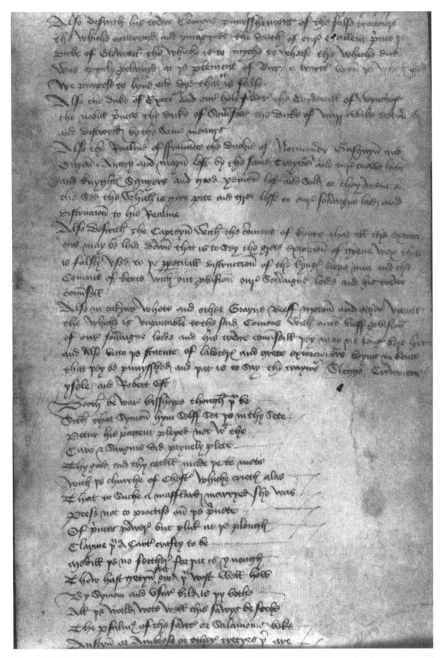

Plate 15. London, British Library, Cotton Roll II. 23, showing the end of a petition of Cade's rebels and the beginning of 'Boothe, be ware, bissoppe thoughe thou be', a verse libel against William Booth. Permission British Library, Cotton Roll II. 23.

Punning on the name of William de la Pole, Duke of Suffolk, the poet prays that God will save the king from 'Southefolkes', because 'The Pole is so parlyus men for to passe'.[168] The poem aligns itself with clamour in all of its varieties. The church of Chester 'crieth "alas" ' to be 'marryede' to such a spouse.[169] The truth of the poem is attested by the bishop's notoriety: 'Alle the worlde wote welle this sawys be sothe'. The bishop is guilty of supporting someone against whom complaint is universal:

> And pray for the party to make his pees,
> That alle the worlde crieth oute on, sotly to say.
> The voyse of the pepille is clepide *vox Dei*;
> It is agayns grace and a gret griff
> To maynetayne a mater of suche myscheffe.
>
> *Vox oppressorum* one the prince playnyth,
> And one the priste eke ... [170]

Here the poet charges Booth with maintenance (with supporting unjust cases at law), citing this complaint ('gret griff') as one expressed by all the world. The voice of the oppressed ones complains ('playnyth') against the prince (Suffolk) and the priest (Booth). The complaint of the people establishes notoriety of treason, and the poet aligns his verses with this clamour:

> Be ware of this warnyng, and wayte welle aboute,
> I counselle the corse not, ne blame not the bille,
> Yt is myche lesse harme to bylle thanne to kylle.
>
> ...
>
> Men seyne that youre secte is opynly knowyne and asspiede,
> Concludede in conciens wonne of the tweyne,
> That ye be ychone with tresoun aliede,
> Or els hit is lucre that maketh you to leyne.
> Pité for to here the people complayne,
> And riken up the ragmanne of the hole rowte,
> That servyth silvyre and levyth the law oute.[171]

The poet hears the complaint of the people and 'reckons up the ragman'. A *ragman roll* was the record of the testimony given by witnesses in shire courts appointed to hear complaints.[172] Just so, the poem is a bill that calls for justice and in doing so it claims legitimacy: the bishop should not blame the bill, for it is 'much less harm to bill than to kill'.

Claims for the legitimacy of such a text as clamour were countered by legislation and prosecution. As early as April 1450 the crown ordered a proclamation against bills to be made in London and Middlesex. The sheriffs were to proclaim

---

[168] Wright (ed.), *Political Poems and Songs*, ii. 228.   [169] Ibid., ii. 225 (my punctuation).
[170] Ibid., ii. 227.   [171] Ibid., ii. 228.
[172] Alford, Piers Plowman: *A Glossary of Legal Diction*, 125.

a prohibition against 'Scedulas, Billas, seu Libellos Diffamatorios, Famosos vulgariter nuncupatos' ('schedules, bills, and diffamatory libels or, in the vulgar tongue, infamous libels').[173] Such items, the proclamation says, were secretly posted up on church walls and in churchyards and other places, or scattered in certain locations, in denigration of the reputation of the king's subjects and to the disturbance of the peace and security of the realm. Henceforth, it was forbidden either secretly or openly to read out, publish, pass on or show, or to make or have made any copy of such an item; rather, any such bill must immediately be torn up or burned. Anyone found doing any of these things would be treated as if he were the author of the bill until he found or produced the author ('tanquam Originalis Scriptor, Dictator, Confector, aut Auctor ejusdem Scedulae, Billae, sive Libelli reputabitur & tenebitur, donec & quousque ipse ejusdem Libelli famosi, Scedulae, sive Billae invenerit atque produxerit Auctorem.') The effect was to define bill-posting as seditious, to attribute to texts claiming status as clamour the highest degree of illegitimacy.

The prohibition of libels and bill-posting was used as a weapon against highly placed political enemies, as well as less significant persons. In 1453 William Oldhall and others were accused of having distributed verse bills in Bury St Edmunds ('diversas billas et scripturas in ritmiis et balladis'). It was alleged that in these bills they said that, counselled by the Duke of Suffolk, the bishops of Salisbury and Chichester, and Lord Say, the king had sold the kingdom of England and France and that the king's uncle in France would reign in England.[174] Oldhall had been Speaker at the parliament of November 1450 in which the commons presented their petition for the removal of certain courtiers. The indictment alleges that the aim of those accused was to deprive the king and set up Richard, Duke of York in his place.

Law-writers were among the less significant persons who were prosecuted for involvement in bill campaigns. We have already seen that it was probably law-writers who composed, copied, and distributed bills for the Cade rebels, noting that this activity is sometimes mentioned in charges against the rebels. We know of other occasions on which law-writers were prosecuted for involvement in libel campaigns. According to the chronicle copied by John Benet, early in 1456 John Holton (or Helton), an apprentice-at-law of Gray's Inn, was hanged for the composition of bills which alleged that Prince Edward was not the king's son.[175] In the previous year Robert Bale, a London scrivener, was imprisoned for having copied or even composed a bill that denigrated the court of aldermen.[176]

The literature of clamour was generated not only by the Yorkists. There is some evidence that counter campaigns were mounted. From the chronicle of the

---

173 Rymer (ed.), *Foedera*, xi. 268.   174 TNA (PRO), KB 9/118/1/30.

175 Harriss and Harriss (eds.), *John Benet's Chronicle*, 216.

176 Kekewich *et al.* (eds.), *John Vale's Book*, 122, n. 213; for Bale, see Ramsay, 'Scriveners and Notaries', 124.

London scrivener Bale, we learn of a campaign in the city against Richard, Duke of York:

Item, the xix day of September in the nyght tyme wer sett upon the Standard in ffletestrete a fore the duk of york being þer lodged in the Bisshop of Salisbury place certain dogges hedes with Scriptures in their mouthes balade wise which dogges wer slayn vengeably in the same nyght.[177]

The allegation that verse libels against the Duke of York were put in the mouths of slaughtered dogs is corroborated by the appearance in John Benet's book of some texts that correspond to this account. In *The Five Dogs of London*, each dog is allocated a proverbial expression and a four-line rhyming stanza in which it complains against its fate and its master's crimes, and each wishes that its master had been slain in its place. Colle, for example, illustrates the truth of the proverb 'Whan lordshype fayleth, gode felowschipe awayleth':

> My mayster ys cruell and can no curtesye,
> ffor whos offence here am y pyghte.
> hyt ys no reson þat y schulde dye
> ffor hys trespace, & he go quyte.[178]

Displaying libels on the corpses of dogs slain in place of their master may have been a gruesome allusion to the bill-posting practices of the rebels. A comparable practice was alleged in a charge brought against some Kentish rebels in 1452.[179] It was alleged that they planned to murder royal officials and place bills on their corpses that explained the reasons for their murder. The explanation was to be that the officials had been murdered because this was how things had been done in the time of Jack Straw. The verses posted in the dogs' mouths therefore calculatedly oppose the gestures and language of the campaign against unpopular courtiers such as the Duke of Suffolk and the queen and her household. They demonstrate that not only were campaigns in York's favour countered through legislation and prosecution, but they were also, on occasion, met with precisely targeted counter campaigns. The Yorkist literature of clamour was answered with Lancastrian counter clamour.

The petitions and libels of the 1450s demonstrate the maturing of clamour writing. In these texts many traditional complaint themes and techniques are recycled. Clamour is expressed in a variety of modes and genres, and becomes a vehicle of expression which is important to different political factions. Evidence for the production and reception of clamour texts shows that a rather wide range of persons was involved in producing this literature, and that its circulation and impact were considerable. This impression is corroborated, too, by the legislation against the practice. Other signs of maturity are those that suggest that clamour

---

[177] Flenley (ed.), *Six Town Chronicles*, 144.
[178] Robbins (ed.), *Historical Poems*, no. 77, pp. 189–90.
[179] TNA (PRO), KB 9/955/2/2. Cf. Harvey, *Jack Cade's Rebellion*, 167.

texts were beginning to be seen as a literature and not simply as occasional pieces. Older texts were recycled; newer ones answered. They were collected and copied by John Piggott, Robert Bale, John Benet, and many others whose names we do not know. The compiler of Cotton Roll II. 23 produced a particularly rich and various collection of clamour literature. The indictment of the 1452 Kentish rebels is particularly suggestive. The prosecutors and (if we believe the charge against them) the rebels themselves understood the posting of bills in the light of a practice of opposition that went back to the example of the times of Jack Straw. The 1381 rebellion was a model for the practice of clamour. The purpose of posting these bills was to announce the authority of precedent, the echoing of clamour down the decades.

4

Transmission, Response, and Development: Clamour Writing 1460–1553

CLAMOUR IN YORKIST AND EARLY TUDOR ENGLAND

> I haue put forth here in printe this prayer and complaynte of the
> plowman which was written not longe after the yere of oure
> Lorde a thousande and thre hundred in his awne olde english.
>
> *The praier and complaynte of the ploweman unto Christe*[1]

The praier and complaynte of the ploweman, a sixteenth-century printed edition of an earlier lollard treatise, is one among many examples of later medieval and early modern texts which, I shall argue in this chapter, transmit, respond to, and develop the traditions of clamour writing.[2] It has gone largely unremarked that a rather large number of Reformation complaint tracts and pamphlets are framed as petitionary texts. In his 1871 edition of three of these texts, J. Meadows Cowper observed in passing that 'the form of a petition or supplication' seems to have been 'a favourite mode of expressing the grievances under which the people groaned', but this observation has never been developed.[3] Among the better known of these texts is Simon Fish's *Supplicacyon for the Beggers*— no doubt it is well known in part because Foxe retails a colourful story about it in his *Acts and Monuments*—but the many other examples remain little known, and these texts have attracted relatively little critical or editorial attention.[4] If the printed pamphlets have been neglected, the manuscript materials have fared little better. Adam Fox's recent work has highlighted the wide social reach and prevalence of libelling culture in the period, and the editorial problems posed by the sheer

---

[1] Parker (ed.), *The praier and complaynte of the ploweman vnto Christe*, 110.
[2] For discussion of this text, see below, 154–6.
[3] Cowper (ed.), *A Supplication of the Poore Commons*, p. xvii.
[4] See Furnivall (ed.), *A Supplicacyon for the Beggers,* where it is bound with editions of three other petitionary texts, and Foxe's story at pp. vi–x. The best survey of this and related material remains White, *Social Criticism in Popular Religious Literature*, esp. 82–131.

quantity of manuscript survivals are now being addressed by online publication.[5] But it remains the case that most examples have been discussed in relation to their immediate contexts rather than as part of a tradition. Fox has brought to our attention the attractive story about William Shakespeare's alleged authorship of a libel against Sir Thomas Lucy, a Warwickshire judge and member of parliament. Shakespeare is reputed to have departed from Warwickshire to London, and to global literary fame, directly as a result of his prosecution for that act.[6] Pauline Croft has traced the more convincing evidence for the way in which the death in 1612 of the Lord Treasurer, Robert Cecil, Earl of Salisbury, was associated with a flood of bills against him.[7]

If this vast corpus of material itself is rather neglected, its connections with earlier writing are even less explored. Scholars have observed parallels with past practices, but have not explored them in detail or elucidated the channels by which tradition was transmitted. The few discussions of the medieval sources of the printed pamphlets have been confined to brief generalizations or else very specific identifications.[8] Pauline Croft registers the lacuna in our knowledge of the historical background to the manuscript libels. She sees the earlier sixteenth century as a time of the flourishing of the libel and handbill, and argues for even more vigorous development after legislative changes mid-century, but admits that 'lack of any systematic study' of the earlier period 'makes it difficult to establish a base line to establish the growth of the practice [of political libelling]', and she does not consider at all the tricky question of the transmission of the medieval material and models.[9] It is not the purpose of this chapter to survey comprehensively the early modern clamour materials and their contexts; to do so would require another, different, book. Rather, it is my purpose to identify some of the most important means by which clamour texts and traditions became available for appropriation and development by later writers, and to explore the ways in which later writers responded to earlier models and built on and developed the literature of clamour.

The complaint practices which flourished in the 1450s continued in use in the following decades of threatened and actual Yorkist rule, providing, in

---

[5] Fox, *Oral and Literate Culture*, 302–34; for an online database of unpublished texts, see Bellany and McRae (eds.), *Early Stuart Libels*. Other work on the seventeenth-century materials includes Bellany, ' "Raylinge Rymes and Vaunting Verse" '; and Cogswell, 'Underground Verse'. Libelling was, of course, a pan-European practice; furthermore, traditions and even some texts had international currency; see Croft, 'Libels', 267, 282–4.

[6] Fox, *Oral and Literate Culture*, 299–300. According to local tradition, Shakespeare's libel against Sir Thomas Lucy punned on the West Midlands pronunciation of his name: 'A parliamente member, a justice of the peace, At home a poore scarecrow, At London an asse, If lowsie is Lucy, as some volke miscalle it, Then Lucy is lowsie [louse-ridden] whatever befalle it'.

[7] For a survey and analysis, see Croft, 'The Reputation of Robert Cecil'.

[8] See, e.g., the introductions in Parker (ed.), *The praier and complaynte of the ploweman vnto Christe*; and Parker (ed.), *Rede Me and Be Nott Wrothe*. For some examples of specific links, see below.

[9] Croft, 'Libels', 266.

principle, recent examples for sixteenth-century writers. The Cade petition text witnessed by Magdalen College, Magdalen Misc. 306 seems to have resurfaced in 1460 in association with the invasion of the Yorkist Earls of March, Warwick, and Salisbury. The complaints in this text that the definition of 'traitor' was arbitrary and motivated by greed and malice ('they sey when the Kynge wulle, schalle be traytours, and when he wulle none schalle be none') must have seemed to constitute a particularly apt response to the attainder of Richard, Duke of York and other Yorkist lords by the 1459 Coventry parliament.[10] In John Vale's book this text is copied with the rubric 'Tharticles of the commones of Kente at the coming of therls of Marche Warrewic and Salisbury with the lordes Faconbrigge and Wenlok from Cales to the batell at Northampton anno 1460'. Given the proliferation of open letters and bills circulated by the Yorkist lords, it is possible that these lords were themselves responsible for recycling the text.[11] At the end of the decade the idiom of the Cade bills was imitated in a petition associated with a rebellion in Lincolnshire led by 'Robin of Redesdale'. This text lists complaints against 'sedicious personnes' who have misled the king, and itemizes the 'peticions of us true and feithefull subgiettes and comunes of this lande'.[12] The rubric associates the petition with sponsorship by the alienated lords George, Duke of Clarence and Richard Neville, Earl of Warwick and others: 'Which articles folowing were divised made and desired by the duc of Clarence, therle of Warrewik, the lorde Willowby and lorde Wellis before the felde of Lyncolnshire men'. Warwick and Clarence are also associated with the distribution of other bills and letters. A letter sent from them to the commons of England in 1470 was fleetingly posted up at various sites around London before being taken down by the mayor. We know about how this text was published from a note by a copyist:

The whiche letre above wretyn divers copies were made and sette upon the standarde in Chepe, upon the stulpes [low stone posts] on London brigge and uppon divers chirche doris in London and in other places in Englonde, before the comyng inne and landing of the seid duc and erle oute of Fraunce, to thenlarging of king Henry oute of the Towre of London and to the upsetting of hym ageyne unto his astate and dignite roiall. In the tyme of Richard Lee, grocer, thanne beyng mair, the whiche toke downe the seide letres and wolde not suffre theime to be openly known ner seen to the commones.[13]

The association of petitions with verse bills which we have observed in the earlier period is once again demonstrated by the *Ballad set on the Gates of Canterbury, 1460*.[14] The poem represents the impending return of the Earls of Warwick, March, and Salisbury as a remedy for the evils besetting the kingdom. The grievances expressed in the petitions are echoed in the poem: 'fals wedlock',

---

[10] Harvey, *Jack Cade's Rebellion*, 189.
[11] Kekewich *et al.* (eds.), *John Vale's Book*, 210–12, 210. For discussion of the context, see 30–1.
[12] Ibid., 212–15, and for discussion, see 44–5.
[13] Ibid., 218–19, quotation from 219.
[14] Robbins (ed.), *Historical Poems*, no. 88, pp. 207–10.

'periury expresse' (l. 13), and 'vnryghtewys dysherytyng with false oppresse' (l. 15), as are the voices of the petitioners and complainants:

> Euery reame cryeth owte of Engelondes treson.
> O falshod, with thy colored presence,
> Euer shulle we syng duryng thy season:
> 'Omne caput languidum, et omne cor merens'.[15]

(ll. 21–4)

The plaintiffs fulfil the prophecy of Isaiah concerning the fall of Judah, a nation riven with evil-doers:

> But euer mornethe Engelond for ham that be hens,
> Wythe languysshyng of herte, rehersyng my scyle,
> 'Omne caput languidum, et omne cor merens'.

(ll. 38–40)

In the closing stanzas the refrain changes, as the poet invites the king to hear and join in a 'new song' when he restores the returning lords to power:

> And so to oure newe songe, Lorde, thyn erys inclyne,
> 'Gloria, laus et honor tibi sit, Rex Christe Redemptor!'

(ll. 63–4)

The hymn celebrating Christ as 'Redemptor' king replaces the grieving lament.[16] The poem is learned and carefully crafted. Part of its craft involves the way it is positioned in relation to petitionary discourse. Not only do the grievances mentioned relate to those of contemporary petitions circulated by the Yorkists, but also the poem is aligned with the practices of bill-posting. According to a rubric in the manuscript, the poem was posted on the gates of the city of Canterbury prior to the invasion of the earls at Sandwich.[17] Also, the poet carefully invokes the anthem as an alternative to the laments expressed by 'Engelond' in mourning. In this way the poet's technique looks forward to the ballads of the next century.

   The closely contemporary poem which Robbins calls *The Battle of Northampton* similarly contrives to replace the discourse of complaint with one of celebration.[18] The poem seeks to characterize the capture of Henry VI at Northampton as a remedy for complaint. Now 'sorow is turned into ioyfulnesse' by divine

---

[15] 'Every head sick, and every heart faint' (Isaiah 1: 5).

[16] Compare how, a decade later, supporters of Edward IV used texts from the Palm Sunday liturgy to characterize the king's return to England as the triumphant entry of a redeeming victor; see Scase, 'Writing and the "Poetics of Spectacle"'.

[17] The manuscript is now lost; see Robbins (ed.), *Historical Poems*, 369, headnote.

[18] Ibid., no. 89, pp. 210–5.

intervention :

> Where-of god of his speciall grace,
> Heryng þe peple crying for mercye,
> Considering þe falsehode in euery place,
> Gaue infleweinz of myrþe into bodyes on hye.
> The which in a berward lighted preuelye,
> Edward, yong of age, disposed in solace,
> In hauking & huntyng to begynne meryly,
> To Northampton with þe bere he toke his trace.
>
> (ll. 17–24)

Edward, Earl of March, has joined with Richard Neville, Earl of Warwick (the bear), in a 'hunt' to put the ravening 'dogs' (Lancastrian lords such as John Talbot, 'Talbot ontrewe' (l. 33), and John, Viscount Beaumont, 'Bauling bewmond' (l. 34)) to flight and to capture the king. The poet figures the earls' good intentions as a paradoxical reversal of the hunt—the quarry (bear) captures the hunter (king):

> But þe hunt he saued from harme þat day—
> He þou3t neuer oþer in all his mynde—
> He lowted downe, & at his fote lay,
> In token to hym that he was kynde.
> The bereward also, þe huntes frende,
> ffel downe on kne, saying with obedience:
> 'Souereigne lord, thenk vs not offence.
> Nor take ye this in none offence.
>
> We haue desired to com to your presence,
> To oure excuse we myght not answere;
> Al þinges were hyd from your audience,
> Where-for we fled away for fere.'
>
> (ll. 57–68)

At last achieving audience with the king (no longer prevented by evil counsellors), the earls have the opportunity to have their defence heard. The proper channels of justice are restored.

The petition of 'Robin of Redesdale' from the Lincolnshire rebellion of 1469 is expressed in an English couplet in Dublin, Trinity College, MS 516, which appropriates the voice of the plaintiff:

> Yf any man askyth ho made this crye
> Say Robyn Rydesdale, Jac rag, and I[19]

The composition of satirical bills of complaint against unpopular individual courtiers continued into the reign of Richard III. William Collyngbourne's lampoon against three of Richard III's ministers, posted on the doors of St Paul's

---

[19] Dublin, Trinity College, MS 516, f. 113ᵛ.

in 1484, earned him hanging, drawing, and quartering—and also posthumous fame. 'The Cat, the Rat and Lovel our dog Rule all England under a hog' refers coarsely to Sir Richard Ratcliffe, a member of the king's council, Francis, Viscount Lovell, chamberlain, and William Catesby, Speaker in the 1484 parliament, while the hog alludes to the white boar emblem used by the king.[20] Collyngbourne's squib seems to have been part of a wider practice of bill-casting. The following year the crown responded to the spread of seditious bills in London and elsewhere by summoning the mayor, aldermen, lords spiritual and temporal, and others, and issuing strict instructions about how the practice was to be handled:

> … we now of late called before us the Maire and Aldermen of our Citie of London, togidder with the moste sadde and discrete persones of the same Citie in grete nombre being present, and many of the lords spirituel and temporel of our land … where we also at the same tyme gafe straitley in charge as well to the said Maire as to all othre our officers, servaunts and feithfull subgietts whersoever they be, that from hensfurth as oft as they find any persone speking of us, or any othre lord or estate of this our land, othrewise than is according to honour, trouth, and the peas and ristfulnesse of this our realme, or telling of tales and tidings, wherby the people might be stird to commocions and unlawfull assembles, or any strife and debate arise betwene lord and lord, or us and any of the lords and estats of this our land, theye take and arrest the same persons unto the tyme … the furnisher, auctor and maker of the said sedicious speche and langage be taken and punyshed according to his deserts. And that whosoever furst finde any sedicious bille set up in any place he take it downe and without reding or shewing the same to any othre persone bring it furthwith unto us or some of the lords or othre of our Counsaill.[21]

The king instructed the mayor and aldermen of York to do likewise. In 1495–6 verse bills were posted and 'cast' (thrown) in Coventry that were regarded as 'seditious' by the authorities. The bills complained about the enclosure of common land and the imprisonment of Laurence Saunders, a guildsman who had apparently incited a riot against the civic authorities:

> The cyte is bond that shuld be fre!
> The right is holden fro þe Cominalte!
> our Comiens þat at Lammas open shuld be cast,
> They be closed in & hegged full fast.
> And he þat speketh for our right is in þe hall—
> And þat is shame for yewe and for vs all.[22]

The gesture of 'casting' open complaints—the Coventry Leet Book records that 'ij seducious billes wer founde i-sette vppon þe Mynster durr … & a-noþer was cast'—neatly opposes the enclosing of the land with hedges that 'open shuld be

---

[20] Robbins, *Historical Poems*, p. xxxviii; Ross, 'Rumour, Propaganda and Popular Opinion', 16, notes that the principal charge against Collyngbourne was treason. For the king's ministers, see Jacob, *The Fifteenth Century*, 634. For the source of the couplet, see below, 148–9.

[21] Raine (ed.), *York Civic Records*, i. 115–16.

[22] Robbins (ed.), *Historical Poems*, no. 25, p. 63, ll. 1–6.

cast' and the enclosing of the plaintiff in prison.[23] This complaint about the evils of hedging points back to the satires in Harley 2253 and forward, as we shall see, to complaints about changes in agricultural practices in the polemical petitions of the sixteenth century.[24]

DEVELOPMENTS IN THE TRANSMISSION OF CLAMOUR

The instruction issued in 1485 to treat the transmitter of slander as its author was not new; it echoes the proclamation of 1450 and, in fact, expands on legislation against seditious language traceable back to the beginnings of our period, to early in the reign of Edward I.[25] (It is notable that the introduction of legislation against defamation coincides with the introduction of written complaint: the crown's attempt to control rumour was of a piece with its desire to manipulate complaint.) The legislation describes the many ways in which complaint against the crown and ministers could be transmitted. The proclamation of 1450 describes in some detail the ways in which a bill could be passed to another person, forbidding anyone who should come by a libel from passing it on:

Proclamari faciatis ac Inhiberi Ne quis aliquam hujusmodi Scedulam sive Billam Seditiosam aut Pacis nostrae Perturbatoriam, seu Libellum famosum, qui vel quae ad Manus suas ante tempus Proclamationis hujusmodi pervenit seu postea perveniet, palam vel occulte alicui Personae Lega, Pronunciet, Publicet, Tradat, seu Demonstret, nec aliquam inde Copiam scribat seu scribi faciat seu notificet, quinimmo incontinenti Comburat seu Dilaceret[26]

[Have it proclaimed and forbidden that anyone openly or secretly should read, read out, publish, deliver, or show, or have copied or impart to any person any schedule or bill of seditious character or disturbing of the peace which came into his hands before the time of this proclamation or may come afterwards; rather he should burn it or tear it up immediately.]

The proclamation describes the numerous possibilities for transmission of complaint, in writing and orally. But it also describes—indeed, attempts to establish—active efforts to impede transmission. When discovered, bills were immediately to be destroyed so that they could not be transmitted, and action was to be taken against those found composing or transmitting them.

Other factors affected the transmission of bills in the longer term. Clamour texts were the products of volatile political circumstances, and as soon as those

---

[23] Robbins (ed.), *Historical Poems*, no. 25, p. 63.

[24] For *The Man in the Moon* and *Satire on the Consistorie Courts*, both of which depict the hayward as a target of satire, see Ch. 1, 38, n. 130.

[25] See above, Ch. 3, 133–4, and see *Statutes of the Realm* i. 35, xxxiv (3 Edward I, 'Of slanderous reports').

[26] Rymer (ed.), *Foedera*, xi. 268.

circumstances changed they were no longer of relevance. For example, the intense interest that attached to the bills against William de la Pole, Duke of Suffolk, must have evaporated soon after his death. Physical circumstances also conspired against their transmission. We have seen that many texts were circulated on sheets or rolls of paper or vellum. This kind of production would have facilitated cheap and speedy multiplication and distribution, but it did not make for—nor was it intended for—long-term preservation. Relatively few of the bills discussed in this book have come down to us in their original, ephemeral, forms.

There were, however, alternative modes of transmission. Apart from interesting those people immediately concerned with the promulgation and transmission of complaint, bills attracted another kind of audience to the copying of bill texts. This audience recorded and described the circumstances of the production of bills, as well as the texts themselves, contributing to the articulation and transmission of clamour tradition by both means. If we may describe those to whom complaint texts are ostensibly addressed—that is, those responsible for dispensing justice—as a 'first audience' of clamour texts, and those targeted to spread the message as potential or actual adherents as a 'second audience', this group was a third audience, even a 'third-party' audience consisting of those whose interests were threatened by political upheaval. It was the audience implied by the open address of clamour texts on matters of common interest.

Earlier in the period it is primarily in the religious houses that we find the recording of clamour texts. The *Twelve Conclusions of the Lollards*, for example, survives only in texts made by alarmed religious: in the *Fasciculi Zizaniorum* compiled by a Carmelite friar; in the reply of the Dominican friar Roger Dymmok; and in the St Alban's chronicler's *Annales*.[27] The *Anonimalle Chronicle* and the *Chronicon Angliae,* our principal sources for the clamour against John of Gaunt, Duke of Lancaster, are chronicles associated with religious houses. In the fifteenth century, especially in the period after 1450, we can trace the emergence of the new 'third-party' audience and new means by which texts were acquired and transmitted. Sir John Fastolf, who, as we have seen, was a gentry landowner whose property interests were threatened by rebellion and threats of resumption, was one member of this audience. John Payn, his servant, acquired a bill text for him and also transmitted an account of his experience to Fastolf's gentry opponents, the Pastons. The Cook family of London were also interested in Cade's demands. By means of their official position, they obtained copies of texts that were of immediate interest to themselves and their fellow-citizens of London.[28] We have seen, too, that as early as the first decades of the fourteenth century bill texts were transmitted to county communities by their parliamentary representatives and through manuscript books such as London, British Library,

---

[27] See discussion of the reception and transmission of this text in Scase, 'The Audience and Framers of the *Twelve Conclusions of the Lollards'*.
[28] Kekewich *et al.* (eds.), *John Vale's Book*, 76–7.

MS Cotton Faustina B. i. The copying and studying of clamour texts by lay persons in the fifteenth century suggests that a new audience has identified itself as directly impacted upon by the processes of complaint and is now able to participate in clamour textualities.

John Benet's book, Dublin, Trinity College, MS 516, offers one example of the preservation and use of clamour texts by 'third-party' audiences. Benet's book contains extensive material copied by Benet himself, together with material in other hands but (probably) assembled by him. The material written in his own hand is thought to have been copied by him from before 1461 to 1471 (by which time the book was bound).[29] Clamour materials in the book include the verses on the five dogs of London (ff. 22^v–23^r); the Robin Redesdale couplet (f. 113^v); 'In the moneth of May' (f. 116^{r-v}); and articles for and against Richard Scrope (ff. 196^v–200^v). The book also includes assorted prophecies and chronicle material, in Latin and English. Something of how Benet came by this material, and what he wanted with it, is suggested by the physical properties of the manuscript. The complaint verses and many of the other items are written in Benet's own hand (an untidy, cursive anglicana—witnessed as Benet's hand by an ownership note on f. 2^v). Some of the material is on single sheets, or sheets of varying sizes, which suggests that the book was based on a gradually accumulated archive of notes. For example, prophetic material on f. 6^{r-v} is written upside-down on the verso, suggesting that the material was copied as a roll. Other insertions occur at f. 54^{r-v} and f. 55^{r-v}. 'In the moneth of May' is written on the recto and verso of one folio (f. 116), followed by a blank leaf (f. 117).[30] The inclusion of texts in hands other than Benet's alongside materials in his own hand suggests a flexible practice. It looks as if he collected ready-copied texts where possible and made his own copies in other cases, that is, he did whatever was efficient and practicable.

Benet's narrative sources included the *Polychronicon* and the *Brut*. For 1440–62 he obtained a London chronicle that includes full accounts of the 1450s insurgency, the posting of the bills against York in the mouths of dead dogs, and the hanging of the bill-poster John Holton, and also narratives of parliaments, great councils, and convocations.[31] His methods, and to some extent his materials, align with the practices of archiving and chronicling associated with the London chronicle traditions of the period, though the volume is distinguished from the London compilations by its particular interest in ecclesiastical affairs.[32] Benet was not resident in London. During the period in which he was copying the manuscript he seems to have been the resident vicar of Harlington, a living in the

---

[29] Harriss and Harriss (eds.), *John Benet's Chronicle*, 157.

[30] According to the editors, ff. 111–19 is a quire (ibid., 155–6). But possibly it was not originally copied as such. I have not been able to investigate this because my examination is based on a microfilm copy.

[31] Harriss and Harriss (eds.), *John Benet's Chronicle*, 195–205, 217.

[32] Ibid., 159–69.

patronage of the prior and convent of Dunstable. He could have obtained some of his material, such as the *Polychronicon* extracts, from the library of Dunstable Priory. As for the transmission of the more recent and topical materials, including the clamour texts, there are several possible scenarios. From an inscription in the volume warning against its removal, we can infer that Benet moved in circles where literary materials were loaned and circulated. We know that his patron John Broughton purchased at least one book in London and was executor for Sir Thomas Cumberworth, described by Ian Doyle as a 'notable Lincolnshire book-owner'.[33] Clearly, Benet, and perhaps his circle or patron, were among those with a close and personal interest in the unfolding of the resumption question and the losses of land and property that followed on attainder for treason. But until more is known about Broughton and other associates, we can be no more specific about Benet's audience and purposes for his book.

Possibly completed some ten years after Benet's book, in the early 1480s, John Vale's book, London, British Library, Additional MS 48031A, is another instructive example of the transmission and reception of complaint materials among this alarmed 'third-party' audience and its clerical servants. Vale's book contains a great many clamour texts. We have already seen that it includes a version of the Cade petition found in Oxford, Magdalen College, Magdalen Misc. 306, a copy of the Cade petition found in London, British Library, Cotton Roll II. 23, and the Robin Redesdale petition. It also includes many bills and letters from the Duke of York and his supporters, together, in some cases, with the crown's replies. It also contains numerous royal letters to the city, petitions, and letters patent. Alongside the diplomatic matter are a skeleton chronicle of events 1431–71 (ff. 119^v–121^r), apparently written by Vale himself, historically precise rubrics, a set of documents often found incorporated in London chronicles (ff. 71^r–119^v), and texts of constitutional and legal theory, including *The Governance of England* by John Fortescue (ff. 148^v–164^r), and Lydgate's history of political conflict in ancient Rome, *The Serpent of Division* (ff. 165^v–175^v).

Vale's book takes us close to the ways in which clamour texts were transmitted, used, and preserved by 'third-party' audiences. Vale obtained some materials from the London stationer John Multon.[34] But of even more importance as a source for the clamour materials was the archive of the Cook family. John Vale served as clerk to Sir Thomas Cook from the early 1460s, and after Sir Thomas's death continued in the service of his widow, Elizabeth (d. 1484). Sir Thomas's father, also Thomas, was a London draper and warden of London Bridge. Sir Thomas himself held office as a member of the Common Council in the 1450s, and as mayor of London in 1462–3. As a consequence of their business and civic

---

    [33] Doyle and Pace, 'A New Chaucer Manuscript', 25, n. 26; for Benet and Broughton, see Harriss and Harriss (eds.), *John Benet's Chronicle*, 157–8, 172–4.
    [34] Kekewich *et al.* (eds.), *John Vale's Book*, 107–11.

roles, the Cook family came by, and needed to archive, a range of documents. We have already seen that the copy of the Cade petition was most likely obtained directly from the rebels for the Common Council, for we know that the younger Thomas Cook, then a member of the Common Council, went as a delegate to Cade on behalf of the city authorities.

But what use did Vale, compiling his volume in the following decades, have for such materials? In some ways the volume has the character of a formulary; for example, often initials are used in place of full names. But this explanation applies only to some of the materials in the volume. Another possibility, suggested in the recent calendar of the volume, is that Vale was 'an amateur historian', collecting material with a view to writing a chronicle himself.[35] Certainly, features of the volume align it with the purposes of the chronicler, including the skeleton chronicle and the documents that are associated with London chronicles. Yet we should not forget that the volume also includes texts of constitutional and legal theory and history. These materials suggest that Vale's (or his patron's) purposes were more immediately practical than those of the amateur historian. Like many of his class, Vale's master had been personally affected by the political upheavals of the period. The house of Philip Malpas, father-in-law of Sir Thomas and a creditor of the Duke of York, was looted by the Cade rebels.[36] In 1468 Cook was charged with treason for allegedly having sent financial aid to the exiled queen Margaret of Anjou and for having concealed a planned Lancastrian invasion. Conviction would have meant the loss of his life and his property, but in the event he was convicted only of the lesser offence of concealing a plot against the king. Imprisoned, fined, and eventually pardoned, Cook tried to remedy his losses during the period in which Henry VI was restored to power (1470–1), petitioning the parliament of November 1470. Forced to flee once Edward IV re-entered the kingdom, Cook had to pay a large ransom and sureties to gain pardon.[37] Clearly, during this time the legal processes and documents associated with complaints of treason and calls for confiscation of lands would have been of intense personal interest to Cook and his household. Vale's project would have provided not simply a formulary or historical archive but an archive that could be searched for legal precedent and argument.

The volumes compiled by Benet and Vale were for personal or household use. They were not intended for, and did not achieve, wide circulation. One chronicle from this tradition did, however, achieve wide and long-lasting circulation. This is the *New Chronicles of England and France*, a work attributed since the sixteenth century to Robert Fabyan (d. 1513), though this attribution has recently been questioned.[38] The *New Chronicles* was completed in 1504, after which time

---

[35] Kekewich *et al.* (eds.), *John Vale's Book*, p. x.   [36] Ibid., 77, 79.   [37] Ibid., 87–95.
[38] Ellis (ed.), *The New Chronicles of England and France*; the following account is based on Gransden, *Historical Writing in England*, ii. 245–8; see also McLaren, 'Fabyan, Robert (*d.* 1513)', and McLaren, *The London Chronicles of the Fifteenth Century*, 265–6, for discussion of the authorship

a continuation covering 1485–1509 was added (possibly by another author). It was published four times in the sixteenth century, first by Richard Pynson (1516), then by William Rastell in 1533, and again in 1542 and 1559. With this chronicle we can trace the ever-widening circle of dissemination of clamour literature. The *New Chronicles* was, like Benet's chronicle, in the tradition of the universal history, beginning with Creation. Its seventh and final book is concerned with the period from the Norman invasion of 1066 to the accession of Henry VII in 1485. The chronicle's sources and model for the years from the reign of Richard I included the London chronicles. The *New Chronicles of England and France* therefore transmit the matter of the London chronicles in print.

The *New Chronicles* played an important role in transmitting the *Lollard Disendowment Bill*. The English text of the *Bill*, in fact, survives because of its transmission in London chronicles: in the fifteenth-century London chronicles in London, British Library, MS Cotton Julius B. ii, and London, British Library, MS Harley 3775, and in the sixteenth-century London chronicles in Longleat MS 53 and the *Great Chronicle of London*.[39] Following this tradition, the bill was incorporated into the *New Chronicles*:

In this yere also [1410], the kynge helde his parlyament at Westmester, duryng the whiche the commons of this lande put vp a bylle to the kyng to take the temporall landes out from spirituell mennes handes or possession … [the text of the bill follows] … To the which byll none answere was made, but that the kyng of this matyr wolde take delyberacion & aduysement, and with that answere it endyd, so that no ferther laboure was made.[40]

The *New Chronicles* also includes a narrative of Cade's petitions, providing a broad paraphrase of the rebels' demands:

[in 1450, on Blackheath, Jack Cade] deuysed a bylle of petycions to the kynge & his counsayll, and shewyd therin what iniuryes and oppressions the poore commons suffred by suche as were aboute ye kynge, a fewe persones in nombre … The kynges counsayll seynge this byll, disalowyd it, and counsayled the kyng … to go agayne his rebellys … [41]

The *New Chronicles* also transmitted the seditious couplet attributed to William Collyngbourne, together with an explanation of its references, and a graphic account of his execution:

… one named Wyllyam Colyngbourne … was caste for sondry treasons; & for a ryme which was layde to his charge, that he shulde make in derysion of the kynge and his counsayll, as folowith:

---

questions; McLaren's assessment varies somewhat between the two publications, and the question of authorship remains unresolved. See further below.

[39] For the manuscripts, see Gransden, *Historical Writing in England*, ii. 238, n. 111; and Hudson (ed.), *Selections*, 203–4. For discussion of the relations among these London chronicles, see McLaren, *The London Chronicles of the Fifteenth Century*, 248–50.

[40] Ellis (ed.), *The New Chronicles of England and France*, 575–6.

[41] Ibid., 622–3.

> The catte, the ratte, and Louell our dogge,
> Rulyth all Englande vnder a hogge.

The whiche was ment, that Catisby, Ratclyffe, and the lorde Louell, ruled the lande vnder the kynge, which bare the whyte bore for his conysaunce. For the whiche and other ... he was put to the moost cruell deth ... [42]

Although questions of the authorship of the *New Chronicles* are extremely difficult, there is firm evidence linking this tradition with training and interests in the legal archive cultivated in an environment extremely similar to Vale's. There are close relations between the *Great Chronicle* and the *New Chronicles*. The two have similarities of content, and part of the manuscript of the *Great Chronicle* (London, Guildhall, MS 3133) and a manuscript of the *New Chronicles* (London, British Library, MS Cotton Nero C. xi) are in the same hand.[43] Recording the appeal of Thomas Cook for treason in 1468, the chronicler of the *Great Chronicle of London* states that he was at that time Cook's apprentice. Here the chronicler acknowledges his motives for his work: he will record the appeal and its result as 'a warning to wise men'.[44] This evidence establishes that the *Great Chronicle,* and the *New Chronicles* by association, were related to the milieu of the Cook household and the chronicling traditions practised by Vale, whoever the author (or authors) may have been. On the basis of the close links between the two chronicles, it has been suggested that Robert Fabyan, traditionally attributed with authorship of the *New Chronicles*, may have written both works, and may, therefore, be the eye-witness narrator of the *Great Chronicle.* This suggestion takes us into difficult and rather speculative territory. Robert Fabyan must have had connections with Thomas Cook. Like Cook, he was a member of the Draper's Company, serving as master of the company, and as an alderman and sheriff of London. Moreover, Sir Thomas Cook is known to have been an associate of John Fabyan, Robert's father.[45] But telling against the attribution to Fabyan is the awkward fact that the author of the *Great Chronicle* does not seem to had access to Vale's materials.[46] Fortunately, these questions of authorship are not crucial for our purposes here. Even if we are not prepared to accept as conclusive the suggestion that Fabyan was the author of both works (or either), it is clear that *The New Chronicles*, cousin of the *Great Chronicle*, had its origins in an environment with very particular uses for clamour materials.

REFORMATION RESPONSES TO CLAMOUR WRITING

The *New Chronicles* bridges the manuscript world of John Vale and the worlds of print and Protestantism, in which new responses to the literature of clamour

---

[42] Ellis (ed.), *The New Chronicles of England and France*, 672.
[43] McLaren, *The London Chronicles of the Fifteenth Century*, 26.
[44] Gransden, *Historical Writing in England*, ii. 231.
[45] Kekewich *et al.* (eds.), *John Vale's Book*, 90.   [46] Ibid., 105.

emerge. By means of the *New Chronicles* in particular, the text and circumstances of the *Disendowment Bill* were transmitted to a wide Tudor audience. Appropriations of this text were among the many responses to clamour tradition in this period. My purpose in the last two sections of this chapter will be to outline some of the most important ways in which clamour writing was transformed and developed during the Reformation, when the tradition became a source of energy and invention for the better-known complaints of the later sixteenth and seventeenth centuries.

Bill-posting in the city of London and elsewhere continued to be a weapon against unpopular ministers. In 1516 bills attacking the king and council for lending money to foreigners were posted on the doors of St Paul's and All Hallows Church, Barking.[47] Bills were sometimes read out by preachers, by which means they reached a large audience. John Lincoln asked the canon of St Mary Spital to read out at an Easter week sermon in 1517 a bill that complained of the poverty of the people.[48] Cardinal Thomas Wolsey, powerful and unpopular lord chancellor to Henry VIII, was a particular target of bill campaigns in the city. After the execution in 1521 of Edmund Stafford, Duke of Buckingham, Wolsey was described as a butcher in libels distributed in London.[49] John Colyns recorded in his commonplace book a verse bill against Wolsey which invites the stones of the city to speak out ('lapides loquentur') against the treatment of 'the buck', instructing him 'nevyr looke þer mouþes to be stoppyd'.[50] In the prologue to the anti-Wolsey satire *Rede Me and Be Nott Wrothe* (*c.*1528), the defiant author figure uses the image of clamorous stones to defend the publication of his work against the timorous objections of the 'treatous' ('treatise'): 'Agaynst whose harde obstynacy to crye The stones in the strete cannot be dom'.[51] The reference is to Luke 19: 40, where Christ replies to the Pharisees' request that the multitude be silenced ('Dico vobis, quia si hi tacuerint, lapides clamabunt'). Over fifty years earlier, Thomas Gascoigne had used the text to describe popular insurrection. If preachers did not protest against corruption in their sermons then the people would 'cry out' in revolt.[52] But, in the London context, the reference in Colyns's bill could conceivably have been read as a reference to the low stone posts ('stulpes') on London Bridge, where, as we have already seen from John Vale's testimony, bills were sometimes displayed.[53] In the middle of the decade Wolsey set up a nightwatch in the city to try to counter the surreptitious spread and display of libels against him.[54] We know that manuscript continued to be

---

[47] Brigden, *London and the Reformation*, 129.   [48] Ibid., 130.
[49] Ibid., 154, referring to Oxford, Bodleian Library, Jesus College, MS 74, f. 126ᵛ.
[50] London, British Library, MS Harley 2252, f. 158ʳ⁻ᵛ. Cf. the poem, also in Colyns's hand, framed as a lament of the Duke of Buckingham (ff. 2ʳ–3ʳ).
[51] Parker (ed.), *Rede Me and Be Nott Wrothe*, 58, ll. 54–5.
[52] Rogers (ed.), *Loci e Libro Veritatum*, 188.
[53] Kekewich *et al.* (eds.), *John Vale's Book*, 219.
[54] Brigden, *London and the Reformation*, 166.

an important means for the transmission of bills. In 1516, apparently, aldermen were asked to check the handwriting of literate persons in their wards to try to find the authors of bills against the king and council.[55] But with the Wolsey affair the traditional themes and distribution patterns of clamour became allied with the new mode of reproduction: print.

A Supplicacyon for the Beggers by Simon Fish was the most significant of the early printed complaints.[56] Fish seems first to have come into conflict with Wolsey as a member of Gray's Inn, where he participated in a play that satirized the cardinal in 1526–7.[57] He continued to rile Wolsey by smuggling copies of Tyndale's New Testament into England and distributing them from his house. He fled to the continent late in 1527, where he wrote the *Supplycacyon* and had it printed at Antwerp in 1528 or 1529 (*STC* 10883). The text was in circulation in London from mid-1529.

A Supplicacyon for the Beggers is in the form of a petition addressed to the king. It expresses the plaints of the poor who are suffering on account of lack of alms:

To the king ovre souereygne lorde.

Most lamentably compleyneth theyre wofull mysery vnto youre highnes, youre poore daily bedemen, the wretched hidous monstres (on whome scarcely for horror any yie dare loke,) the foule, vnhappy sorte of lepres, and other sore people, nedy, impotent, blinde, lame, and sike, that live onely by almesse, howe that theyre nombre is daily so sore encreased, that all the almesse of all the weldisposed people of this youre realme is not halfe ynough for to susteine theim, but that for verey constreint they die for hunger.[58]

According to Fish, the reason for the increase in the numbers of beggars, and the insufficiency of alms, is that in the reigns of the king's predecessors another kind of 'beggar' crept into the realm:

… an other sort (not of impotent, but) of strong, puissaunt, and counterfeit holy, and ydell, beggers and vacabundes … the Bisshoppes, Abbottes, Priours, Deacons, Archedeacons, Suffraganes, Prestes, Monkes, Chanons, Freres, Pardoners and Somners.[59]

These 'beggars' extort money from the poor, and have in their hands a third of the realm and a tenth of the crops and livestock. The remedy is not to create many more hospitals to help the poor—by no means, 'for euer the fatte of the hole foundacion hangeth on the prestes berdes'.[60] The remedy requested, rather, is to set these religious 'beggars' to work, so that they no longer deprive 'vs sore, impotent, miserable people, youre bedemen'. Such a move would restore the rule of law and the power of the king.[61]

---

[55] Brigden, *London and the Reformation*, 129, n. 5. Probably the point of the investigation was to identify all possible suspects (those who could write) rather than to identify individual hands.
[56] Furnivall (ed.), *A Supplicacyon for the Beggers*.
[57] For the following account, see Helt, 'Fish, Simon (*d.* 1531)'.
[58] Furnivall (ed.), *A Supplicacyon for the Beggers*, 1.   [59] Ibid.
[60] Ibid., 13.   [61] Ibid., 14.

A Supplicacyon for the Beggers clearly appropriates the strategies and arguments of earlier complaints. Fish complains that payments exacted by the clergy are an oppressive tallage, under the yoke of which previous Britons had not had to labour:

> Oh greuous and peynfull exactions thus yerely to be paied! from the whiche the people of your nobill predecessours, the kinges of the auncient Britons, euer stode fre.[62]

In ventriliquizing the voice of the poor who are oppressed by their masters, Fish revives the tradition of using peasant plaint. He allies the tradition with the language of true and needy beggars, the stock-in-trade of many earlier anticlerical writings, including Langlandian and lollard texts.[63] As we saw in the last chapter, the lollards mobilized this language in the form of parliamentary complaint in the *Twelve Conclusions*, the *Petition to the King and Parliament*, and the *Lollard Disendowment Bill*, the last of which, as we have seen, was transmitted to sixteenth-century reformers via the London chronicle tradition. The *Disendowment Bill* calculates that removing the temporalities of the Church would yield £ 20,000 or more for the king to use to defend the realm. Fish develops this point. Is it any wonder, he asks, that the king finds it so hard to obtain taxes to defend the realm when the people are so impoverished by payments to the Church? The great conquerors in history, the Danes, Saxons, King Arthur, the Greeks, Romans, and Turks, would never have succeeded under such conditions.[64] He calculates that the clergy's temporalities and spiritualities combined amount to half of the wealth of the realm, a wholly disproportionate amount considering that, by his calculation, only one in every four hundred persons is a clerk. The *Disendowment Bill* petitions the king and noble lords in parliament, appealing for them to use the temporalities of the Church to found a hundred almshouses, as well as fifteen universities, and additional earls, knights, squires, and beneficed priests and clerks. Fish considers and rejects such a remedy:

> But whate remedy to releue vs youre poore, sike, lame, and sore, bedemen? To make many hospitals for the relief of the poore people? Nay truely. The moo the worse; for euer the fatte of the hole foundacion hangeth on the prestes berdes. Dyuers of your noble predecessours, kinges of this realme, haue gyuen londes to monasteries to giue a certein somme of money yerely to the poore people, wherof, for the aunciente of the tyme, they giue neuer one peny … [65]

Whereas the *Disendowment Bill* proposes the removal of temporalities in order to found more almshouses under the control of 'goode and trewe sekulers', Fish rejects any need for more almshouses altogether. By his reckoning, putting clergy

---

[62] Furnivall (ed.), *A Supplicacyon for the Beggers*, 3.

[63] For Langland and earlier writings, see Scase, Piers Plowman *and the New Anticlericalism*, 64–78; and for lollard appropriations, see Aston, 'Caim's Castles'. Hudson, *The Premature Reformation*, 501, describes Fish's text as 'a polemic entirely couched in Lollard terms'.

[64] Hudson (ed.), *Selections*, 136; Furnivall (ed.), *A Supplicacyon for the Beggers*, 2–3.

[65] Furnivall (ed.), *A Supplicacyon for the Beggers*, 13–14.

and religious to work would reduce the burden on the poor and thus the numbers needing alms, and the current funds available for alms would suffice.

Fish also doubts that parliament is the means by which remedy could be achieved. He expresses his doubt by following the tradition of the petition that distances itself ironically from the processes of parliamentary complaint. Unlike the *Disendowment Bill*, Fish's *Supplicacyon* is addressed only to the king, not to the king and lords in parliament. Moreover, although Fish frames the *Supplicacyon* as a petition from and on behalf of the poor ('Most lamentably compleyneth theyre wofull mysery vnto youre highnes, youre poore daily bedemen … '), he later reframes the formulaic third person address as reported speech, when he shifts to writing *about* the complaint of the poor, addressing the king in the second person and writing in the first person: 'Is it any merueille that youre people so compleine of pouertie?'[66] The reason for this distancing of the *Supplicacyon* from the parliamentary petition is explained when Fish calls into question the effectiveness of parliamentary and judicial process. He alleges that anyone who brings a suit against the clergy is accused of heresy and excommunicated, and is thereby prohibited from bringing actions in court. He doubts whether laws for reform could be passed effectively, given the composition and workings of parliament:

What remedy: make lawes ageynst theim? I am yn doubt whether ye be able: Are they not stronger in your owne parliament house then your silf? whate a nombre of Bisshopes, abbotes, and priours, are lordes of your parliament? are not all the lerned men in your realm in fee with theim, to speake yn your parliament house for theim ageinst your crowne, dignite, and comon welth of your realme; a fewe of youre owne lerned counsell onely excepted? whate lawe can be made ageinst theim that may be aduaylable?[67]

Fish put the *Supplicacyon* into circulation in London at a time of considerable hostility to Wolsey and controversy over the role of parliament. After the cardinal's resignation and loss of power in October 1529, parliament was summoned for the first time since 1523, giving an opportunity for complaint against the powers and corruptions of the Church, but also leading to claims from the clergy in the lords that such criticisms of the clergy were heretical—the supremacy of the crown over parliament and the clergy was at stake.[68] According to John Foxe, copies of Fish's *Supplicacyon* were distributed in London on the first day of the parliament.[69] It is not entirely clear that we should give absolute credence to this story, for Foxe has several rather improbable stories about the reception of the text in England, but, if true, it would be consistent with the other ways in which

---

[66] Furnivall (ed.), *A Supplicacyon for the Beggers*, 1, 3.

[67] Ibid., 8.

[68] Lehmberg, *The Reformation Parliament*, 76–89; and for contemporary criticisms alleging self-interestedness among members of parliament, see 8; Brigden, *London and the Reformation*, 175–8.

[69] Helt, 'Fish, Simon (*d*.1531)'.

Fish's text aligns with those of previous polemical petitions. Even if it is fictional, the existence of the story testifies that the *Supplicacyon* was associated with the old tradition of publishing clamour texts while parliament was in session.

Fish's *Supplicacyon* gave rise to a series of petitionary polemics. Thomas More, Wolsey's successor as lord chancellor, replied to Fish immediately, issuing even before the November parliament his *Supplycacyon of soulys made by syr Thomas More … Agaynst the supplycacyon of beggars*.[70] This text, printed by William Rastell in the autumn of 1529 (*STC* 18092), answered petition with petition. Against the complaints of the poor, More pitted the petitions of the dead in purgatory for the clergy to say prayers for them, countering Fish's assertion that the entire doctrine of purgatory had no foundation and served only to enrich the clergy.

The praier and complaynte of the ploweman unto Christe, with which this chapter began, develops the voice of the poor plaintiff oppressed by clerical exactions, giving it a historical dimension. Issued in February 1531 by the printer Martinus de Keyser of Antwerp (*STC* 20036), and again in England in 1532 (anonymously, by Thomas Godfrey, *STC* 20036.5), *The praier and complaynte of the ploweman unto Christe* seems to have been a lollard treatise written in the fourteenth or fifteenth century, edited with new framing and editorial material.[71] It has been edited by its sixteenth-century editor in such a way that it addresses many of the same targets as Fish's *Supplicacyon*. Just as Fish challenges the clergy's authority for saying prayers for souls in purgatory, so *The praier and complaynte* is made to speak to this issue, challenging the clergy's claims for the value of their prayers. Short, infrequent, prayers from good servants are more pleasing to God than long, 'quaynte' prayers by those who are hypocrites:

> … and Lord I trow that praye a man neuer so many quaynte prayers yif he ne kepe not thyne hestes he ne ys not thy good seruant. But yif he kepe thyne hestes than he ys thy good seruant and so me thinketh Lorde that preynge of longe preyers ne ys not the seruyse that thou desirist. But kepinge of thyne hestes: and than a lewed man maye serue God as well as a man of religion. And so Lorde oure hope ys that thou wilt as sone yhere a plowmans prayer and he kepe thyne hestes as thou wilt do a mans of religion: though that the plowman ne maye nat haue so much syluer for his prayer as men of religion. For they kunnen not so wel preysen her preyers as these other chapmen: But Lorde oure hope ys that oure preyer be neuer the worse though it be not so well sold as other mens preyers.[72]

This is the first and only point in the treatise when the writer's voice aligns with that of a ploughman.[73] But by giving the treatise the title *The praier and*

---

[70] Manley *et al.* (eds.), *The Complete Works of Thomas More*, vii. 107–228.

[71] For discussion of issues of authenticity and the broader problem of whether Reformation lollard texts are forgeries, see Hudson, ' "No Newe Thyng" ', 246.

[72] Parker (ed.), *The praier and complaynte of the ploweman vnto Christe*, 123.

[73] I cannot agree with the text's recent editor, that 'the author of *The praier and complaynte* never forgets his persona as Plowman' (Parker (ed.), *The praier and complaynte of the ploweman vnto Christe*, 17–18); Parker does not mention that the title must be editorial, and many of the

complaynte of the ploweman unto Christe, the sixteenth-century editor has framed the whole tract as peasant plaint. Whereas Fish has the poor complain to the king about the extortionate practices of the clergy, this text values the lament of the oppressed peasant above the petitions of the clergy (for those in purgatory) that are 'well sold'. Effectively, it offers a riposte to More's *Supplycacyon of Soulys*.

As we saw at the beginning of this chapter, the editor of *The praier and complaynte of the ploweman* claims, 'I haue put forth here in printe this prayer and complaynte of the plowman which was written not longe after the yere of oure Lorde a thousande and thre hundred in his awne olde english'. His express purpose in publishing this old complaint is to show that the current persecutions carried out by the clergy are 'no new thinge'. Christ and his apostles were charged with 'new [heretical] lerninge'. Yet they taught nothing 'which was not taught in the law and the prophetes more then a thousande yeres before', and they invited their audiences to 'serch the olde scriptures' to find the authority for their teachings for themselves. He offers to print and distribute 'any more soch holy reliques' if he comes by any. [74]

Equally important is the fact that the ploughman's complaint is 'no new thinge' either. To authenticate the old age of the text, the editor has ostentatiously retained the old orthography and vocabulary, providing a glossary of obsolete words. By publishing an old text, the editor perhaps seeks to avoid any charge that this complaint could be a heretical criticism of the clergy. Royal proclamations were issued in March and June 1530 prohibiting certain 'blasphcmous and pestiferous English books, printed in other regions and sent into this realm', and Fish's *Supplicacyon* was specified as one of these prohibited heretical books in the second proclamation.[75] Published in England in a second edition in 1532 by Thomas Godfrey, *The praier and complaynte of the ploweman* was the first Protestant book originally published abroad to be printed in England, and it was not proscribed until 1546.[76] The text's recent editor finds its evasion of proscription perplexing. He proposes that the propagandist value of the tract may have outweighed its heresy, or that it 'slipped through the cracks' of 'ideological confusion'.[77] But part of the answer at least may have been that the text is explicitly an *old* complaint. *The praier and complaynte of the ploweman* is markedly not addressed to the king by or on behalf of those suffering oppressions under the clergy, but is a very old prayer spoken

narratorial features he cites as characteristic of the ploughman are not specific to ploughmen, for example, the shepherding metaphors, and references to lewedness. I agree with Anne Hudson that 'the ploughman hardly exists outside the title' (Hudson, 'The Legacy of *Piers Plowman*', 257, cited and opposed by Parker (ed.), *The praier and complaynte of the ploweman vnto Christe*, 88, n. 18).

[74] Parker (ed.), *The praier and complaynte of the ploweman vnto Christe*, 108–10.
[75] Hughes and Larkin (eds.), *Tudor Royal Proclamations, Volume One*, 193–7, 194.
[76] Parker (ed.), *The praier and complaynte of the ploweman vnto Christe*, 47, 48.
[77] Ibid., 51.

by a ploughman, and written in English over two hundred years previously. By ostentatiously advertising the antiquity of the ploughman's peasant plaint, *The praier and complaynte of the ploweman unto Christe* imaginatively follows Fish's lead and continues the complaint tradition while avoiding the charge of heresy.

The strategy of re-using old complaint material is recommended explicitly in *A proper dyaloge, betwene a Gentillman and an Husbandman*, a text possibly by Jerome Barlowe and William Roye, thought to have been published in Antwerp in 1529 or 1530 (*STC* 1462.3). This text frames the lollard disendowment treatise now called *The Clergy may not hold Property* with a sixteenth-century debate.[78] The husbandman produces this work, which is described as a remnant of a tract over a hundred years old, written in the 'tyme of kinge Rycharde the seconde', and the gentleman approves of it:

> Yf soche auncyent thynges myght come to lyght
> That noble men hadde ones of theym a syght
> The world yet wolde chaunge perauenture.
> For here agaynst the clergye can not bercke
> Sayenge as they do 'thys is a newe wercke
> Of heretykes contriued lately'.[79]

The gentleman notes that the clergy have condemned Fish's *Supplicacyon* as unprecedented criticism of them. Recent critics have pointed out that the strategy here is to rebut claims that reformist doctrine is new, and therefore heretical, teaching—Anne Hudson, for example, refers to 'the search for precedent'.[80] But we should perhaps recognize the search for a voice safely distanced from contemporary clamour. The 'clergy can not bercke' against this voice because it is not contemporary complaint against them. Anything written in the time of Richard II or earlier was definitively not contemporary complaint and must even have pre-dated Arundel's *Constitutions* that defined heresy in 1409. In fact, *A proper dyaloge* seems to have been proscribed none the less, if it was indeed one and the same as the tract entitled *A.B.C. ayenst the Clergye* as Margaret Aston has argued.[81] But the editor of the *The praier and complaynte* evidently followed its hint with some success.[82]

---

[78] Parker (ed.), *A proper dyaloge*; Aston, 'Lollardy and the Reformation', 223, n. 14, 233; Hudson, '"No Newe Thyng"', 229.

[79] Parker (ed.), *A proper dyaloge*, ll. 685–7, 1156–61.

[80] Hudson, '"No Newe Thyng"', 234, n. 24; Aston, 'Lollardy and the Reformation', 223–4; Simpson, *The Oxford English Literary History, Volume Two*, 331–2.

[81] Aston, 'Lollardy and the Reformation', 220–1, n. 4.

[82] Contrast Simpson's observation that 'later [i.e. Reformation] Protestant polemic generally had greater clarity of address [than that in medieval texts], very often directed as it was to parliament or the king himself' (Simpson, *The Oxford English Literary History, Volume Two*, 343).

COMPLAINT FROM THE DISSOLUTION TO THE FALL OF SOMERSET

The Act of Suppression of the monasteries of March 1536 gave rise to a series of complaints about the impact of reform. Petitionary texts complaining of social and economic oppressions were drawn up both in the cause of reversing the suppression, and in the cause of the reform of government. The rebels of the Pilgrimage of Grace (October–December 1536) included among their grievances the impact on the poor of the closures of the religious houses: 'the service of our God is not wel [maintained] but also the [commons] of yor realme by unrelieved'. On account of general poverty, livestock are 'utterly decayed', and the fifteenth to be levied on sheep and cattle is 'an importunate charge to theym considering the povertie that they be in all redye'. In addition, the petitioners suspect that the king's council includes named persons 'which hath procuryed the premisses most especially for theyr own advantage'.[83] The petitionary structure and strategy, the arguments, and even the language of the text echo those of the Cade petitions—for example, the petition in Cotton Roll II. 23 describes taxation by purveyance of grain, beef, and mutton as 'vnportable to the said Commons'—and behind them the long tradition of peasant plaint.[84] Another 1536 draft or consultative petition, addressed to the pilgrims at Pontefract, describes the extortion of money from both king and people by Thomas Cromwell, Wolsey's successor, as 'pillage', and the description of his influence in the judicial system echoes the Cade petitions' assertion 'when the Kynge wulle, schalle be traytours, and when he wulle none schalle be none':

… hys servandes and ek hys servandes servandes thynkes to have the law in every playse here oyrderyd at their commandment, and wyll tayk upon thayme to commande scheryffe, justysays of peyse, coram, and of secyon in their mayster's name at their plesure, wytnes Brabsun and Dakynes, so that what so ever thay wyll have doyne must be lawfull, and who contrarys thaym shall be accusyd off tresun, be he never so trew a man.[85]

The petition finally drawn up at Pontefract calls for reformation in parliament ('reformation for the election of knightes of shire and burgess, and for the use among the lordes in parliament hows after theyr auncient custome'), building on the old grievance, as expressed in a Cade petition 'the peple may not have here fre eleccion in chesyng knyghtys of the Shyre'.[86]

---

[83] Fletcher and MacCulloch, *Tudor Rebellions*, 142–3.
[84] Harvey, *Jack Cade's Rebellion*, 191.
[85] Ibid., 189; Fletcher and MacCulloch, *Tudor Rebellions*, 147.
[86] Fletcher and MacCulloch, *Tudor Rebellions*, 148; Harvey, *Jack Cade's Rebellion*, 187.

Such texts could be viewed as further examples of the adaptation of peasant plaint as transmitted by the earlier rebel petitions; we have seen that rebels of the 1450s were aware of, and imitated, precedents. Yet further examples are associated with Kett's rebellion of 1549. Only one series of articles survives, yet the existence of many other petitions is attested by royal responses to them, and we know that later in the sixteenth century Stow had available to him earlier petitions in manuscript.[87] But chronicles and associated historical archives could also have played an important part in the transmission of models. The author of the draft Pontefract petition refers to the lessons of chronicles on whether it is legitimate to intervene in the composition of the king's council, 'who reydes the crownakylls of Edwarde the ii what iuperdy he was in ... and ... Rycharde the ii was deposyd for folowing the cunsell of susche lyke'.[88]

Responses to Fish's *Supplicacyon* after the dissolution of the monasteries show awareness of the rebels' petitions and position themselves carefully in relation to them. Fish's *Supplicacyon* was first printed in England in 1546, when it was bound together with *A Supplication of the Poore Commons* (*STC* 10884).[89] This text clearly signals that it is a development of Fish's petition:

Not many yeres tofore, your Highnes poore subiectes, the lame, and impotente creatures of this realme, presented your Highnes with a piteful and lamentable complaint, imputyng the head and chiefe cause of their penury and lacke of reliefe, vnto the great & infinite nombre of valiant and sturdy beggers which had, by their subtyll and crafty demaner in begging, gotten into their handes more then the third part of the yearely reuenewse and possessions of this your Highnes realme ...[90]

The petitioners signal their support for the reform of the religious—thus distancing their text from the position of the Pilgrimage of Grace petitions. But they too complain of the sufferings of the poor, asserting that, despite the king's abolition of these sturdy beggars, Fish's old petition is even more relevant in contemporary England:

For, although the sturdy beggers gat all the deuotion of the good charitable people from them, yet had the pore impotent creatures some relefe of theyr scrappes, where as nowe they haue nothyng. Then had they hospitals, and almeshouses to be lodged in, but nowe they lye and storue in the stretes. Then was their number great, but nowe much greater. And no merueil, for ther is in sted of these sturdy beggers, crept in a sturdy sorte of extorsioners. These men cesse not to oppresse vs, your Highnes pore commons, in such sort that many thousandes of vs, which here before lyued honestly vpon our sore labour and trauayl, bryngyng vp our chyldren in the exercise of honest labore, are now constrayned some to begge, some to borowe, and some to robbe & steale, to get food for vs and our poore wiues & chyldren. And that whych is most lyke to growe

87 Shagan, 'Protector Somerset and the 1549 Rebellions', 39–41.
88 Fletcher and MacCulloch, *Tudor Rebellions*, 146.
89 Helt, 'Fish, Simon (*d*.1531)'.
90 Cowper (ed.), *A Supplication of the Poore Commons*, 61–2.

to inconuenience, we are constrained to suffer our chyldren to spend the flour of theyr youth in idlenes, bringyng them vp other to bear wallettes, other eles, if thei be sturdy, to stuffe prisons, and garnysh galow trees.[91]

The reason that the poor now have neither alms nor labour, that their sons, lacking food, must provide flavoursome 'food' for the penal system—must stuff prisons and garnish gallows trees—is that extortionate rents are charged by the new landlords for farms and tenements. The rich who purchase the former abbey lands from the king challenge the tenancies of the occupiers and demand much higher rents than did the old monastic landlords. *A Supplication of the Poore Commons* also engages, as did Fish's tract and the 1536 rebels' petitions, with controversy over the role of parliament as a forum for complaint. The new landlords assert that they have the authority of parliament to disregard the contracts tenants made with the abbeys. But, the petitioners warn, the king should beware: 'let them not perswade your Highnes that al is good that is concluded in your Hygh Court of Parliament'. Like Fish's *Supplicacyon*, *A Supplication of the Poore Commons* is addressed directly to the king from the 'pore comones of this your Maiestes realme', rather than to the king in parliament.[92]

Several other complaints issued at this time address parliament directly. One author adopts a false identity when he writes as if a petitioner to parliament. *The complaint of Roderyck Mors somtyme a gray fryre vnto the parlament house of Ingland hys naturall countrey for the redresse of certein wycked lawes evell custumes and cruell decrees* was printed in Strasbourg by Wolfgang Köpfel, possibly in 1542, and again in 1548 in London by A. Scoloker and W. Seres, under a false imprint.[93] In the following decade John Bale revealed that the true author of this text and of another complaint, *The Lame⟨n⟩tacyon of a Christen agaynst the cytye of London for some certayne greate vyces vsed therin*, printed in Antwerp in 1545, was the London mercer Henry Brinklow.[94] In the *Complaynt of Roderyck Mors*, Brinklow claims to be Roderyck Mors, an exiled Franciscan friar, driven abroad for speaking God's truth ('a man banysshed my natyue contry only by the cruelty of the forkyd cappes of Ingland for speakyng Gods truth').[95]

Even very recently, the story that Brinklow/Mors was a former Franciscan friar has been accepted at face value, but we must, I think, recognize that his claim is much more probably an appropriation of an old complaint tradition.[96] The false identity gave Brinklow security and authority. The Act for the Advancement of True Religion passed by parliament in 1542–3 prohibited publication of any unlicensed works in English, requiring that all printed books henceforth bear the

---

[91] Cowper (ed.), *A Supplication of the Poore Commons*, 79.   [92] Ibid., 89, 61.
[93] Cowper (ed.), *Henry Brinklow's Complaynt of Roderyck Mors*. The 1542 edn. is *STC* 3759.5; the date of publication is conjectured by *STC*; the edn. of 1548 is *STC* 3760.
[94] Ryrie, 'Brinklow (Brinkelow), Henry (*d*. 1545/6)'.
[95] Cowper (ed.), *Henry Brinklow's Complaynt of Roderyck Mors*, 6.
[96] e.g., in his recent biographical sketch, Simpson says that Brinklow was 'briefly a Franciscan friar' (*The Oxford English Literary History, Volume Two*, 566).

printer's name, dwelling place, and the year of publication.[97] In choosing this persona, Brinklow was adopting the old complaint persona of the 'feigned friar'. As we saw in Chapter 3, the Latin antifraternal poem 'Sedens super flumina' is voiced by a disillusioned apostate from the orders, and Peter Pateshull, distributer of pro-lollard bills against the friars in late fourteenth-century London, was also reputed an apostate friar.[98] The persona gave Brinklow, like his medieval predecessors, a particular authority. Antifraternal verses and bills, supposedly written by apostate friars, were ostensibly authored by those who had no vested interest in attacks on the mendicant orders—quite the opposite, in fact—and first-hand knowledge of their corruption. Brinklow's target was, like that of *A Supplication of the Poore Commons,* primarily the negative effects of the dissolution of the monasteries. An exiled friar would not be expected to have a vested interest in making a case for the advantages of the old monasteries. When 'Roderyck Mors' makes unfavourable comparisons between the regime before the dissolution and that after it, calling for parliament to reverse the harm caused by laws enacted by their predecessors, it carries some authority:

> … seing so many cruel lawes in hevy yockys vpon the showlders of the peple of my natyue contry (specyaly vpon the comons), and agayn consydering how lytle the poore be regarded and prouyded for I can but rekyn my selfe bownd to open and disclose vnto the sayd cownsell of the Parlament part of the forsayde yockys. The euerlyuinge God graunt that thei may be as redy to see them redressyd as their predecessers were to bryng the peple into such calamyte by the makyng of them. For the which cause I haue made this litle worke, to cause them to haue instruccyon, that thei may se a reformacyon … [99]

The old persona of the former friar therefore offers a convenient alias behind which to cloak criticism, and an authoritative petitionary position.

An informacion and peticion agaynst the oppressours of the pore commons of this Realme, by Robert Crowley, printed some six years later, in 1548 by John Day, advances similar arguments about the impact of the dissolution. Crowley takes as his text Isaiah 58: 9: 'When you suffre none oppression to bee amongest you, and leaue of youre idle talke: then shal you cal vpon the Lord and he shal hear you, you shal crie and he shal say, Behold I am at hand', calling on the lords and commons of parliament to follow this injunction and complete the reformation for the poor.[100] Crowley makes similar points to those made by 'Roderyck Mors', suggesting that the new regime is a replica of the old, only worse, transferring the language formerly applied against the monastic possessioners to the new

---

[97] 34/35 Henry VIII, ch. 1, *Statutes of the Realm,* iii, 894–7, section vi, p. 895.

[98] See 97. For the tradition, see Scase, Piers Plowman *and the New Anticlericalism,* 171; and Scase, ' "Heu! Quanta desolatio Angliae praestatur" ', 30.

[99] Cowper (ed.), *Henry Brinklow's Complaynt of Roderyck Mors,* 6.

[100] Crowley, *An informacion and peticion agaynst the oppressours of the pore commons,* titlepage (*STC* 6086).

'possessioners':

Nowe herken you possessioners, and you rich men lyfte vp your ears, ye stuards of the Lord marke what complayntes are layede agaynste you in the hygh court of the lyueynge God.[101]

Parliament should not be silent on such matters, Crowley asserts, even if these grievances seem 'not worthy to be spoken of in so noble an assemble as this most honorable parliament', and parliamentarians must redress extortion and usury and other priestly practices authorized by parliament.[102]

Unlike Brinklow, Crowley had his text printed in London, rather than abroad, and identified himself as the petitioner using his real name:

To the moste honorable Lords of the Parliament wyth the commones of the same: theyr moste humble and dayely Oratoure Roberte Crowley, wysheth the assistence of Gods holy spirite … [103]

The reason for Crowley's confident reclamation of the genre in his own name lies with the change of government that followed on the death of Henry VIII. Under Protector Somerset, evangelicals expected, and got, liberalization of policy. Legislation passed in 1547 by the first parliament of the reign of Edward VI greatly liberalized publication laws in respect of criticism of the Church (though not in respect of criticism of the crown): a new statute restored the definition of treason to what it had been in 1352, exempting all other acts 'by wordes, writing, cip[h]ring, dedes or otherwise'.[104] It was in this more liberal climate that Crowley established his own printing press in London, and in 1550 issued the first printed edition of *Piers Plowman*.[105]

Somerset's fall led to the resumption of clandestine complaint. When, in January 1550, Somerset was deposed, bills were circulated in London that called for support for the lord protector. As a counter-measure, proclamations were issued by the London lords prohibiting the casting of bills in Somerset's support.[106] Some documents survive among the State Papers which are apparently original bills from this campaign. They show debts to previous rebel petitions; and adaptations of the form. They are not themselves staged as petitions; instead

[101] Crowley, *An informacion and peticion agaynst the oppressours of the pore commons*, sig. A.

[102] Ibid., sig. B ii–B iiii, quotation from B ii.

[103] Ibid., sig. A ii.

[104] 1 Edward VI, ch. 12, *Statutes of the Realm*, iv. 18–22, quotation at 19. Simpson, *The Oxford English Literary History, Volume Two*, 334, sees the act as liberalization, but it might be more accurate to say that while it did indeed diminish the protection of the Church, it more tightly focused control on protection of the crown's authority.

[105] Simpson, *The Oxford English Literary History, Volume Two*, 343 attributes the printing to the 'permissive environment' brought about by the 'deregulation' of 1547. For the impact of the protectorate on religious literature, see also Mueller, 'Literature and the Church', though Mueller (and the entire Cambridge History volume) says almost nothing about the complaint texts of the period; for a thematic survey of the prolific printed literature of the reign, see Davies, *A Religion of the Word*.

[106] For Somerset's career, see Beer, 'Seymour, Edward, duke of Somerset (*c*.1500–1552)', and for the proclamations against the bills, see Brigden, *London and the Reformation*, 499.

they position themselves in relation to Somerset's role as petitioner on behalf of the authors and their audience.

One of these bills, signed by 'the kinges true and loving subiect … Henry A.', and addressed to 'moste loving and trew ynglyshmen which love god and your kyng', attacks those members of the council who oppose Somerset, accusing them of aiming to disrupt the processes of reform out of self-interest.[107] 'Henry A.' invites his readers to recognize that reactionary 'traytours' are conspiring to interfere with the processes of reform. They have plotted the death of the lord protector, who 'accordyng to his promise wold haue redressyd things in the courte of parliament which he shortly entendyd to haue sett to thentent that the poore commons myght be godly eased and thinges well redressyd'. The motivation for their plotting is a combination of self-interest and a desire to counter the Reformation: 'partly for their insatiate covetise and ambicioun and partly to plant agayn the doctryne of the devill and antychrist of Rome'. Readers are exhorted to consider the accusations against Somerset carefully, and not to be 'caried away with the peyntyd eloquence of a sorte of crafty traytours'; they should 'dilligently ponder and waye what they be and what their accustomed condiciouns be', and how the accusers have risen from the 'dunghill', and are more fitted to keep swine 'then to occupye the offices which they do occupye and now serue to the vtter impoverishyng and vndoyng of all the commons of this realme'. The document shows knowledge of political and constitutional theory. It complains that these traitors who call themselves the 'body' of the council in fact comprise a monstrous body ('then may ye call yt a monstruous councell for truly euery body is nothing without the head') and as such, this body may be destroyed by God ('the lord shall destroye such a body at his pleasure'); as for London ('callyd Troye vntrue'), 'Marlyne' (? Merlin) has predicted the execution of twenty-three aldermen in one day. On the back of the bill, in the middle (where one would expect an address if the document were a letter) is written 'Rede it and gyue it ffurth'.

A briefer bill, unsigned but implicitly from the commons to their own kind (for example, it refers to 'we the poore comens', and 'vs the poore comynalte'), complains about 'certen Lordes and gentilmen and there mastres' who wish to depose the protector, and calls on 'good people' to rebel ('Let vs ryse with all owre power … let vs fyght'). A note on the verso says 'the copie of the bill sowed [?] amongest the comons'.[108] Susan Brigden wonders whether these texts could be 'black propaganda', that is, texts issued by Somerset's opponents to prove that he was a threat to order.[109] Features of this second example might support her suspicion, in this case at least (I incline to the belief that the 'Henry A.'

---

[107] Plates 16–17, TNA (PRO), SP 10/9/12. The document is on paper measuring *c*.29.5 cm high × *c*.20 cm wide. I have worked from microfilm and photographs and have not been able to measure the document precisely.

[108] TNA (PRO), SP 10/9/13. This bill measures *c*.13.5 cm high × *c*.20 cm wide.

[109] Brigden, *London and the Reformation*, 499.

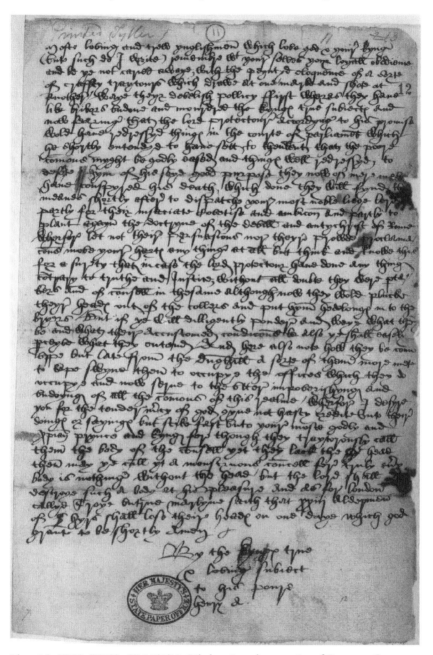

Plate 16. TNA (PRO), SP 10/9/12. Libel against the enemies of Protector Somerset. Reproduced by kind permission of the Keeper of the National Archives.

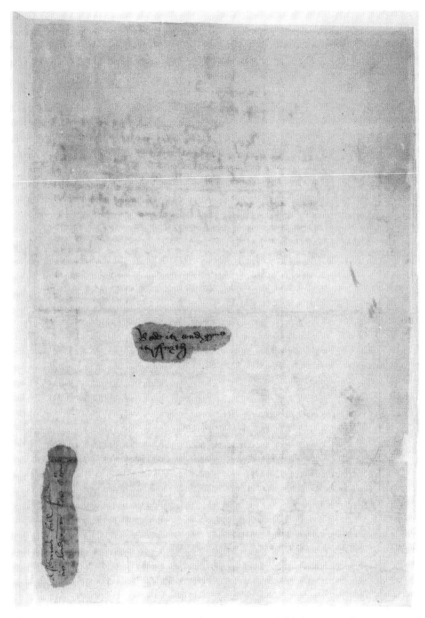

Plate 17. TNA (PRO), SP 10/9/12, dorse. Reverse of libel against the enemies of Protector Somerset, showing instruction 'Rede it and gyue it ffurth'. Reproduced by kind permission of the Keeper of the National Archives.

bill is genuine). The clarity and directness with which the document incites insurrection are not at all typical of rebel petitions, which, as we have seen, seek to show constitutional legitimacy. The text seems suspiciously to promulgate the stereotype of the rebel which was regularly mobilized as a threat by polemicists of all stripes.

In the same year that the pro-Somerset bills circulated and were suppressed, the name Piers Plowman was seized upon as a pseudonym for a further evangelical complaint to parliament. *Pyers plowmans exhortation vnto the lordes knightes and burgoysses of the Parlyamenthouse* (*STC* 19905) negotiates a finally nuanced position in relation to previous complaint. Like the supplications of both Fish and 'Roderyck Mors', *Pyers plowmans exhortation* appropriates the old complaint against the religious and applies it to those enriched by the dissolution:

… euen as in the time of oure greatest errour & ignorance, the fatte priestes wold neuer confesse that any thing concerninge our religion was amis, worthy to be reformed euen so now at this daye there be many fatte marchauntes which wold haue no reformation in the comon wealth … [110]

The 'fatte' priests have been replaced by 'fatte marchauntes' who now are in quite as much need of complaint and reformation.

The writer aligns the present complaint with other petitions presented to parliament:

And for these purposes I haue drawen furth certeyne rude Bylles to be exhibited to you of þe Parliamenthouse trustinge that by your wysdomes learninge & knowledge sayd of the same rude bylles may be reduced into the due forme of good statutes … [111]

The language and description of parliamentary process here align the text with the parliamentary bill.[112] In the 1540s the term *petition* was beginning to be distinguished from *bill*. *Petition* was the term for a text that sought an act of parliament on a private matter, whilst a document that led to a public act was termed a *bill*. Crowley's *An informacion and peticion* aligns with the private petition, whereas the use of *bill* in *Pyers plowmans exhortation* suggests that the text seeks enactment as public legislation. Further alignment with this process is suggested by the speaker's apology for his lack of rhetorical skill. The speaker associates the 'rudeness' of his text with the preliminary stages of a bill in parliament. He invites members of parliament to turn his text into 'the due forme of goode statutes', aligning it with bills in the parliamentary process which would often go through a process of reading, intense scrutiny, and careful revision

---

[110] *Pyers plowmans exhortation vnto the lordes knightes and burgoysses of the Parlyamenthouse*, 2–3, pagination mine here and below, counting from the title-page as p. 1 (only two signatures are visible in the copy I have used; the volume is closely cropped). See Plate 18.

[111] Ibid., 16.

[112] The following account of how bills were drafted, processed, and referred to at this date is based on Lehmberg, *The Later Parliaments of Henry VIII*, 252–68.

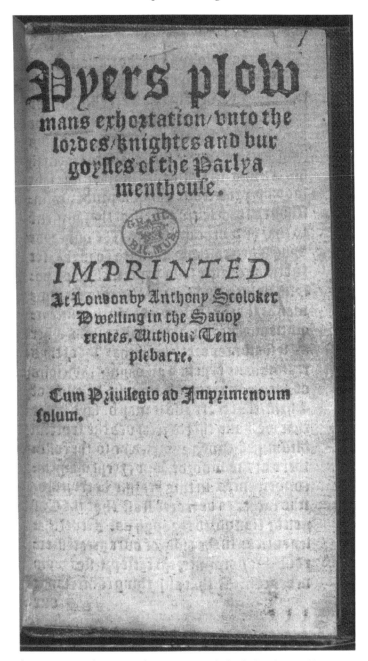

Plate 18. *Pyers plowmans exhortation vnto the lordes knightes and burgoysses of the Parlyamenthouse*, title-page. Permission British Library, 238.a.11.

before being enacted. Of course, the material form of the text points up the fact that these are simply rhetorical tactics. Real draft bills were hand-written so that they might easily be emended, and were communicated to members of parliament by being read out, rather than being distributed in immutable printed copies.[113]

The choice of a ploughman as plaintiff in texts of this period creates a number of problems, but in the case of this text we can say that the selection of Piers Plowman as petitioner is carefully judged.[114] *Pyers plowmans exhortation* develops and modifies the uses of the poor and unlearned petitioner figure in *The praier and complaynte of the ploweman unto Christe*. Like previous supplicants the petitioner doubts that his bill will be effective. But he has a rather different reason for his doubts (ostensibly). His petition may be ineffective not because parliament is corrupt but because, as an uneducated man, he lacks art:

… for I being altogether ignoraunt of the arte of rethorycke haue not conningly set furth this matter but onely layde before you the naked trueth in rude wordes … [115]

Unable to move parliament by using his own rhetorical skills, he invites his audience to imagine how their children would supplicate before them, if only they could foresee how the wrath of God will descend to avenge the oppression of the poor:

… wolde they not altogether knele vppon their knees with the teares running downe by their chekes rufullye loking towardes you of the parliamenthouse and holding vp their handes, desier you altogether with one voyce that you with all diligence and hast possible wolde se to the reformacion hereof … [116]

Rather than (or as well as) representing a voice from the past, this is a contemporary voice which is also knowingly prophetic about the present and its future—Piers Plowman can see what parliamentarians and their children cannot.

The choice of the ploughman as plaintiff aligns precisely with the analysis of economic and social malaise that the bill puts forward. Like *A Supplication of the Poore Commons*, *Pyers plowmans exhortation* builds on Fish's *Supplicacyon*. Fish had claimed that a third of the land of the realm and a third of the yearly revenues were in the hands of the religious orders and the clergy. *Pyers plowmans exhortation* develops the statistically based petition—that goes all the way back to the *Disendowment Bill*—into a reasoned policy document. It extrapolates (somewhat questionably) from Fish's one third statistic to explain current economic and social problems. Before the dissolution of the monasteries,

---

[113] Lehmberg, *The Later Parliaments of Henry VIII*, 243, 257.

[114] Hudson, 'The Legacy of *Piers Plowman*', describes the choice of ploughmen as protagonists as 'puzzling': 'none of the authors thought it worthwhile to explain their figure, or to start by establishing his authority' (259).

[115] *Pyers plowmans exhortation vnto the lordes knightes and burgoysses of the Parlyamenthouse*, 19.

[116] Ibid., 24.

a third of the population was monks, canons, friars, chantry priests, pardoners, hermits, and others. The other two thirds of the population worked manually ('that is to say manured þe ground to bryng furth corne and victuall').[117] Now, as a consequence of the dissolution, the labouring class has become much larger and poorer. Formerly, a husbandman with two or three sons could educate one of them for a clerical career, but now they must all seek manual labour. The population of those needing work will also increase now that all the population can marry (admittedly, Pyers says, in the past the clergy were not chaste—but they did not have so many children as they do nowadays). The amount of work has decreased because a few rich men now have control of the land:

> … a fewe riche men haue ingrossed vp so many fermes & shepe pastures & haue decayed so many whole townes that thousandes of the poore comens can not get so muche as one ferme nor scant any litell house to put their head in …

The new rich landowners are changing to less labour-intensive kinds of farming. Rich landowners are putting the land over to sheep, which yields profit 'with very litell charge of seruaunces': where there were formerly 500 labourers, there will now be twelve shepherds or four or five cattleherds.[118] The ploughman belongs to this class of labourers, whose livelihoods have been undermined by the new agricultural practices. He is a representative of the hugely inflated class of impoverished workers of the land whom the new landowners oppress.

Closely contemporary with *Pyers plowmans exhortation*, *The Decaye of England (Certayne causes gathered together, wherin is shewed the decaye of England … approued by syxe olde Prouerbes)* is also built around the impact of the Reformation on the ploughman.[119] *The Decaye of England* relies even more heavily than *Pyers plowmans exhortation* on quantitative analysis, and it adds the economic wisdom of the 'old proverb' to make its claim for redress. Six apparently riddling old proverbs are explicated:

> The more shepe, the dearer is the woll.
> The more shepe, the dearer is the motton.
> The more shepe, the dearer is the beffe.
> The more shepe, the dearer is the corne.
> The more shepe, the skanter is the whit meate.
> The more shepe, the fewer egges for a peny.[120]

The petitioners explain how it is that more sheep can lead to less wool and scarcity of food, providing quantitative evidence to underpin the arguments of

---

[117] *Pyers plowmans exhortation vnto the lordes knightes and burgoysses of the Parlyamenthouse*, 8–9.
[118] Ibid., 9, 3, 13.
[119] *STC* 9980, 9980.5 (2nd edn.); Cowper (ed.), *The Decaye of Englande*. Furnivall (102) in an editorial note dates the treatise 1550–3 on the grounds that it was printed by Hugh Singleton who was at work from 1550 and that it is addressed to the king (i.e. Edward VI, d. 1553). *STC* dates both editions 1552.
[120] Cowper (ed.), *The Decaye of Englande*, 96.

Pyers plowmans exhortation against the new agricultural practices. There are forty fewer ploughs in Oxfordshire now than there were in the reign of Henry VII. Each plough used to support six people, therefore 240 people who used to be supported and pay 'skot & lot to our God & to our Kyng' have now been replaced by sheep. In addition, each plough would yield a surplus of thirty quarters of grain per year for sale, which, multiplied by a loss of forty ploughs, means 1,200 quarters less grain produced each year in each shire, which would feed 540 people a year. And if, as suspected, there are actually eighty fewer ploughs in each shire, then 1,080 people in each shire have lost their living. Similar calculations apply to the towns and villages. The remedy requested is that the number of ploughs kept should be restored to what it was in the reign of Henry VII:

… we desyre of God and the Kynges Maiestye, yf it shal please his Highnes to be so good & gracyous vnto his poore subiectes, that there might be in euery shyre & hundred, as many plowes vsed, occupyed, and maynteyned, as many housholds kept, as was by kyng Henry the Seuenth tyme, fyrst commynge. And then vnfayned, as we do thynke, we sholde haue corne ynough, cattell ynough, and shepe ynough; then wil shepe and woll be in more mens handes; we shall haue also white meate ynough, and all thynges necessary.[121]

The Decaye of England takes a long-traditional stance in relation to the old device of ventriloquizing peasant plaint. The text is framed as a private 'petition' from a special interest group ('the peticion of these his graces poore subiectes'; 'Our complaynt is for Oxford-shyre, Buckyngham-shyre, & Northampton-shyre; and as for all other shyres, we refer it to the playntyues.').[122] But *The Decaye of England* aims to show that remedy will be 'for a common wealth for his graces subiectes, & to the greate encrease of this noble realme of England'.[123] In accordance with this aim, although the petitioners ask that their ignorance be pardoned, suggesting their association with poor labourers, they also identify themselves as 'his graces poore subiectes', and 'the Kinges Magestyes subiectes' rather than identifying with a particular social group.[124] The petitioners supplicate not out of self-interest but as would anyone who heard the plaints of all of the population save the few rich landowners:

Furthermore, yf it shall please the Kinges Highnes, and hys noble counsell, for to haue a further tryall of thys matter, and to assure it to be true, take al craftes men dwelling in cyties & townes, daye laborers that laboreth by water or by lande, cottygers & other housholders, refusynge none, but only them that hath al this aboundance, that is to saye, shepe or wollmasters, and inclosers, the lamentacions of the Kinges Maiestyes subiectes will make any true herted body to seke & call for remedy, which we beseche the Lorde to amende.[125]

Thus the petition, for all of its novelty, draws on the old tradition with which this book began, the tradition of peasant plaint.

---

[121] Cowper (ed.), *The Decaye of Englande*, 98–9, 100.   [122] Ibid., 95, 96.
[123] Ibid., 95.   [124] Ibid., 95–6.   [125] Ibid., 101.

5

Literature, Complaint, and the *Ars Dictaminis*

> To Loue y putte pleyntes mo,
> hou Sykyng me haþ siwed so,
> ant eke Þoht me þrat to slo
> wiþ maistry, ȝef he myhte,
> ant Serewe sore in balful bende
> þat he wolde for þis hende
> me lede to my lyues ende
> vnlahfulliche in lyhte.
>
> Hire loue me lustnede vch a word
> ant beh him to me ouer bord,
> ant bed me hente þat hord
> of myne huerte hele,
> 'ant bisecheþ þat swete ant swote,
> er þen þou falle ase fen of fote,
> þat heo wiþ þe wolle of bote
> dereworþliche dele.'
>
> *Blow Northerne Wynd*[1]

De modo dictandi litteras, supplicationes, et billas … in gallicis, ore fait a dire quant vous fiez a seignours en manere de lettre, quant en manere de bille, quant en manere de supplicatione, et qest la difference parentre eux.

De modo dictandi[2]

[The composition of letters, petitions, and bills … in French, that is to say when to write to lords in the epistolary manner, when in the manner of a bill, when in the manner of a supplication, and what the difference is between them.]

In this witty sequence from the early fourteenth-century lyric *Blow Northerne Wynd*, the lover's complaint is compared with 'pleyntes' put in court. The lover's traditional suffering (loss of his heart, sighing, sorrowing, danger of dying) is

---

[1] Brook (ed.), *The Harley Lyrics*, 48–50, ll. 55–78.
[2] Cambridge, Cambridge University Library, MS Ee.4.20, f. 167ʳ.

expressed in the language proper to legal actions. The lover complains that the lady has 'hent in honde on huerte þat myn wes'; she has 'disseised' him of his heart. Like some plaintiffs in the courts of the early fourteenth century, the lover invokes the language of peasant plaint to express the injustice he suffers. His sufferings are represented as threats of lifetime servitude ('bende ... to my lyues ende'), threats which, he claims, are 'unlawful' and 'against the power of Peace'. The plaintiff obtains no relief. Love can only advise that the poet supplicate to his lady for remedy ('ant bisecheþ þat swete ant swote ... þat heo wiþ þe wolle of bote'). Formerly, to suffer the pains of love, and to participate in love poetry, was a marker that distinguished the courtier from the uncourtly.[3] But in this poem, ironically, the lover's position is close to that of the villein. Like the villein, the poet suffers arbitrary seizure of his goods, and bondage to a lord.[4] And the plaint of the lover, like the plaint of the peasant, achieves no justice. His complaint in the court of love having failed, the poet is left only with the prospect of petitioning his mistress—is left with love poetry as his only means of complaining of his loss.

When this poet invokes the forms and institutions of judicial process, he makes explicit a structure of relationships between different kinds of plaint and theorizes his poem's place within it. The love lyric is like a plaint put in court; it is also like peasant plaint that is unable to achieve a remedy. The lyric is an early example of the ways in which judicial plaint restructures literature. Once there was the possibility that some writings could be viewed as legally admissible complaint, it followed that the status of all writings could, in principle, be defined by the new framework. The new categories and distinctions provided a framework for retheorizing and restructuring writing. In this final chapter I propose to examine the practices of complaint writing in relation to the arts of analysis and composition of the plaint.

The theorization, analysis, and composition of plaint were part of the *ars dictaminis*. The discipline encompassed the writing of letters missive, and the composition of bills of complaint and petitions, and all of these arts were taught together in England, with business and legal writing being taught alongside the writing of diplomatic and other non-legal letters.[5] One means by which the *ars*

---

[3] Cf. the classic statement by C. S. Lewis: '[The] service of love ... thus becomes, from one point of view the flower, from another the seed, of all those noble usages which distinguish the gentle from the villein: only the courteous can love, but it is love that makes them courteous.' Lewis, *The Allegory of Love*, 2.

[4] For a different reading, see Scattergood, 'Authority and Resistance', 191–2, who sees this as a poem that deals indirectly with problems of bastard feudalism and retinues.

[5] Some have drawn attention to the fuzziness of the boundary more generally. For example, in the view of Giles Constable, 'there is no clear line of demarcation between public and official "documents" and unofficial and private "letters" in the Middle Ages' (Constable, *Letters*, 22–33; cf. Camargo, *Ars Dictaminis*, 37; Camargo, *Medieval Rhetorics*, 22.) The *ars dictaminis* was usually associated with the composition of prose, but there were overlaps with the arts of versification (Camargo, *Ars Dictaminis*, 17, 48).

dictaminis was taught was by formularies and treatises. *De modo dictandi*, an example of such a formulary from later fourteenth-century England, has many precedents. H. G. Richardson lists several examples of treatises 'which seem to have been originally composed about the middle of the thirteenth century'.[6] From *c*.1350 treatises of English origin become more plentiful, examples including the dictaminal treatises compiled in England by John de Briggis, Thomas Sampson, and Thomas Merke, between 1351 and 1409, one by one Simon O, dated 1400–25, and another in London, British Library, MS Harley 670 of *c*.1435.[7] Models of the *libellus* in Roman and ecclesiastical law may also have been used. Some treatise authors drew on continental formularies which provided examples of the *libelli* of Roman law, and some of the authors who wrote for secular courts may have been trained to write the *libelli* used in ecclesiastical courts.[8] We know that formularies of canon law which contained libels were passed down in the fourteenth and fifteenth centuries. For example, Robert Easingwold, proctor of the court of York, left to his former clerk in his will 'books of the practice of the court, namely libels, positions, articles, exceptions and so on'.[9] The *ars dictaminis* involved distinguishing different kinds of petitionary text, knowing the circumstances appropriate to their use, being able to analyse, label, and know the function of the parts of a text (the analysis of a document was based on the analysis of the parts of speech), and imitating models.[10] The rubric from the late fourteenth-century *De modo dictandi*, quoted above, essentially announces that this treatise will teach this art; it will explain the differences between letters, petitions, and bills, will offer guidance on when the different kinds should be used, and will teach the vocabulary of dictaminal analysis. As a textual practice concerned with the forms, vocabulary, and performative functions of complaint texts, and their relations and distinctions, clamour writing is, I shall argue in this chapter, a vigorously innovative practice of the *ars dictaminis*. I shall propose that it was essentially by means of a kind of dictaminal experimentation and development that the relations between literature and complaint were explored.

The history of dictaminal experimentation and development offered in this chapter involves some revision of the picture offered by recent work on the *ars dictaminis*. Recently, scholars have proposed that a crucial change in dictaminal practice was a shift to the use of English by the royal writing offices around the second quarter of the fifteenth century, which, it has been argued, facilitated the spread of models for emulation widely throughout society. In the fourteenth

---

⁶ Richardson, 'Business Training', 275, and n. 84.

⁷ Murphy, 'Rhetoric', 8, 15–19; Pantin, 'Treatise on Letter-Writing', 329; Salter, Pantin and Richardson (eds.), *Formularies*, ii. 440–2.

⁸ Richardson and Sayles (eds.), *Procedure without Writ*, pp. lvii–lix.

⁹ Owen, *Medieval Canon Law*, 30–42, quotation at 32.

¹⁰ Murphy, 'Rhetoric', 1–8.

century the usual languages of letter-writing were French and Latin (what are possibly the earliest surviving letters in English date from the 1390s).[11] After 1420 the use of English in letters and documents spread rapidly.[12] After this date, too, English replaces French as the usual language of chancery bills; according to Haskett, most are in French before 1432, and most are in English after 1443.[13] This development has been explained in terms of royal policy. A key event, it has been argued, was the adoption of English for royal communications by Henry V in 1420. John Fisher has suggested that the chancery texts written in English offered authoritative vernacular models for rendering the style and idioms taught by the French and Latin dictaminal treatises.[14] In Malcolm Richardson's view, the practice of chancery clerks stood at the apex of a structure of apprenticeship and learning by emulation, suffusing the legal quarter, and even extending into private correspondence that was not written by professional clerks.[15]

Our analysis of the relations between literature and complaint offers a rather different perspective on the developments of the fifteenth century. As we have seen, the development of judicial plaint has an impact on literary composition from the earliest days of the written plaint. Plaint procedure introduced categories of plaint text and also contestation over those categories. It extended the forms and varieties of text which could count as legal plaint, and also led to the creation of categories of inadmissible and illegal plaint, providing a framework within which plaint traditions could take on new and contested status. The writings we have examined from the later thirteenth century and the first half of the fourteenth century illustrate a variety of experiments with the plaint. *Blow Northerne Wynd* explores, in the register of the love lyric, a practice of analysis, distinction, experiment, and the employment of analytical vocabulary that we have observed in many examples in Chapters 1 and 2. We have seen that texts from the period to *c.*1340 such as *Poem on Disputed Villein Services*, *Trailbaston*, *Song of the Husbandman*, *Versus compositi de Roger Beler*, and *Song on the Venality of the Judges* are informed by the framework of the legal plaint.

The first surviving vernacular clamour texts that are petitionary in phrase and structure date from the 1380s. The Mercers' petition of 1387/8 is an excellent

---

[11] Richardson, 'The *Dictamen*', 209–10. For the earliest letters in English, see Davis, 'The *Litera Troili*', 237, n. 4; he follows Kingsford, though with a caveat that there may be older letters preserved in later copies.

[12] Richardson, 'The *Dictamen*', 212.

[13] Haskett, 'Country Lawyers?', 14; cf. Baildon (ed.), *Select Cases*, p. xxiv, who dates the change to the reign of Henry V.

[14] Fisher, *Emergence of Standard English*, 42–52.

[15] Richardson, 'The *Dictamen*', 220–1; cf. Richardson, 'Fading Influence'. Camargo, 'Waning of the Medieval *Ars Dictaminis*', surveys the varying later histories of *dictamen* in England, France, and Italy.

example. The text follows the structure of petitions as taught in the dictaminal treatises and modelled in the formularies. It opens with an address, followed by identification of the petitioner, and then a lengthy exposition:

⟨T⟩o the moost noble & Worthiest Lordes moost ryghtful & wysest conseille to owre lige Lorde the Kyng, compleynen, if it lyke to yow, the folk of the Mercerye of London, ⟨as⟩ a membre of the same citee, of many wronges subtiles & also open oppressions, ydo to hem by longe tyme here bifore passed.

Of whiche oon was where the eleccion of Mairaltee is to be to the fre men of the Citee bi gode & paisible auys of the wysest & trewest at o day in the yere frelich, there, nought-withstondyng the same fredam or fraunchise, Nichol Brembre wyth his vpberers purposed hym, the yere next after John Northampton, Mair of the same Citee with stronge honde, as it is ful knowen, & though debate & strenger partye ayeins the pees bifore purueyde was chosen Mair in destruccion of many ryght. [16]

As we saw in Chapter 2, this petition parallels the Anglo-Norman petitions issued on the same occasion by the other London guilds and possibly it was the model for the other eleven petitions against Brembre.[17] From the dictaminal perspective its model in turn is clearly other Anglo-Norman petitions. John Wolde's and John Reche's petition to the lords of the council in parliament begins with a similar address ('Aus honurables et sages seigneurs du conseil de cest present parlement'), identification of the petitioners ('suppliont Johan Wolde et Johan Reche'), followed by the exposition (recital of the problem) ('que, come ils estoient seiséz en lour demesne … que les ditz suppliantz furont oustéz des ditz tenementz par un Johan Marshalle, Agnes Crosby et Thomas Bradwas par colour des lettres patentes nostre seigneur le Roy').[18] The second part of the Mercers' petition also follows the canon of form and the formulaic phrases of petitionary rhetoric, as for example identified by Haskett in chancery petitions. The supplication is signalled by a relative ('For thy, graciouse lordes'). This is formulaic; compare two of Haskett's examples: 'Que plese a vostre tresgraciouse seigniorie', and 'Where fore like yt to your right myghty lordship'.[19] Then follows the request for consideration ('lyke it to yow to take hede'), the request for process (a trial before 'an indifferent Juge & Mair'), a request for examination ('that we mowe come in answer to excuse vs [should they be falsely indicted]'), a remedy ('oon the grettest remedye … that the statut … mowe stonde in strengthe & be excecut'), and an explicit.[20]

Several other examples of efforts to compose clamour texts in the vernacular which we have already encountered are associated with intense dictaminal

---

[16] Chambers and Daunt (eds.), *Book of London English*, 33–4.   [17] See 68–9, 77.

[18] Legge (ed.), *Anglo-Norman Letters and Petitions*, 16–17; date first decade of the fifteenth century.

[19] Haskett, 'Medieval Chancery Bills', 27, 24; both texts are dated 1439. On chancery as a judicial institution, see Haskett, 'Court of Chancery'.

[20] The reference is to a statute that forbad victuallers to hold judicial office, see Chambers and Daunt (eds.), *Book of London English*, 245, n. *ad loc.*

experimentation. With the lollard petitions discussed in Chapter 3 we have several examples of clamour texts that survive in parallel English and Latin versions. These provide particularly good opportunities to observe early attempts to render dictaminal conventions in English. The formula of address in the lollard *Petition* has parallels with the particularly florid modes of address adopted for petitions to the monarchy towards the end of the century—perhaps from as early as mid-century. The *Petition* participates in this dictaminal innovation in its Latin version, and finds an English translation. In Latin, the text is addressed 'illustrissimo Regi nostro tam Anglie quam Francie ac Domino Duci ceterisque magnatibus Regni Anglicani tam secularibus quam ecclesiasticis viris in parliamento congregatis'. In the English version, this is rendered with a precise equivalent, 'to oure most noble and most worþi King Richard, kyng boþe of Englond and of Fraunce, and to þe noble Duk of Lancastre, and to oþere grete men of þe rewme, boþe to seculers and men of holi Chirche, þat ben gaderid in þe Parlement'. The superlative *illustrissimus*, applied to the king in the *Petition*, finds an English equivalent of *most noble* in the address to both king and duke in the English version. The Latin version of the term is applied to the duke in a letter from the friars against the Wycliffites of 1382, where John of Gaunt is addressed 'illustrissimo principi ac domino serenissimo domino Johanni Dei gratia praeclarissimo regi Castelliae et Legionis, ac nobilissimo duci Lancastriae'.[21] It is thought that the king promoted these modes of address.[22] With the *Lollard Disendowment Bill*, as we have seen, we seem to have two independent attempts at composition in English, one possibly the original draft, the other, arguably, re-translated from Latin into English. These versions offer us the opportunity to compare two different attempts at rendering the new dictaminal conventions in English. For example, the openings 'To the moste excellent redoubte lorde the Kyng, and to alle the noble lordes of this present parlement' (?original), and 'The most excellent and dowȝty lord, oure lege Lord the Kyng, and to alle the Lordys of the reme of this present Parlement' (Sharp text) both offer attempts at the florid address in English.[23]

---

[21] Stein (ed.), 'The Latin Text of Wyclif's *Complaint*', 88; Arnold (ed.), *Select English Works of John Wyclif*, iii. 508; Shirley (ed.), *Fasciculi Zizaniorum*, 292.

[22] e.g., letters from the king to the University of Oxford, Shirley (ed.), *Fasciculi Zizaniorum*, 312, 314. On Richard's promotion of particularly florid forms of address, see Saul, 'Richard II and the Vocabulary of Kingship'. In Mark Ormrod's view, Saul's dating of the change to the 1390s is too late; he would place it mid-century (Mark Ormrod, private communication, 18 Sept. 2003.) John But's addition to the A version of *Piers Plowman* is another example of a Middle English text that seems to show awareness of these forms; see Scase, ' "First to Reckon Richard" '. In view of the appearance of florid modes of address in letters to Gaunt, and taking into consideration Gaunt's influential position at this time, I suggest that it is possible that Gaunt himself was behind this initiative.

[23] Riley (ed.), *Chronica Monasterii S. Albani. Annales Monasterii S. Albani, a Johanne Amundesham*, i. 453; Hudson (ed.), *Selections*, 135. Lollard interest in the possibilities of vernacular dictaminal composition at this period is also evidenced by the *Epistola Sathanae ad Cleros*, a Middle

These creative dictaminal projects were crucial to enabling the formation of a literature of clamour. The clamour literature of the 1450s and after, which we explored in Chapters 3 and 4, derives its particular maturity and complexity in part because it was close to being a monolingual literature. There was now a very close relation between the formal literature of judicial fora and the literature of clamour. The use of the vernacular was no longer marked as excluded from a hearing, or from record. We have seen that from the mid-fifteenth century the commons presented petitions to parliament in English, and petitions were enrolled and circulated in English. Copies of the rebel petitions were sought out and recorded in English. Legal arguments and defences seem to have been drafted in English. No longer marked as the plaint which is excluded from legal fora, henceforth the claims to legitimacy of English clamour were strengthened.

The history of the emergence of English as a legitimate vehicle for judicial communication and record has overlooked clamour materials, or else misinterpreted their significance. Clamour writings provided the earliest models for English *dictamen*, models that pre-date the adoption of the vernacular for the purposes of official communication and legal record by the royal writing offices. As we have seen, it has been traditional to view the Mercers' petition as one of the two earliest vernacular petitions to parliament, when the evidence suggests rather that it was produced as a clamour text. Discussion of the *Twelve Conclusions* and the *Lollard Disendowment Bill* has never resolved the question of whether these texts were 'real' petitions. This study suggests that it is the idea of clamour that stimulated the writing of these texts. The fact that clamour gave status and legitimacy, in principle, to complaint texts of all kinds, I would argue, stimulated these creative experiments in English *dictamen*.

The energies and sources of creativity of the clamour experiment were essentially literary and poetic. As we have seen, long before the royal writing offices began to adopt English as the language of royal communications, poets were responding to the impact of judicial plaint. The awareness of plaint demonstrable in the earlier poems considered here suggests that poets and their audiences were familiar with the conventions of the judicial plaint. We can sometimes find material evidence to corroborate this deduction. Some of the scribes of the early poetry anthologies seem to have participated in both legal and literary production. As we saw in Chapter 1, *Against the King's Taxes* occurs in a cartulary. Carter Revard has identified forty-one legal instruments and two fragmentary legal documents in the hand of the scribe of London, British Library, MS Harley 2253.[24]

English text in the tradition of the letter from Satan. Lollards also composed, or at least circulated, Latin versions of this text. See Scase, ' "Let him be kept in most strait prison" '.

[24] Revard, 'Scribe and Provenance'. The unusual anglicana hand used by the scribe of Oxford, Bodleian Library, MS Digby 86, another early West Midlands literary anthology, may suggest that

From the start, while clamour writing nourished and stimulated the growth of a sense that vernacular writing could have legitimacy, it in turn drew on the resources of vernacular literature as well as literature in Latin and French. The Mercers' petition is a good example of the close and mutually stimulating relations between clamour writing and vernacular literary production. As we have seen, the scribe of the Mercers' petition was probably Adam Pinkhurst, clerk for the Mercers (his hand appears in the Mercers' accounts). Pinkhurst copied some of the most important manuscripts of vernacular poetry: the Ellesmere and Hengwrt manuscripts of the *Canterbury Tales*, the Ilchester manuscript of *Piers Plowman*, a Gower, and a *Troilus* (now fragmentary). He may even have been the Adam, scribe of *Troilus*, to whom Chaucer addressed 'Chaucers wordes unto Adam, his owne scriveyn'.[25]

Chaucer's *Troilus* is a good example of the interest of literary writers at precisely this date in finding vernacular equivalents for dictaminal conventions. Norman Davis has famously shown that Troilus's letter to Criseyde (*Troilus*, v. ll. 1317–421) applies dictaminal principles to the hints Chaucer found in his narrative sources:[26]

Litera Troili

Right fresshe flour, whos I ben have and shal,
Withouten part of elleswhere servyse,
With herte, body, lif, lust, thought, and al,
I, woful wyght, in everich humble wise
That tonge telle of herte may devyse,
As ofte as matere occupieth place,
Me recomaunde unto youre noble grace.

Liketh yow to witen, swete herte,
As ye wel knowe, how longe tyme agon
That ye me lefte in aspre peynes smerte,
Whan that ye wente, of which yet boote non
Have I non had, but evere wors bigon

---

he was experimenting with trying to adapt a legal script to produce a more formal script suitable for a book (Tschann and Parkes (eds.), *Facsimile of Oxford, Bodleian Library, MS Digby 86*, pp. xl–xli.)

[25] 'Adam scriveyn, if ever it thee bifalle Boece or Troylus for to wryten newe … ', ll. 1–2 (Benson (ed.), *Riverside Chaucer*, 650). For the manuscripts in Pinkhurst's hand, see Mooney, *Late Medieval English Scribes*, and 'Chaucer's Scribe'. As we have seen, John Whitelock's bill is written in a similar hand, a hand more typical of literary than legal texts at this date. Perhaps this suggests that the scribe—and perhaps drafter—of the bill was also, like Pinkhurst, engaged in the production of English literary texts.

[26] Benson (ed.), *Riverside Chaucer*, 471–585; Davis, 'The *Litera Troili*', 236: 'what gives Chaucer's version of Troilus's letter much of its shape and point is his use, indeed exploitation, of the conventions of ordinary letter-writing of the time in English'. Davis takes the view that Chaucer was following the model of the Anglo-Norman formularies. Camargo accepts and builds on Davis's analysis, suggesting in addition that Chaucer was influenced by the constructions of Latin model epistles, and the reordering of sections taught by the dictaminal manuals (Camargo, *Middle English Verse Love Epistle*, 65–78).

Fro day to day am I, and so mot dwelle,
While it yow list, of wele and wo my welle.

For which to yow, with dredul herte trewe,
I write, as he that sorwe drifeth to write,
My wo, that everich houre encresseth newe,
Compleynyng, as I dar or kan endite.

(v. ll. 1317–34)

'Right fresshe flour', the opening phrase, translates the formulaic salutation
with a compound intensifier and adjective, for example 'tresgracious', 'tressages',
'tresexcellent', 'treshaut', 'treshonurable' in an Anglo-Norman formulary; and
'trescher', 'tresame' in letters of the 1370s from the Stonor collection.[27] The
equivalent in Latin is the superlative adjective, for example, a letter from Henry IV
to the Doge of Venice has 'Amice precarissime'.[28] The vocative address formula
is an innovation of fourteenth-century letters in French (replacing the dative
address 'to … ').[29] Other formulas align Troilus's letter with the petition. First,
he requests consideration, beseeching Criseyde to read the letter and to forgive
any errors 'Yow firste biseche I' (v. ll. 1338–44). He describes his suffering, and
specifies remedies—her return, or at least a letter (v. ll. 1366–400). And he
requests process: a judgement of any case against him (v. ll. 1387–91). These
elements correspond to the canon of form of judicial plaint, for example, to
sections of the chancery bill as analysed by Haskett.[30]

Critics have found Chaucer's vernacularization of dictaminal conventions and
formulas here embarrassingly precocious, since it anticipates the use of those
conventions in any actual English letters. The earliest letters that Davis could
find that conform with those conventions date from 1392 and 1393; as he points
out, *Troilus*, dating from the mid-1380s, antedates these by about seven years, a
curiosity that he could not explain ('that these epistolary conventions appear first
in a fictional letter written by Chaucer is a strange accident of history').[31] But
if we cannot find comparable *letters* evincing an interest in *dictamen* in English,
the Mercers' petition, written by a *Troilus* scribe, clearly shares this interest in
English *dictamen*.

[27] The formulary examples are all from petitions dated 1390–1412 in Legge (ed.), *Anglo-Norman Letters and Petitions*, 1–41; Kingsford (ed.), *Stonor Letters and Papers*, i. 7–17. For *right* as an intensifier, and medieval examples in forms of address, see *OED right*, adv. 9. b and 9. c; this usage of *right* as an intensifier is not recognized in *MED*.

[28] Hall (ed.), *Formula Book*, 140.   [29] Ibid., 139.

[30] In Haskett's analysis, the early fifteenth-century chancery bill has eleven sections (Haskett, 'Medieval Chancery Bills', 12–13). In the analysis of Fisher, Richardson, and Fisher, a petition to chancery has five sections: Address, Identification of the Petitioner, Exposition, Petition, Valediction (Fisher, Richardson, and Fisher (eds.), *An Anthology of Chancery English*, 21–2).

[31] Davis, 'The *Litera Troili*', 244. For a discussion of dating, see Benson (ed.), *Riverside Chaucer*, 1020; one crucial piece of evidence is the use by Thomas Usk (d. 1388) of the text in his *Testament of Love*; recent work (see Summers, *Late-Medieval Prison Writing*, 27) dates the *Testament c*.1385–6, which would mean that *Troilus* was either finished (or in progress, if Usk saw an uncompleted text) at that date.

The connection between the Mercers' petition and *Troilus* is not the only example of a link between English literary projects and dictaminal experiments in English at this time. There are a great many examples of the ways in which the project of composing vernacular clamour texts stimulated and was stimulated by English literary projects, but we have space here to consider only a few representative examples. Another English language bill-writer who knew *Troilus* and had other vernacular literary interests was Thomas Usk. Usk, at one time a scrivener in the service of John Northampton for whom he wrote bills, was the author of the *Testament of Love*, a text closely indebted to *Troilus*, and an English clamour text. Usk was arrested by Brembre in 1384, and while in the mayor's custody listed complaints against Brembre's enemies in the form of an appeal. He provided his complaint in an English text written, he says, in his own hand.[32] His appeal was mobilized in several judicial contexts. He was called as witness for the prosecution at the trial of John Northampton in August 1384, and the appeal was the basis for a jury presentment used to initiate a further hearing in September.[33] During the Appellants' crisis in 1388, it was again mobilized, along with a number of other jury presentments against John Northampton. On this occasion—now that Brembre was on trial—the purpose seems to have been to get redress for the earlier actions instigated against Northampton by Brembre.[34] Strohm analyses this series of documents in which Usk's appeal is transmitted in terms of the 'effacement' of Usk the author.[35] We might also observe that this process corresponds precisely to the production and mobilization of clamour texts.

Thomas Hoccleve offers us another example of a petition-writer whose poetry evinces interest in vernacularizing the forms and phrases of dictaminal writing. As is well known, Hoccleve, scribe at the office of the privy seal, had a professional interest in *dictamen*. Hoccleve's *Formulary* (London, British Library, Additional MS 24062) contains over a thousand models, organized according to type and with a table of contents to help the user access relevant material. As well as including instruments such as warrants, writs, and pardons issued by the privy seal, the collection includes diplomatic letters. These materials are all in French or Latin.[36] It is in his literary pursuits that Hoccleve experiments with finding vernacular versions of dictaminal forms and phrases. Some of Hoccleve's experimentation is associated with his translation of French literary sources. His translation of Christine de Pisan's *L'epistre au Dieu d'Amours* offers him a

---

[32] Chambers and Daunt (eds.), *Book of London English*, 22–31, 22. ('The Appeal of Thomas Usk against John Northampton'); for Usk's career, see Summers, *Late-Medieval Prison Writing*, 24–7.

[33] Strohm, *Hochon's Arrow*, 154.   [34] Ibid., 155–7.   [35] Ibid., 157.

[36] See the description in Burrow, *Thomas Hoccleve*, 192–4. Richardson and Sayles, 'Parliamentary Documents', 153, speculate that a petition from the clergy to the king and lords in parliament found in the formulary may be a French translation of a Latin original.

particularly interesting opportunity to experiment with vernacularizing plaint.[37] The epistle is the outcome of a legal process, in which women have complained to Cupid about the ways in which men use complaint against them—to deceive them, or to blame them falsely. Hoccleve's 'L'epistre de Cupide' includes a long description of the lover's plaint (ll. 22–35) and of how women are betrayed by it:

> Hir wordes spoken been so sighyngly,
> And with so pitous cheere and contenance,
> That euery wight þat meeneth trewely
> Deemeth þat they in herte han swich greuance.
>
> (ll. 22–5)[38]

Cupid reports that ladies have sown 'seed of conpleynte in our audience' (l. 11), and that they 'moost conpleyne' about England ('Albyon', l. 16). Cupid's letter is a command to punish these men and banish them from his court (ll. 463–9). 'L'epistre de Cupide' follows Christine de Pisan's epistolary parody, finding equivalents in English. The letter follows Christine's use of the dative address:

> A tous nos vrais loiaulx servans subgiez,
> Salut, Amour, Familiarité!
>
> (ll. 6–7)[39]

Translating into equivalent English formulas it follows the protocols of royal letters, for example, placing Cupid's name first.[40] Proper to the protocols of royal letters, it begins with a salutation:

> Cupido, vnto whos commandement
> The gentil kynrede of goddes on hy
> And peple infernal been obedient,
> And the mortel folk seruen bisyly,
> Of goddesse Sitheree sone oonly,
> To all tho þat to our deitee
> Been sogettes, greetynges senden we.
>
> (ll. 1–7)

Textual evidence suggests that Hoccleve revised the text to increase the use of the first person plural, preferring it where Christine de Pisan uses the more intimate singular.[41]

---

[37] Contrast Knapp, *Bureaucratic Muse*, 64–5, who sees Cupid as guarding 'standards that are at once both ethical codes of conduct and literary techniques'; he does not recognize that the women in the poem are like legal complainants: in Knapp's terms they make 'charges' and 'critiques' about men's false complaint (65).

[38] Ellis (ed.), *Thomas Hoccleve: 'My Compleinte'*, 93–107.

[39] Furnivall and Gollancz (eds.), *Hoccleve's Works: The Minor Poems*, 243–8.

[40] See analysis in Fisher, Richardson, and Fisher (eds.), *An Anthology of Chancery English*, 6–7. For analysis of Hoccleve's text in relation to the conventions of royal communications, see Camargo, *Middle English Verse Love Epistle*, 96–8.

[41] Fisher, Richardson, and Fisher (eds.), *An Anthology of Chancery English*, 8. For the textual evidence concerning 'L'epistre', see Ellis (ed.), *Thomas Hoccleve: 'My Compleinte'*, 17.

Chaucer and Hoccleve both use clamour to think in complex ways about the purposes and legitimacy of their poetry. For example, the clamour for the resumption of wealth into the king's hand stimulates them to reflect on the agency of poetry when they write begging poems. The petitions for resumption of the king's wealth led to the restriction on payment of Hoccleve's annuity, and this prompts Hoccleve to reflect on the efficacy of plaint poetry. In *The Regiment of Princes*, Hoccleve rejects the tradition of writing a complaint against Fortune:

> What schal I do? Best is I stryve nat
> Ageyn þe peys of Fortunes balance,
> For wel I woot that hir brotil constance
> A wyght no whyle souffre can sojourne
> In o plyt; thus nat wiste I how to tourne.[42]

The Old Man advises the poet to seek relief from his poverty by petitioning the Prince to have his patent charged to the Hanaper; he can write his petition in English if his Latin or French are not good enough (ll. 1849–80). The Old Man explicitly acknowledges Hoccleve's poetic project of vernacularizing plaint, putting it in a humorous light. The poet objects that the restriction on annuities prevents any amelioration of his position—plaint is useless. The Old Man advises him to write another work instead for the Prince, in hope of obtaining his grace (ll. 1901–11). Chaucer's 'Fortune' is comparable and may be one of Hoccleve's models. Fortune petitions princes to relieve the plaintiff of his pain, either by taking action themselves or by petitioning 'his beste frend' (l. 78).[43] It has been suggested that the appeal to 'three of you or tweyne' (l. 76) may refer to a privy council ordinance issued in 1390 that required the consent of the privy council to grants and awards from the king.[44]

Chaucer's 'Pity' is one of the most complex examples of the ways in which vernacular poetry interfaces with clamour. Chaucer experiments with vernacularizing plaint rhetoric, using the formulas of address to distinguish the beginning of the written bill that the lover has to present to Pity:

> Humblest of herte, highest of reverence,
> Benygne flour, coroune of vertues alle
> Sheweth unto youre rial excellence
> Youre servaunt ...
>
> (ll. 57–60)[45]

---

[42] Blyth (ed.), *Thomas Hoccleve: The Regiment of Princes*, ll. 59–64.

[43] Benson (ed.), *Riverside Chaucer*, 652–3. Burrow, 'Poet as Petitioner', finds this one of the exceptional uses by Chaucer of the art of the begging poem for 'practical purposes' (69).

[44] Scattergood, 'The Short Poems', 506.

[45] Benson (ed.), *Riverside Chaucer*, 640–1. Nolan, 'Structural Sophistication', 366, compares the address to Pity with those in legal bills. Camargo, *Middle English Verse Love Epistles*, 94, says this is the closest Chaucer comes to imitating the *form* of a document; here, except for his use of the salutation, Chaucer relies on legal forms rather than epistolary conventions. However, it is worth noting that the salutation is one example of the cross-fertilization of petition and epistle.

Ironically, Pity is dead and the speaker does not know to whom to complain
(l. 28). In the written bill of complaint to Pity, the lover identifies himself
humbly: 'Youre servaunt, yf I durste me so calle'. Chaucer uses the formulaic
petitionary verb 'sheweth'(l. 59) here and after end of the 'bill': 'What nedeth to
shewe parcel of my peyne?' (l. 106, the 'parcel' refers to the traditional itemisation
of grievances). In the 'bill' within 'Pity', the expository section is marked with
the phrase 'Hit stondeth thus' (l. 64), and the petition section is introduced with
the relative 'wherfore' after the exposition:

> Shal Cruelte be youre governeresse?
> Allas, what herte may hyt longe endure?
> Wherfore, but ye the rather take cure
> To breke that perilouse alliaunce,
> Ye sleen hem that ben in your obeisaunce.
>
> (ll. 80–4)

The bill within 'Pity' concludes with a request that the petition be granted 'for
Goddis love': 'Have mercy on me, thow Herenus quene … For Goddis love have
mercy on my peyne' (ll. 92–8).[46] But Chaucer does not only experiment with
petitionary form and phrasing here. He also engages with clamour writing by
invoking the theme of the failures attendant on petitioning for justice. Those who
impede the lover's complaint are falsely conspiring against the royal authority of
Pity. Confronted by a confederacy of courtiers and the death of Pity, the plaintiff
'put [his] complaynt up ageyn' (l. 54). In the unused bill, the case is presented
as one of interest to the 'renoun' of Pity (l. 63). Cruelty threatens to oust Pity
from her 'heritage' (l. 89) and 'place' (l. 90), for there is an alliance 'ayenst your
regalye' (l. 65). This is the language of maintenance, even treason: it evokes a
scenario in which justice is imperilled, and in which poetry is a valid alternative
when treasonous foes plot against the king: 'Thus for your deth I may wel wepe
and pleyne' (l. 118). Here Chaucer inflects the themes of the clamour text in a
courtly register, finding a language in which to think about the purposes and
effectiveness of poetry.

   Another kind of experimentation employs the analytical vocabulary of the *ars
dictaminis*. *De modo dictandi*, with which this chapter opened, is one of many
examples of treatises that provide terms for distinguishing different kinds of plaint.
The same manuscript, Cambridge, Cambridge University Library, MS Ee.4.20,
includes a treatise headed 'Salutationes sive modo dictandi in gallicis cum litteris
billis et supplicationibus diversas personas et causas concernentibus' (f. 155ʳ,
'Salutations, or, letter-writing in French, with letters, bills, and supplications

---

46 For Nolan, 'Structural Sophistication', 368, this valediction marks the end of the inner bill.
He draws attention to difficulties in the closing stanzas, suggesting that now the poet is addressing
his lady (369). Another way of reading it would be to see the final stanzas as the lover complaining
about the uselessness of complaining to Pity: 'What nedeth to shewe parcel of my peyne?' (l. 106);
'I dar not to yow pleyne' (l. 108); 'Ye rekke not' (l. 110).

concerning various persons and cases'). London, British Library, MS Harley 4971 has a treatise headed 'Bille et supplicationes secundum novum modum' ('Bills and petitions according to the new style').[47] London, British Library, MS Harley 3988 includes a French dictaminal treatise associated with Thomas Sampson, the Oxford *dictamen* teacher, which, by the end of the fourteenth century, was being added to by a clerk of the privy seal or signet office. The additional part promises that, having dealt with 'litteris missiuis', the reader will here go on to 'billis et supplicacionibus' (f. 64).[48]

As we have seen, writers employ this dictaminal vocabulary in clamour texts. The poem against William de la Pole, 'Ye that have the kyng to demene', describes itself as a 'bille', as does 'Boothe, be ware, bissoppe thoughe thou be', which also aligns itself with the 'ragmanne [roll]'. *Pyers plowmans exhortation* aligns itself with 'certeyne rude Bylles', while Crowley adopts the analogy of the private petition in his title *An informacion and peticion ageynst the oppressours of the pore commons*. This kind of experimentation with dictaminal vocabulary is also found in texts which represent the processes of amorous petition and complaint. In Gower's *Cinquante Ballades*, ballade XX, the poet's letter ('ceo lettre ci') is messenger for 'mon trespovere cri' and his heart (ll. 25–8). Ballade XXIIII is 'cette supplicacion'; the refrain asks God that the poet does not petition in vain 'Dieus doignt qe jeo ne prie pas en vain'. Ballade XXVI is 'ceste escript', ballade XXVII is 'Ceo lettre', and ballade XLII a 'complaint' for all lovers: 'As toutz amantz jeo fais ceste compleignte' (l. 27). Ballade XLIII, written in a woman's voice, is also 'Ceste compleignte' (l. 26). This vocabulary is also used by Gower in English. In the *Confessio Amantis*, the lover's 'Supplicacion' to Venus (viii. l. 2184) is written in a 'lettre' (written in tears instead of ink, viii. ll. 2212–3, 2216).Venus refers to it as 'thi bille ... In which to Cupide and to me somdiel thou hast compleigned thee' (viii. ll. 2324–6). This vocabulary is used by Gower together with formal terms from French poetics, such as *balade* and *dit*.[49]

Chaucer and Hoccleve also use dictaminal vocabulary analytically. In Chaucer's *Anelida and Arcite*, the betrayed queen, Anelida, makes a 'compleynynge' which 'of hir owne hond she gan it write, And sente hit to her Theban knyght, Arcite' (ll. 208–10).[50] In the Merchant's Tale, Damyan tells May of his love by writing a 'lettre' of 'al his sorwe In manere of a compleynt or a lay' (ll. 1880–1); the word 'manere' recalls the vocabulary of the formularies as do the terms 'compleynt' and 'lettre'.[51] Damyan's letter is also described as a 'bille' (l. 1937); it is as if he 'putte a bille of Venus werkes ... to any womman

---

[47] Cf. Baker and Ringrose, *Catalogue* entry on Cambridge University Library, MS Ee.4.20.

[48] Cf. Salter, Pantin, and Richardson (eds.), *Formularies*, ii. 408–13; and Richardson, 'Business Training', 269.

[49] Macaulay (ed.), *Gower: The French Works*; Ballades XXIII (25) and XXVIII (23–4) are 'ceo dit'; ballade XXIX is 'ceste balade' (26); Macaulay (ed.), *The English Works of John Gower*, ii.

[50] Benson (ed.), *Riverside Chaucer*, 375–81.   [51] Ibid., 154–68.

for to gete hire love' (ll. 1971–3). When Hoccleve defends his translation of Christine de Pisan's *L'epistre au Dieu d'Amours* in *The Series*, 'A Dialoge', against the charge that he wrote against women, he offers the defence that he spoke 'complainingly':

> Whan I it spak I spak conpleynyngly
> I to hem thoghte no repreef ne shame.
>
> (ll. 772–3)

A recent editor glosses 'conpleynyngly' thus: 'he followed Christine's "Epistle" in uttering a complaint not against but on behalf of women (Hammond reads "conpleynyngly" "under protest")'.[52] But the simplest interpretation is that 'conpleynyngly' refers to the women's perspective: Hoccleve (Cupid) was 'speaking in the manner of plaint' (that is, in the manner of the women plaintiffs).

The application of dictaminal analysis to plaint poetry provides a framework for innovations in rubrication in some manuscript books of poetry. Charles d'Orléans's French poems include some that are rubricated 'Lectre en complainte', while a section of the French poems is categorized 'Complaintes'.[53] It seems likely that scribes were responding to internal cues when they labelled texts. In Chaucer's 'Mars', the bird narrator refers to Mars's 'compleynt', which he will 'seyn and singe' (ll. 150, 152).[54] Early scribes call the poem a complaint: Shirley's colophon in Cambridge, Trinity College, MS R.3.20 reads 'this complaint'.[55] Again, in texts which lack the envoy, Chaucer's 'Purse' is, when it is classified, labelled (on formal criteria) as a 'balade'. With the envoy, where the poem is described as a 'supplicacion', the poem is identified as a complaint: 'La complaint de Chaucer a sa Bourse voide', 'the complaint of Chaucer unto his purse'; and in one manuscript as a 'supplication'.[56]

One of the most thoroughgoing and novel experiments with the use of dictaminal rubrics and side-notes is Oxford, Bodleian Library, MS Fairfax 16, a commercially produced manuscript thought to have been commissioned by John Stanley (d. *c*.1469), a courtier in the service of Henry V and Henry VI.[57] This manuscript is a virtual formulary of love plaint texts, including Chaucer's 'Mars' and 'Venus', *Anelida and Arcite*, 'Pity', 'Fortune', 'Purse', and dream visions; Hoccleve's 'L'epistre de Cupide' and 'Balade to Henry V'; Lydgate's *Temple of Glass* and *Complaint of the Black Knight*; and a sequence of lyrics associated

---

[52] Ellis (ed.), *Thomas Hoccleve: 'My Compleinte'*, 159, n. to l. 772.
[53] Champion (ed.), *Charles d'Orléans: Poésies*, i. 258, 272.
[54] Benson (ed.), *Riverside Chaucer*, 643–7.   [55] Ibid., 1079.   [56] Ibid., 1191.
[57] Reproduced in facsimile in Norton-Smith (ed.), *Bodleian Library, MS Fairfax 16*. For the manuscript's provenance, see pp. vii, xiii.

with Charles d'Orléans and his circle.[58] A table of contents, title rubrics, running headings, and side-notes organize the texts. Chaucer's 'Mars' is entitled 'Complaynt of Mars and Venus' (f. 15^r), and Mars's complaint has the side-note: 'The Compleynt of Mars' (f. 17^r). This layout is echoed by that of the 'Complaint of Venus'. Lydgate's *Complaint of the Black Knight* is headed 'Complaynte of a louers lyfe' (f. 20^v), and the knight's overheard complaint, described internally as a 'lamentacioun' (l. 166), and 'compleynyng' (l. 215), is rubricated 'Compleynt' (f. 23^v).[59] The lady's petition in Lydgate's *Temple of Glass* has a side-note 'Supplicacio mulieris amantis' (f. 67^r), and the response 'Thansuere of Venus' (f. 67^v), while her lady's prayer is indicated with 'Oracio amantis supradicte' (f. 69^r). The lover's petition to Venus has an interlinear heading 'Supplicacio amantis' (f. 72^v), and her reply has the side-note 'Responsio veneris' (f. 75^r).[60] Chaucer's dream visions are not provided with significant paratextual notes, but 'Fortune' has headings that analyse the poem according to forensic process: 'La Respons du Fortune au pleintif'; 'Le pleintif encontre Fortune'; 'Fortune encontre le pleintif'; 'Le pleintif encontre Fortune'; and 'lenvoy du Fortune' (ff. 191^r–192^v). The manuscript rubrics in 'Fortune' interpret the structure as a sequence comparable with the legal documents deposited in cases in chancery. This sequence is followed by a further sequence of short texts labelled *balade*, *envoy*, and *complaynt* (ff. 192^v–195^r).[61]

The sequence of lyrics associated with Charles d'Orléans and his circle exhibits the most thoroughgoing use of dictaminal vocabulary in Fairfax 16. The sequence is the second item in the final booklet, where it follows a lover's 'mass', itself set out with headings appropriate to a religious service. The love poems are categorized into types: some of them lyric types (labelled *balade*); others dictaminal types. Ten poems are labelled 'compleynt' (ff. 319^r, 319^v, 320^v, 321^r, 321^v, 322^r (two), 322^v, 324^r (two), 325^r); three are labelled 'lettyr' (ff. 320^r, 323^v, 324^v); one is labelled 'supplicacioun' (f. 323^r); one 'parlement' (f. 327^r); and one 'lenvoye' (f. 329^r).[62] The table of contents at the front of the book (f. 2$^{r–v}$), written in the main scribal hand, is based on these and the other rubrics. Chaucer's

---

[58] For a full list of contents, see Norton-Smith (ed.), *Bodleian Library, MS Fairfax 16*, pp. xxiii-xxix, and for a discussion of its probable exemplars, see p. viii.

[59] MacCracken (ed.), *The Minor Poems of John Lydgate: Part II*, 382–410.

[60] For a useful discussion of what Lydgate's *Temple* may have meant to fifteenth-century readers, see Boffey, ' "Forto compleyne she had gret desire" '.

[61] Contrast the suggestion of Norton-Smith concerning the paratextual features here; he suggests that the omission of colophons may indicate the grouping of Chaucer's 'Fortune', 'Scogan', 'Purse', and 'Bukton' in 'an integral collection' (Norton-Smith (ed.), *Bodleian Library, MS Fairfax 16*, p. viii).

[62] Camargo, *Middle English Verse Love Epistle*, 114–18, suggests that the labels *complaint* and *supplication* give themes generic status. But arguably the response is rather to the conventional formulas and to the functionality implied by the internal references.

'Mars', 'Venus', *Anelida and Arcite*, 'Pity', 'Purse', 'Lak of Stedfastnesse', some anonymous love plaints, Lydgate's *Black Knight*, and from the final sequence 'ii complayntez þat þe louere made to his lady', 'vii complayntez þat þe louere made to his lady', and a further 'ii complayntes þat þe louere made to his lady' are all listed as complaints. The list also offers a *supplication* to the king in verse, 'The supplicacioun to þe kyng in balayd wise' (Hoccleve's ballade to Henry V), two *envoys* ('The sendyng of Chawcer to Bukton', and 'The sendyng of Chawcer to Scogan'), several *letters* ('The letter of Cupyde gode of love', two examples of 'a letter þat þe lover made to his lady'), and one hybrid text: 'a letter and a complaynt that þe louer made to his lady'). These dictaminal labels give unity to þe whole book and a framework for its use by readers. They make the volume analogous in structure to a dictaminal formulary, implying that readers could use the material in it in similarly practical ways, for the purposes of emulation and imitation.[63]

These examples are elaborate instances of a literary practice that spans the entire period of this book. Even before the flowering of the vernacular *dictamen* project, the definition of judicial plaint institutes an implicit dictaminal analysis which applies to all modes of plaint and provides a means of relating them to one another. We have encountered many examples in the course of our history of complaint literature in this book. In the earliest text considered in this book, miserable Adam and his fellow-peasants go off to the royal court singing and come home 'weeping, lamenting without end'. *Song of the Church* uses the *Lamentations of Jeremiah* to express the plaint of tax-payers. The *Epistola ad Regem Edwardum III* deploys numerous biblical plaints from, among other sources, Ecclesiasticus, the Psalms, and Exodus. *Song of the Husbandman* records that a 'mon' has replaced the peasants' song. 'The taxe hath tened vs alle' ('The Course of the Revolt') imagines the murder of Sudbury as a clamorous cry. The Wycliffites return to biblical models in their libels, drawing on Jeremiah, and the lamentations of the exiled Israelites. 'In the moneth of May' relates the love plaint (with its spring opening) to the funeral liturgy ('*Placebo* and *Dirige*') and to the petitions against William de la Pole. *Ballad set on the Gates of Canterbury, 1460*, relates a sorrowful text from Isaiah to the Palm Sunday anthem 'Gloria, laus et honor'. The bill recorded by John Piggott relates the popular lamentation ('well away') to clamour. 'Ye that have the kyng to demene' invokes the 'singing' of the executed at Smithfield. *The praier and complaynte of the ploweman* contrasts the short prayers of the poor with the petitions on behalf of souls in purgatory which are 'sold' by chantry-priests. With the *Decaye of England*, we come full circle. The 'lamentacions of the Kinges Maiestyes subiectes', in the latest text in our survey, recall the lament of miserable Adam. Judicial plaint offers all of the authors of these texts, from the thirteenth-century poet to the Reformation pamphleteer, a framework within which to create the literature of complaint.

---

[63] Camargo, *Middle English Verse Love Epistle*, 118, notes that these poems are 'polished clean of any particular occasion'—a characteristic, we should note, of texts in a formulary.

List of Abbreviations

MED   *Middle English Dictionary*
OED   *Oxford English Dictionary*
PROME   *The Parliament Rolls of Medieval England*
RP   *Rotuli Parliamentorum*
STC   *A Short-title Catalogue of Books printed … 1475–1640*
TNA   (PRO) The National Archives (Public Record Office)

List of Works Cited

PRIMARY SOURCES IN MANUSCRIPT

CAMBRIDGE
Cambridge University Library
Ee.4.20

DUBLIN
Trinity College
Trinity College 516

LONDON
British Library
Additional 34888
Cotton Roll II. 23
Cotton Roll IV. 50
Cotton Vespasian B. xvi
Harley 2252
Harley 3988
Harley 4971

The National Archives (Public Record Office)
C 1/68/63
C 49/9
C 49/10
JUST 1/335
JUST 1/337
JUST 1/521
JUST 1/850
KB 9/46
KB 9/118/1
KB 9/203
KB 9/204/1
KB 9/955/2
KB 27/26
KB 27/81
KB 27/609
KB 27/624
KB 39/47/1
SC 8/20/997

SC 8/20/998
SC 8/20/999
SC 8/20/1000
SC 8/20/1001B
SC 8/20/1002
SC 8/20/1003
SC 8/20/1004
SC 8/20/1005
SC 8/20/1006
SC 8/94/4664
SC 8/262/13079
SP 10/9

OXFORD
Bodleian Library
Digby 98
Eng. hist. b. 119
Fairfax 16
Magdalen College
Magdalen Misc. 306

PRIMARY SOURCES IN PRINTED AND ELECTRONIC MEDIA

Thomas Arnold (ed.), *Select English Works of John Wyclif*, 3 vols. (Oxford: Clarendon Press, 1871).

Isabel S. T. Aspin (ed.), *Anglo-Norman Political Songs*, Anglo-Norman Texts, Vol. IX (Oxford: Basil Blackwell, 1953).

George James Aungier (ed.), *Croniques de London depuis l'an 44 Hen. III. jusqu'à l'an 17 Edw. III*, Camden Society, 1st ser., Vol. 28 (London, 1844).

William Paley Baildon (ed.), *Select Cases in Chancery AD 1364 to 1471*, Selden Society, Vol. 10 (London: Quaritch, 1896).

Helen Barr (ed.), *The Piers Plowman Tradition* (London: Dent, 1993).

Alastair Bellany and Andrew McRae (eds.), *Early Stuart Libels*, http://www.earlystuartlibels.net/htdocs/index.html (accessed 11 October 2005).

Larry D. Benson (ed.), *The Riverside Chaucer*, 3rd edn. (Oxford: Oxford University Press, 1988).

Charles R. Blyth (ed.), *Thomas Hoccleve: The Regiment of Princes* (Kalamazoo, MI: Western Michigan University, 1999).

William Craddock Bolland (ed.), *Select Bills in Eyre AD 1292–1333*, Selden Society, Vol. 30 (London: Quaritch, 1914).

Bracton Online (*Bracton: De Legibus Et Consuetudinibus Angliae*), http://hlsl.law.harvard.edu/bracton/index.htm (accessed 16 December 2005).

G. L. Brook (ed.), *The Harley Lyrics: The Middle English Lyrics of MS. Harley 2253* (Manchester: Manchester University Press, 1956).

Calendar of the Patent Rolls preserved in the Public Record Office, Henry V. Volume 1, AD. 1413–1416 (London: Her Majesty's Stationery Office, 1910).

R. W. Chambers and Marjorie Daunt (eds.), *A Book of London English* (Oxford: Clarendon Press, 1931).

Pierre Champion (ed.), *Charles d'Orléans: Poésies*, 2 vols., Les Classiques Français du Moyen Âge, Vols. 34, 56 (Paris, 1923–4).

C. A. Cole (ed.), *Memorials of Henry the Fifth, King of England*, Rolls Series, Vol. 11 (London: Her Majesty's Stationery Office, 1858).

J. Meadows Cowper (ed.), *The Decaye of Englande by the Great Multitude of Shepe,* Early English Text Society, e.s. 13 (London: N. Trübner, 1871).

_____ (ed.), *A Supplication of the Poore Commons,* Early English Text Society, e.s. 13 (London: N. Trübner, 1871).

_____ (ed.), *Henry Brinklow's Complaynt of Roderyck Mors*, Early English Text Society, e.s. 22 (London: N. Trübner, 1874).

H. S. Cronin (ed.), *Rogeri Dymmok, Liber Contra XII Errores et Hereses Lollardorum* (London: Kegan Paul, Trench, Trübner and Co. for the Wyclif Society, 1922).

Robert Crowley, *An informacion and peticion agaynst the oppressours of the pore Commons of this Realme* ([London: John Day, 1548]).

Norman Davis (ed.), *Paston Letters and Papers of the Fifteenth Century*, 2 vols. (Oxford: Clarendon Press, 1971, 1976).

R. W. Dyson (ed. and trans.), *Three Royalist Tracts, 1296–1302* (Bristol: Thoemmes Press, 1999).

Caroline D. Eckhardt (ed.), *Castleford's Chronicle or The Boke of Brut*, 2 vols., Early English Text Society, o.s. 305–6 (Oxford: Oxford University Press, 1996).

Henry Ellis (ed.), *The New Chronicles of England and France ... by Robert Fabyan ... Reprinted from Pynson's Edition of 1516* (London: printed for F. C. and J. Rivington etc., 1811).

Roger Ellis (ed.), *Thomas Hoccleve: 'My Compleinte' and other Poems* (Exeter: University of Exeter Press, 2001).

John H. Fisher, Malcolm Richardson, and Jane L. Fisher (eds.), *An Anthology of Chancery English* (Knoxville: University of Tennessee Press, 1984).

Ralph Flenley (ed.), *Six Town Chronicles of England* (Oxford: Clarendon Press, 1911).

Frederick J. Furnivall (ed.), *A Supplicacyon for the Beggers ... by Simon Fish*, Early English Text Society, e.s. 13 (London: N. Trübner, 1871).

—— and I. Gollancz (eds.), *Hoccleve's Works: The Minor Poems*, Early English Text Society, e.s. 61 and 73, rev. and repr. in 1 vol. by Jerome Mitchell and A. I. Doyle (Oxford: Oxford University Press, 1970).

James Gairdner (ed.), *The Historical Collections of a Citizen of London in the Fifteenth Century*, Camden Society, n.s., Vol. 17 (London, 1876).

—— (ed.), *Three Fifteenth-Century Chronicles with Historical Memoranda by John Stowe*, Camden Society, n.s., Vol. 28 (London, 1880).

—— (ed.), *The Paston Letters 1422–1509 AD*, 3 vols. (Westminster: A. Constable & Co., 1896).

V. H. Galbraith (ed.), *The Anonimalle Chronicle 1333 to 1381* (Manchester: Manchester University Press, 1927).

—— (ed.), *The St Albans Chronicle 1406–1420* (Oxford: Clarendon Press, 1937).

Andrew Galloway (trans.), *History or Narration Concerning the Manner and Form of the Miraculous Parliament at Westminster in the Year 1386, in the Tenth Year of the Reign of King Richard the Second after the Conquest, Declared by Thomas Favent, Clerk*, in Emily Steiner and Candace Barrington (eds.), *The Letter of the Law: Legal Practice and Literary Production in Medieval England* (Ithaca, NY: Cornell University Press, 2002), 231–52.

G. N. Garmonsworthy (ed.), *Ælfric's Colloquy*, 2nd edn. (London: Methuen, 1947).

Hubert Hall (ed.), *A Formula Book of English Official Historical Documents: Part One, Diplomatic Documents* (Cambridge: Cambridge University Press, 1908).

Alan Harding (ed.), 'Early Trailbaston Proceedings from the Lincoln roll of 1305', in R. F. Hunnisett and J. B. Post (eds.), *Medieval Legal Records edited in memory of C. A. F. Meekings* (London: Her Majesty's Stationery Office, 1978), 143–51.

G. L. Harriss and M. A. Harris (eds.), *John Benet's Chronicle for the years 1400 to 1462*, Camden Miscellany, Vol. 24, Camden 4th ser., Vol. 9 (London: Royal Historical Society, 1972), iii. 151–233.

F. S. Haydon (ed.), *Eulogium Historiarum*, 3 vols., Rolls Series, Vols. 1–3 (London: Longman, Brown, Green, Longmans, and Roberts, 1858–63).

L. C. Hector and Barbara F. Harvey (eds. and trans.), *The Westminster Chronicle 1381–1394* (Oxford: Clarendon Press, 1982).

Francis Charles Hingeston (ed.), *The Chronicle of England by John Capgrave*, Rolls Series, Vol. 1 (London: Longman, Brown, Green, Longmans, and Roberts, 1858).

Anne Hudson (ed.), *Selections from English Wycliffite Writings* (Cambridge: Cambridge University Press, 1978).

Paul L. Hughes and James F. Larkin (eds.), *Tudor Royal Proclamations, Volume One: The Early Tudors (1485–1553)* (New Haven: Yale University Press, 1964).

Margaret Lucille Kekewich, Colin Richmond, Anne F. Sutton, Livia Visser-Fuchs, and John L. Watts (eds.), *The Politics of Fifteenth-Century England: John Vale's Book* (Stroud: Alan Sutton, 1995).

John Kerrigan (ed.), *Motives of Woe: Shakespeare and 'Female Complaint', A Critical Anthology* (Oxford: Clarendon Press, 1991).

C. L. Kingsford (ed.), *Chronicles of London* (Oxford: Clarendon Press, 1905).

_____ (ed.), *The Stonor Letters and Papers 1290–1483*, 2 vols., Camden Society, 3rd ser., Vols. 29–30 (London, 1919).

I. S. Leadam and J. F. Baldwin (eds.), *Select Cases before the King's Council 1243–1482*, Selden Society, Vol. 35 (Cambridge, MA: Harvard University Press, 1918).

M. D. Legge (ed.), *Anglo-Norman Letters and Petitions from All Souls MS 182*, Anglo-Norman Texts, Vol. III (Oxford: Basil Blackwell, 1941).

G. C. Macaulay (ed.), *The Complete Works of John Gower: The French Works* (Oxford: Clarendon Press, 1899).

_____ (ed.), *The English Works of John Gower*, 2 vols., Early English Text Society, e.s. 80–1 (London: Kegan Paul, Trench, Trübner, 1900–1).

Henry Noble MacCracken (ed.), *The Minor Poems of John Lydgate*: *Part II: The Secular Poems*, Early English Text Society, o.s. 192 (London: Oxford University Press, 1934).

May McKisack (ed.), *Historia Mirabilis Parliamenti*, Camden Miscellany, Vol. 14, Camden Society, 3rd ser., Vol. 37 (London, 1926).

Frederic Madden (ed.), *Matthaei Parisiensis, Monachi Sancti Albani, Historia Anglorum*, 3 vols., Rolls Series, Vol. 44 (London: Longmans, Green & Co., 1866, 1869).

Frank Manley, Germain Marc' Ladour, Richard Marius, and Clarence H. Miller (eds.), *The Complete Works of St Thomas More*, Vol. 7 (New Haven: Yale University Press, 1990).

G. H. Martin (ed. and trans.), *Knighton's Chronicle 1337–1396* (Oxford: Clarendon Press, 1995).

Joseph Moisant (ed.), *De speculo regis Edwardi III* (Paris: Picard, 1891).

Cary J. Nederman (ed. and trans.), *Political Thought in Early Fourteenth-Century England: Treatises by Walter of Milemete, William of Pagula, and William of Ockham* (Tempe, AZ: Arizona Centre for Medieval Studies in collaboration with Brepols, 2002).

Nonarum Inquisitiones in Curia Scaccarii temp. regis Edwardi III (London: Record Commission, 1807).

John Norton-Smith (ed.), *Bodleian Library, MS Fairfax 16* (London: Scolar Press, 1979).

H. S. Offler (ed.), *Guillelmi de Ockham, Opera Politica*, Vol. 1 (Manchester: Manchester University Press, 1940).

Douglas H. Parker (ed.), *Jerome Barlowe and William Roye, Rede Me and Be Nott Wrothe*, (Toronto: University of Toronto Press, 1992).

_____ (ed.), *A proper dyaloge, betwene a Gentillman and an Husbandman* (Toronto: University of Toronto Press, 1996).

_____ (ed.), *The praier and complaynte of the ploweman vnto Christe* (Toronto: University of Toronto Press, 1997).

The Parliament Rolls of Medieval England, gen. ed. Chris Given-Wilson, ed. Paul Brand (1275–1307), Seymour Phillips (1307–37), Mark Ormrod (1337–77), Geoffrey

Martin (1377–9), Chris Given-Wilson (1380–1421), Anne Curry (1422–53), and Rosemary Horrox (1455–1504). CD-ROM edn. (Leicester: Scholarly Digital Editions, 2005).

Luke Owen Pike (ed. and trans.), *Year Books of the Reign of King Edward the Third Years XIV and XV*, Rolls Series, Vol. 31 (London: Her Majesty's Stationery Office, 1889).

Josiah Pratt (ed.), *The Acts and Monuments of John Foxe*, 8 vols., 4th edn. (London: The Religious Tract Society, n.d.).

Nicholas Pronay and John Taylor (eds.), *Parliamentary Texts of the Later Middle Ages* (Oxford: Clarendon Press, 1980).

Pyers plowmans exhortation vnto the lordes knightes and burgoysses of the Parlyamenthouse (London: Anthony Scoloker, [1550]).

Angelo Raine (ed.), *York Civic Records*, Vol. 1, The Yorkshire Archaeological Society Record Series, Vol. 98 (Yorkshire Archaeological Society, 1939 for 1938).

H. G. Richardson and G. O. Sayles (eds.), *Rotuli Parliamentorum Anglie Hactenus Inediti MCCLXXIX-MCCCLXXIII*, Camden Society, 3rd ser., Vol. 51, for the Royal Historical Society (London, 1935).

—— (eds.), *Select Cases of Procedure without Writ under Henry III*, Selden Society, Vol. 60 (London: Quaritch, 1941).

H. T. Riley (ed.), *Chronica Monasterii S. Albani. Thomae Walsingham, quondam monachi S. Albani, Historia Anglicana*, 2 vols., Rolls Series, Vol. 26 (London: Longman, Green, Longman, Roberts, and Green, 1864).

—— (ed.), *Chronica Monasterii S. Albani. Johannis de Trokelowe, et Henrici de Blandforde, Monachorum S. Albani, necnon quorundam anonymorum, Chronica et Annales*, Rolls Series, Vol. 28.3 (London: Longman, Green, Reader and Dyer, 1866).

—— (ed.), *Chronica Monasterii S. Albani. Annales Monasterii S. Albani, a Johanne Amundesham, monacho*, 2 vols., Rolls Series, Vols. 5, 28 (London: Her Majesty's Stationery Office, 1870–1).

Rossell Hope Robbins (ed.), *Historical Poems of the Fourteenth and Fifteenth Centuries* (New York: Columbia University Press, 1959).

J. E. T. Rogers (ed.), *Loci e Libro Veritatum: Passages selected from Gascoigne's Theological Dictionary illustrating the condition of Church and State 1403–1458* (Oxford: Clarendon Press, 1881).

Harry Rothwell (ed.), *The Chronicle of Walter of Guisborough*, Camden Society, 3rd ser., Vol. 89 (London, 1957).

Rotuli Parliamentorum, 7 vols. (London: Record Commission, 1783–1832).

Thomas Rymer (ed.), *Foedera, conventiones, literae, et cujuscunque generis acta publica*, 20 vols. (London: A. & J. Churchill, 1704–35).

H. E. Salter, W. A. Pantin, and H. G. Richardson (eds.), *Formularies which bear on the History of Oxford, c.1204–1420*, 2 vols., Oxford Historical Society, n. s., Vols. 4–5 (Oxford: Clarendon Press, 1942).

G. O. Sayles (ed.), *Select Cases in the Court of King's Bench*, Vol. 7, Selden Society, Vol. 88 (London: Quaritch, 1971).

A. V. C. Schmidt (ed.), *William Langland, The Vision of Piers Plowman*, new edn. (London: Dent, 1987).

Walter W. Shirley (ed.), *Fasciculi Zizaniorum Magistri Johannis Wyclif*, Rolls Series, Vol. 5 (London: Longman, Green, Brown, Longmans, and Roberts, 1858).

Eric Gerald Stanley (ed.), *The Owl and the Nightingale* (Manchester: Manchester University Press, 1960).

Statutes of the Realm, 11 vols. (London: George Eyre and Andrew Strahan for the Record Commission, 1810–28).

William Stubbs (ed.), *Select Charters and other illustrations of English Constitutional History*, 8th edn. (Oxford: Clarendon Press, 1905).

Idelle Sullens (ed.), *Robert Mannyng of Brunne: 'The Chronicle'* (Binghampton, NY: State University of New York, 1996).

Edward Maunde Thompson (ed.), *Chronicon Angliae, ab anno Domini 1328 usque ad annum 1388*, Rolls Series, Vol. 64 (London: Longman, Trübner, Parker, Macmillan, Black and Thom, 1874).

——— (ed.), *Robertus de Avesbury, De Gestis Mirabilibus Regis Edwardi Tertii*, Rolls Series, Vol. 11 (1889), repr. (London: Her Majesty's Stationery Office, 1965).

Judith Tschann and M. B. Parkes (eds.), *Facsimile of Oxford, Bodleian Library, MS Digby 86*, Early English Text Society, s.s. 16 (Oxford: Oxford University Press, 1996).

Thorlac Turville-Petre (ed.), *Alliterative Poems of the Later Middle Ages: An Anthology* (London: Routledge, 1989).

Barry Windeatt (ed.), *The Book of Margery Kempe* (Harlow: Longman, 2000).

Thomas Wright (ed.), *Political Songs of England, from the reign of John to that of Edward II*, Camden Society, o.s., Vol. 6 (London, 1839).

——— (ed.), *Political Poems and Songs*, 2 vols., Rolls Series, Vol. 14 (London: Longman, Green, Longman and Roberts, 1859, 1861).

——— (ed.), *The Chronicle of Pierre de Langtoft*, 2 vols., Rolls Series, Vol. 47 (London: Longmans, Green, Reader and Dyer, 1866, 1868).

SECONDARY SOURCES

John A. Alford, Piers Plowman: *A Glossary of Legal Diction* (Cambridge: D. S. Brewer, 1988).

Christopher Allmand, *Henry V*, new edn. (New Haven: Yale University Press, 1997).

The Anglo-Norman Dictionary, http://www.anglo-norman.net (accessed 29 March 2006).

Margaret Aston, 'Lollardy and Sedition' (1960), repr. with additional note and postscript in *Lollards and Reformers: Images and Literacy in Late Medieval Religion* (London: The Hambledon Press, 1984), 1–47.

——— 'Lollardy and the Reformation: Survival or Revival?' (1964), repr. in *Lollards and Reformers: Images and Literacy in Late Medieval Religion* (London: The Hambledon Press, 1984), 219–42.

——— *Thomas Arundel: A Study of Church Life in the Reign of Richard II* (Oxford: Clarendon Press, 1967).

——— 'Caim's Castles' (1984), repr. in *Faith and Fire: Popular and Unpopular Religion 1350–1600* (London: The Hambledon Press, 1993), 95–131.

——— 'Devotional Literacy', in *Lollards and Reformers: Images and Literacy in Late Medieval Religion* (London: The Hambledon Press, 1984), 101–33.

J. H. Baker, 'The Three Languages of the Common Law' (1998), repr. in *The Common Law Tradition: Lawyers, Books and the Law* (London: The Hambledon Press, 2000), 225–46.

John H. Baker and J. S. Ringrose, *A Catalogue of English Legal Manuscripts in Cambridge University Library* (Woodbridge: The Boydell Press, 1996).

Barrett L. Beer, 'Seymour, Edward, duke of Somerset (*c*.1500–1552)', *Oxford Dictionary of National Biography* (Oxford: Oxford University Press, 2004), http://www.oxforddnb.com/view/article/25159 (accessed 29 October 2005).

J. G. Bellamy, *The Criminal Trial in Later Medieval England: Felony before the Courts from Edward I to the Sixteenth Century* (Stroud: Sutton Publishing, 1998).

Alastair Bellany, ' "Raylinge Rymes and Vaunting Verse": Libellous Politics in Early Stuart England, 1603–1628', in Kevin Sharpe and Peter Lake (eds.), *Culture and Politics in Early Stuart England* (Basingstoke: Macmillan, 1994), 285–310.

Ruth Bird, *The Turbulent London of Richard II* (London: Longmans, Green & Co., 1949).

Thomas N. Bisson, *Tormented Voices: Power, Crisis, and Humanity in Rural Catalonia 1140–1200* (Cambridge, MA: Harvard University Press, 1998).

Julia Boffey, ' "Forto compleyne she had gret desire": The Grievances Expressed in Two Fifteenth-century Dream Visions', in Helen Cooney (ed.), *Nation, Court and Culture: New Essays on Fifteenth-Century English Poetry* (Dublin: Four Courts, 2001), 116–28.

R. H. Bowers, 'Versus compositi de Roger Belers', *Journal of English and Germanic Philology*, 56 (1957), 440–2.

Leonard E. Boyle, 'William of Pagula and the *Speculum Regis Edwardi III* ', *Medieval Studies*, 31 (1969), 329–36.

Paul Brand, *The Origins of the English Legal Profession* (Oxford: Blackwell, 1992).

—— 'The Languages of the Law in Later Medieval England', in D. A. Trotter (ed.), *Multilingualism in later Medieval Britain* (Cambridge: D. S. Brewer, 2000), 63–76.

Susan Brigden, *London and the Reformation*, repr. with corrections (Oxford: Clarendon Press, 1994).

Nicholas Brooks, 'The Organisation and Achievements of the Peasants of Kent and Essex in 1381', in Henry Mayr-Harting and R. I. Moore (eds.), *Studies in Medieval History presented to R. H. C. Davies* (London: The Hambledon Press, 1985), 247–70.

J. A. Burrow, 'The Poet as Petitioner', *Studies in the Age of Chaucer*, 3 (1981), 61–75.

—— *Thomas Hoccleve*, Authors of the Middle Ages, 4 (Aldershot: Ashgate Publishing, 1994).

Martin Camargo, *Ars Dictaminis, Ars Dictandi* (Turnhout: Brepols, 1991).

—— *The Middle English Verse Love Epistle* (Tübingen: Max Niemeyer Verlag, 1991).

—— *Medieval Rhetorics of Prose Composition: Five English Artes Dictandi and their Tradition*, Medieval and Renaissance Texts and Studies (Binghampton, NY, 1995).

—— 'The Waning of the Medieval *Ars Dictaminis*', *Rhetorica*, 19 (2001), 135–40.

James P. Carley, ' "Cum excuterem puluerem et blattis": John Bale, John Leland, and the *Chronicon Tinemutensis coenobii* ', in Helen Barr and Ann M. Hutchison (eds.), *Text and Controversy from Wyclif to Bale: Essays in honour of Anne Hudson* (Turnhout: Brepols, 2005), 163–87.

Neil Cartlidge, 'Festivity, Order, and Community in Fourteenth-Century Ireland: The Composition and Contexts of BL MS Harley 913', *The Yearbook of English Studies*, 33 (2003), 33–52.

Pierre Chaplais, *English Diplomatic Practice in the Middle Ages* (London: Hambledon and London, 2003).

S. B. Chrimes, 'Richard II's Questions to the Judges, 1387', *The Law Quarterly Review*, 72 (1956), 365–90.

Thomas Cogswell, 'Underground Verse and the Transformation of Early Stuart Political Culture', in Susan D. Amussen and Mark A. Kishlansky (eds.), *Political Culture and Cultural Politics in Early Modern England: Essays presented to David Underdown* (Manchester: Manchester University Press, 1995), 277–300.

Giles Constable, *Letters and Letter-Collections*, Typologie des Sources du Moyen Âge Occidental, fasc. 17 (Turnhout: Brepols, 1976).

Marilyn Corrie, 'Kings and Kingship in British Library MS Harley 2253', *The Yearbook of English Studies*, 33 (2003), 64–79.

Pauline Croft, 'The Reputation of Robert Cecil: Libels, Political Opinion and Popular Awareness in the early Seventeenth Century', *Transactions of the Royal Historical Society*, 6th ser., 1 (1990), 43–69.

——— 'Libels, Popular Literacy and Public Opinion in Early Modern England', *Historical Research*, 68 (1995), 266–85.

W. A. Davenport, *Chaucer: Complaint and Narrative* (Cambridge: D. S. Brewer, 1988).

——— 'Fifteenth-Century Complaints and Duke Humphrey's Wives', in Helen Cooney (ed.), *Nation, Court and Culture: New Essays on Fifteenth-Century English Poetry* (Dublin: Four Courts, 2001), 129–52.

Catherine Davies, *A Religion of the Word: The Defence of the Reformation in the reign of Edward VI* (Manchester: Manchester University Press, 2002).

Richard G. Davies, 'Alexander Neville, Archbishop of York, 1374–1388', *The Yorkshire Archaeological Journal*, 47 (1975), 87–101.

Norman Davis, 'The *Litera Troili* and English Letters', *Review of English Studies*, n. s., 16 (1965), 233–44.

R. B. Dobson, 'Neville, Alexander (*c*.1332–1392)', *Oxford Dictionary of National Biography* (Oxford: Oxford University Press, 2004), http://www.oxforddnb.com/view/article/19922 (accessed 29 December 2005).

A. I. Doyle and George B. Pace, 'A New Chaucer Manuscript', *PMLA*, 83 (1968), 22–34.

Georges Duby, *The Three Orders: Feudal Society Imagined*, trans. by Arthur Goldhammer (Chicago: University of Chicago Press, 1980). First published as *Les trois ordres ou l'imaginaire du féodalisme* (Éditions Gallimard, 1978).

Christopher Dyer, 'Memories of Freedom: Attitudes Towards Serfdom in England, 1200–1350', in M. L. Bush (ed.), *Serfdom and Slavery: Studies in Legal Bondage* (London: Longman, 1996), 277–95.

J. G. Edwards, '*Confirmatio Cartarum* and Baronial Grievances in 1297', *English Historical Review*, 58 (1943), 147–71.

Thomas J. Elliott, 'Middle English Complaints against the Times: To Contemn the World or to Reform it?', *Annuale Medievale*, 14 (1973), 22–34.

George F. Farnham, *Leicestershire Medieval Village Notes*, Vol. 4 (1930).

John H. Fisher, *The Emergence of Standard English* (Lexington: University Press of Kentucky, 1996).

Anthony Fletcher and Diarmid MacCulloch, *Tudor Rebellions*, 5th edn. (Harlow: Longman, 2004).

Adam Fox, *Oral and Literate Culture in England 1500–1700* (Oxford: Oxford University Press, 2000).

Paul Freedman, *Images of the Medieval Peasant* (Stanford, CA: Stanford University Press, 1999).

Natalie M. Fryde, 'Edward III's Removal of his Ministers and Judges, 1340–1', *Bulletin of the Institute of Historical Research*, 48 (1975), 149–61.

John Gillingham, 'Slaves of the Normans? Gerald de Barri and Regnal Solidarity in Early Thirteenth-Century England', in Pauline Stafford, Janet L. Nelson, and J. Martindale (eds.), *Law, Laity and Solidarities: Essays in honour of Susan Reynolds* (Manchester: Manchester University Press, 2001), 160–71.

C. J. Given-Wilson, 'Purveyance for the Royal Household, 1362–1413', *Bulletin of the Institute of Historical Research*, 56 (1983), 145–63.

Anthony Goodman, *John of Gaunt: The Exercise of Princely Power in Fourteenth-Century Europe* (London: Longman, 1992).

Antonia Gransden, *Historical Writing in England*, 2 vols., repr. (London: Routledge, 1996).

Great Britain, Royal Commission on Historical Manuscripts, *Third Report of the Royal Commission on Historical Manuscripts* (London: Her Majesty's Stationery Office, 1872).

____ *Eighth Report of the Royal Commission on Historical Manuscripts*, 3 vols. in 1 (London: Her Majesty's Stationery Office, 1881).

Richard Firth Green, *A Crisis of Truth: Literature and Law in Ricardian England* (Philadelphia: University of Pennsylvania, 1999).

____ 'Medieval Literature and Law', in David Wallace (ed.), *The Cambridge History of Medieval English Literature* (Cambridge: Cambridge University Press, 1999), 407–31.

R. A. Griffiths, *The Reign of King Henry VI* (1981), repr. (Stroud: Alan Sutton, 1998).

Roy Martin Haines, *Archbishop John Stratford: Political Revolutionary and Champion of the Liberties of the English Church ca.1275/80–1348* (Toronto: Pontifical Institute of Medieval Studies, 1986).

____ 'Stratford, John (*c.*1275–1348)', *Oxford Dictionary of National Biography* (Oxford: Oxford University Press, 2004), http://www.oxforddnb.com/view/article/26645 (accessed 29 December 2005).

Ralph Hanna, 'Two Lollard Codices and Lollard Book-Production', in *Pursuing History: Middle English Manuscripts and their Texts* (Stanford, CA: Stanford University Press, 1996), 48–59.

Alan Harding, *The Law Courts of Medieval England* (London: George, Allen & Unwin, 1973).

____ 'Plaints and Bills in the History of English Law, mainly in the period 1250–1350', in Dafydd Jenkins (ed.), *Legal History Studies 1972: Papers presented to the Legal History Conference, Aberystwyth, 18–21 July 1972* (Cardiff: University of Wales Press, 1975), 65–86.

____ 'The Revolt Against the Justices', in R. H. Hilton and T. H. Aston (eds.), *The English Rising of 1381* (Cambridge: Cambridge University Press, 1984), 165–93.

____ *Medieval Law and the Foundations of the State* (Oxford: Oxford University Press, 2002).

G. L. Harriss, *King, Parliament, and Public Finance in Medieval England to 1369* (Oxford: Clarendon Press, 1975).

I. M. W. Harvey, *Jack Cade's Rebellion of 1450* (Oxford: Clarendon Press, 1991).

Timothy S. Haskett, 'The Presentation of Cases in Medieval Chancery Bills', in W. M. Gordon and T. D. Fergus (eds.), *Legal History in the Making: Proceedings of the Ninth*

British Legal History Conference Glasgow 1989 (London: The Hambledon Press, 1991), 11–28.

Timothy S. Haskett, 'Country Lawyers? The Composers of English Chancery Bills', in Peter Birks (ed.), *The Life of the Law: Proceedings of the Tenth British Legal History Conference Oxford 1991* (London: The Hambledon Press, 1993), 9–23.

——— 'The Medieval English Court of Chancery', *Law and History Review*, 14 (1996), 245–313.

G. L. Haskins, 'Three Early Petitions of the Commonalty', *Speculum*, 12 (1937), 314–18.

——— 'The Petitions of Representatives in the Parliaments of Edward I', *The English Historical Review*, 53 (1938), 1–20.

J. S. W. Helt, 'Fish, Simon (*d.* 1531)', *Oxford Dictionary of National Biography* (Oxford: Oxford University Press, 2004), http://www.oxforddnb.com/view/article/9486 (accessed 18 May 2005).

H. J. Hewitt, *The Organization of War under Edward III, 1338–62* (Manchester: Manchester University Press, 1966).

R. H. Hilton, 'A Thirteenth-century Poem on Disputed Villein Services', *The English Historical Review*, 56 (1941), 90–7.

——— 'Peasant Movements in England before 1381' (1949), repr. in E. M. Carus-Wilson (ed.), *Essays in Economic History*, Vol. 2 (London: Edward Arnold, 1962), 73–90.

——— 'Freedom and Villeinage in England', *Past and Present*, 31 (1965), 3–19.

Anne Hudson, 'A Lollard Sect Vocabulary?' (1981), repr. in *Lollards and their Books* (London: The Hambledon Press, 1985), 165–80.

——— ' "No Newe Thyng": The Printing of Medieval Texts in the Early Reformation Period' (1983), repr. in *Lollards and their Books* (London: The Hambledon Press, 1985), 227–48.

——— 'The Legacy of *Piers Plowman*', in John A. Alford (ed.), *A Companion to* Piers Plowman (Berkeley and Los Angeles: University of California Press, 1988), 251–66.

——— *The Premature Reformation* (Oxford: Clarendon Press, 1988).

John Hudson, *The Formation of the English Common Law: Law and Society in England from the Norman Conquest to Magna Carta* (Harlow: Longman, 1996).

Paul R. Hyams, 'The Action of Naifty in the Early Common Law', *The Law Quarterly Review*, 90 (1974), 326–50.

——— 'The Proof of Villein Status in the Common Law', *The English Historical Review*, 89 (1974), 721–49.

——— *Kings, Lords and Peasants in Medieval England: The Common Law of Villeinage in the Twelfth and Thirteenth Centuries* (Oxford: Clarendon Press, 1980).

W. Illingworth, 'Copy of a Libel against Archbishop Neville, temp. Rich. II. … ', *Archaeologia; or, Miscellaneous Tracts relating to Antiquity*, 16 (1812), 80–3.

E. F. Jacob, *The Fifteenth Century 1399–1485* (Oxford: Clarendon Press, 1961).

A. H. Johnson, *The History of the Worshipful Company of the Drapers of London,* 5 vols. (Oxford: Clarendon Press, 1914–22).

William Chester Jordan, *The Great Famine: Northern Europe in the Early Fourteenth Century* (Princeton, NJ: Princeton University Press, 1996).

Maureen Jurkowski, 'Lawyers and Lollardy in the Early Fifteenth Century', in Margaret Aston and Colin Richmond (eds.), *Lollardy and the Gentry in the Later Middle Ages* (Stroud: Sutton Publishing, 1997), 155–82.

Steven Justice, *Writing and Rebellion: England in 1381* (Berkeley and Los Angeles: University of California Press, 1994).

Richard W. Kaeuper, 'Law and Order in Fourteenth-century England: The Evidence of Special Commissions of Oyer and Terminer', *Speculum*, 54 (1979), 734–84.

George Kane, 'Some Fourteenth-century "Political" Poems', in Gregory Kratzmann and James Simpson (eds.), *Medieval English Religious and Ethical Literature: Essays in honour of G. H. Russell* (Cambridge: D. S. Brewer, 1986), 82–91.

Katherine Kerby-Fulton and Steven Justice, 'Reformist Intellectual Culture in the English and Irish Civil Service: The *Modus Tenendi Parliamentum* and its Literary Relations', *Traditio*, 53 (1998), 149–205.

Charles Lethbridge Kingsford, *English Historical Literature in the Fifteenth Century* (Oxford: Clarendon Press, 1913).

Ethan Knapp, *The Bureaucratic Muse: Thomas Hoccleve and the Literature of Late Medieval England* (University Park, PA: The Pennsylvania State University Press, 2001).

Gabrielle Lambrick, 'The Impeachment of the Abbot of Abingdon in 1368', *The English Historical Review*, 82 (1967), 250–76.

Gaillard T. Lapsley, 'Archbishop Stratford and the Parliamentary Crisis of 1341', in Helen M. Cam and Geoffrey Barraclough (eds.), *Crown, Community and Parliament in the Later Middle Ages: Studies in Constitutional History by Gaillard T. Lapsley* (Oxford: Basil Blackwell, 1951), 231–72.

R. E. Latham (ed.), *Revised Medieval Latin Word-list from British and Irish Sources* (London: Oxford University Press for the British Academy, 1965).

Stanford E. Lehmberg, *The Reformation Parliament 1529–1536* (Cambridge: Cambridge University Press, 1970).

—— *The Later Parliaments of Henry VIII 1536–1547* (Cambridge: Cambridge University Press, 1977).

C. S. Lewis, *The Allegory of Love: A Study in Medieval Tradition* (London: Oxford University Press, 1936).

Sheila Lindenbaum, 'London Texts and Literate Practice', in David Wallace (ed.), *The Cambridge History of Medieval English Literature* (Cambridge: Cambridge University Press, 1999), 284–309.

D. McCulloch and E. D. Jones, 'Lancastrian Politics, the French War, and the Rise of the Popular Element', *Speculum*, 58 (1983), 95–138.

Marjorie K. McIntosh, 'The Privileged Villeins of the English Ancient Demesne', *Viator*, 7 (1976), 295–328.

Mary-Rose McLaren, *The London Chronicles of the Fifteenth Century: A Revolution in English Writing* (Cambridge: D. S. Brewer, 2002).

—— 'Fabyan, Robert (*d.* 1513)', *Oxford Dictionary of National Biography* (Oxford: Oxford University Press, 2004), http://www.oxforddnb.com/view/article/9054 (accessed 20 October 2005).

—— 'The English Peasantry and the Demands of the Crown, 1294–1341', *Past and Present*, Supplement 1 (1975).

—— 'The County Community and the Making of Public Opinion in Fourteenth-century England', *Transactions of the Royal Historical Society*, 5th ser., 28 (1978), 27–43.

—— 'Law and Lordship: Royal Justices as Retainers in Thirteenth- and Fourteenth-century England', *Past and Present*, Supplement 4 (1978).

_____ 'Parliament and the Constituencies, 1272–1377', in R. G. Davies and J. H. Denton (eds.), *The English Parliament in the Middle Ages* (Manchester: Manchester University Press, 1981), 61–87.

_____ 'Poems of Social Protest in Early Fourteenth-century England', in W. M. Ormrod (ed.), *England in the Fourteenth Century: Proceedings of the 1985 Harlaxton Symposium* (Woodbridge: The Boydell Press, 1986), 130–44.

Helen Maurer, *Margaret of Anjou: Queenship and Power in Late Medieval England* (Woodbridge: The Boydell Press, 2003).

Middle English Dictionary, http://ets.umdl.umich.edu/m/med/ (accessed 14 February 2005).

Douglas Moffat, 'Sin, Conquest, Servitude: English Self-Image in the Chronicles of the Early Fourteenth Century', in Allen J. Frantzen and Douglas Moffat (eds.), *The Work of Work: Servitude, Slavery and Labor in Medieval England* (Glasgow: Cruithne Press, 1994), 146–68.

Linne R. Mooney, *Late Medieval English Scribes Database*, http://www.medievalscribes.com/scribes.html (accessed 15 December 2004).

_____ 'Chaucer's Scribe', *Speculum*, 81 (2006), 97–138.

Janel Mueller, 'Literature and the Church', in David Loewenstein and Janel Mueller (eds.), *The Cambridge History of Early Modern English Literature* (Cambridge: Cambridge University Press, 2002), 257–309.

Miriam Müller, 'The Aims and Organisation of a Peasant Revolt in Early Fourteenth-century Wiltshire', *Rural History*, 14 (2003), 1–20.

James J. Murphy, 'Rhetoric in Fourteenth-century Oxford', *Medium Aevum* 34 (1965), 1–20.

Anthony Musson, *Public Order and Law Enforcement: The Local Administration of Criminal Justice 1294–1350* (Woodbridge: The Boydell Press, 1996).

_____ *Medieval Law in Context: The Growth of Legal Consciousness from Magna Carta to the Peasants' Revolt* (Manchester: Manchester University Press, 2001).

Anthony Musson and W. M. Ormrod, *The Evolution of English Justice: Law, Politics and Society in the Fourteenth Century* (London: Macmillan Press, 1999).

A. R. Myers, 'Parliamentary Petitions in the Fifteenth Century', *The English Historical Review*, 52 (1937), 385–404, 590–613.

Cary J. Nederman and Cynthia J. Neville, 'The Origins of the "Speculum Regis Edwardi III" of William of Pagula', *Studi Medievali*, 3rd ser., 38 (1997), 317–29.

Richard Newhauser, 'Historicity and Complaint in the *Song of the Husbandman*', in Susanna Fein, (ed.), *Studies in the Harley Manuscript: The Scribes, Contents, and Social Contexts of British Library MS Harley 2253* (Kalamazoo, MI: Western Michigan University, 2000), 203–17.

Pamela Nightingale, *A Medieval Mercantile Community: The Grocers' Company and the Politics and Trade of London 1000–1485* (New Haven: Yale University Press, 1995).

Charles J. Nolan, 'Structural Sophistication in "The Complaint unto Pity" ', *The Chaucer Review*, 13 (1979), 363–72.

Clementine Oliver, 'A Political Pamphleteer in Late Medieval England: Thomas Fovent, Geoffrey Chaucer, Thomas Usk, and the Merciless Parliament of 1388', in David Lawton, Wendy Scase, and Rita Copeland (eds.), *New Medieval Literatures*, Vol. 6 (Oxford: Oxford University Press, 2003), 167–98.

Mark Ormrod, 'The Use of English: Language, Law, and Political Culture in Fourteenth-century England', *Speculum*, 78 (2003), 750–87.

Dorothy M. Owen, *Medieval Canon Law: Teaching, Literature and Transmission* (Cambridge: Cambridge University Press, 1990).

Oxford English Dictionary, http://www.oed.com (accessed 14 December 2005).

W. A. Pantin, 'A Medieval Treatise on Letter-Writing with Examples from the Rylands Latin MS. 394', *Bulletin of the John Rylands Library*, 13 (1929), 326–82.

S. J. Payling, 'Willoughby, Sir Richard (*c*.1290–1362)', *Oxford Dictionary of National Biography* (Oxford: Oxford University Press, 2004), http://www.oxforddnb.com/view/article/29601 (accessed 29 December 2005).

Kenneth Pennington, *Popes, Canonists and Texts, 1150–1550* (Aldershot: Ashgate, 1993).

John Peter, *Complaint and Satire in Early English Literature* (Oxford: Clarendon Press, 1956).

T. F. T. Plucknett, 'The Origin of Impeachment', *Transactions of the Royal Historical Society*, 4th ser., 24 (1942), 47–71.

Gaines Post, *Studies in Medieval Legal Thought: Public Law and the State, 1100–1322* (Princeton, NJ: Princeton University Press, 1964).

Edward Powell, *Kingship, Law and Society: Criminal Justice in the reign of Henry V* (Oxford: Clarendon Press, 1989).

A. J. Prescott, 'The Accusations against Thomas Austin', in Paul Strohm, *Hochon's Arrow: The Social Imagination of Fourteenth-century Texts* (Princeton, NJ: Princeton University Press, 1992), 161–77.

Michael Prestwich, *War, Politics and Finance under Edward I* (London: Faber & Faber, 1972).

Donald B. Queller, *The Office of Ambassador in the Middle Ages* (Princeton, NJ: Princeton University Press, 1967).

Nigel Ramsay, 'Scriveners and Notaries as Legal Intermediaries in Later Medieval England', in Jennifer Kermode (ed.), *Enterprise and Individuality in Later Medieval England* (Stroud: Alan Sutton, 1991), 118–31.

Doris Rayner, 'The Forms and Machinery of the "Commune Petition" in the Fourteenth Century', *The English Historical Review*, 56 (1941), 198–233.

Zvi Razi and Richard Smith, 'The Origin of the English Manorial Court Rolls as a Written Record: A Puzzle', in Zvi Razi and Richard Smith (eds.), *Medieval Society and the Manor Court* (Oxford: Clarendon Press, 1996), 36–68.

A. C. Reeves, 'Booth, William (*d*. 1464)', *Oxford Dictionary of National Biography* (Oxford: Oxford University Press, 2004), http://www.oxforddnb.com/view/article/2896 (accessed 6 October 2005).

Carter Revard, 'Scribe and Provenance', in Susanna Fein (ed.), *Studies in the Harley Manuscript: The Scribes, Contents, and Social Contexts of British Library MS Harley 2253* (Kalamazoo, MI: Western Michigan University, 2000), 21–109.

H. G. Richardson, 'Business Training in Medieval Oxford', *The American Historical Review* 46 (1941), 259–80.

H. G. Richardson and G. O. Sayles, 'Parliamentary Documents from Formularies', *Bulletin of the Institute of Historical Research*, 9 (1933–4), 147–62.

Malcolm Richardson, 'The *Dictamen* and its Influence on Fifteenth-century English Prose', *Rhetorica*, 2 (1984), 207–26.

Malcolm Richardson, 'The Fading Influence of the Medieval *Ars Dictaminis* in England after 1400', *Rhetorica*, 19 (2001), 225–47.

Rossell Hope Robbins, 'Poems dealing with Contemporary Conditions', in Albert E. Hartung (gen. ed.), *A Manual of the Writings in Middle English 1050–1500*, Vol. 5 (New Haven: The Connecticut Academy of Arts and Sciences, 1975).

Alan Rogers, 'Parliamentary Appeals of Treason in the Reign of Richard II', *The American Journal of Legal History*, 8 (1964), 95–124.

Jens Röhrkasten, 'Beler, Sir Roger (*d*. 1326)', *Oxford Dictionary of National Biography* (Oxford: Oxford University Press, 2004), http://www.oxforddnb.com/view/article/1985 (accessed 29 December 2005).

Charles Ross, 'Rumour, Propaganda and Popular Opinion during the Wars of the Roses', in Ralph A. Griffiths (ed.), *Patronage, the Crown and the Provinces in Later Medieval England* (Gloucester: Alan Sutton, 1981), 15–32.

Alec Ryrie, 'Brinklow ⟨Brinkelow⟩, Henry (*d*. 1545/6)', *Oxford Dictionary of National Biography* (Oxford: Oxford University Press, 2004), http://www.oxforddnb.com/view/article/3437 (accessed 18 May 2005).

Nigel Saul, 'The Commons and the Abolition of Badges', *Parliamentary History*, 9 (1990), 302–15.

—— 'Richard II and the Vocabulary of Kingship', *The English Historical Review*, 110 (1995), 854–77.

—— *Richard II* (New Haven: Yale University Press, 1997).

G. O. Sayles, *The Functions of the Medieval Parliament of England* (London: The Hambledon Press, 1988).

Wendy Scase, *Piers Plowman and the New Anticlericalism* (Cambridge: Cambridge University Press, 1989).

—— ' "First to Reckon Richard": John But's *Piers Plowman* and the Politics of Allegiance', *The Yearbook of Langland Studies*, 11 (1997), 49–66.

—— ' "Strange and Wonderful Bills": Bill-Casting and Political Discourse in Late Medieval England', in Rita Copeland, David Lawton, and Wendy Scase (eds.), *New Medieval Literatures*, Vol. 2 (Oxford: Clarendon Press, 1998), 225–47.

—— 'Writing and the "Poetics of Spectacle": Political Epiphanies in *The Arrivall of Edward IV* and Some Contemporary Lancastrian and Yorkist Texts', in Jeremy Dimmick, James Simpson, and Nicolette Zeeman (eds.), *Images, Idolatry, and Iconoclasm in Late Medieval England: Textuality and the Visual Image* (Oxford: Oxford University Press, 2002), 172–84.

—— ' "Heu! Quanta desolatio Angliae praestatur": A Wycliffite Libel and the Naming of Heretics, Oxford, 1382', in Fiona Somerset, Jill C. Havens, and Derrick G. Pitard (eds.), *Lollards and their Influence in Late Medieval England* (Woodbridge: The Boydell Press, 2003), 19–36.

—— 'The Audience and Framers of the *Twelve Conclusions of the Lollards*', in Helen Barr and Ann M. Hutchison (eds.), *Text and Controversy from Wyclif to Bale: Essays in Honour of Anne Hudson* (Turnhout: Brepols, 2005), 283–301.

—— 'Imagining Alternatives to the Book: The Transmission of Political Poetry in Late Medieval England', in John Thompson and Stephen Kelly (eds.), *Imagining the Pre-Modern Book* (Turnhout: Brepols, 2005), 237–50.

_____ ' "Satire on the Retinues of the Great" (MS Harley 2253): Unpaid Bills and the Politics of Purveyance', in Anne-Marie D'Arcy and Alan F. Fletcher (eds.), *'The Key of All Good Remembrance': Studies in Late Medieval and Early Renaissance Texts in honour of John Scattergood* (Dublin: Four Courts, 2005), 305–20.

_____ ' "Let him be kept in most strait prison": Lollards and the *Epistola Luciferi*', in Peregrine Horden (ed.), *Freedom of Movement in the Middle Ages* (Stamford: Paul Watkins, forthcoming).

V. J. Scattergood, *Politics and Poetry in the Fifteenth Century* (London: Blandford Press, 1971).

_____ 'The Short Poems', in A. J. Minnis (ed.), with V. J. Scattergood and J. J. Smith, *Oxford Guides to Chaucer: The Shorter Poems* (Oxford: Clarendon Press, 1995), 455–512.

_____ 'Authority and Resistance', in Susanna Fein (ed.), *Studies in the Harley Manuscript: The Scribes, Contents, and Social Contexts of British Library MS Harley 2253* (Kalamazoo, MI: Western Michigan University, 2000), 163–201.

Ethan H. Shagan, 'Protector Somerset and the 1549 Rebellions: New Sources and New Perspectives', *The English Historical Review*, 114 (1999), 34–63.

John W. Sherwell, *A Descriptive and Historical Account of the Guild of Saddlers of the City of London* (privately published, 1889).

A Short-title Catalogue of Books printed in England, Scotland and Ireland and of English Books printed abroad: 1475–1640, ed. by A. W. Pollard and G. R. Redgrave, rev. by W. A. Jackson, F. S. Ferguson, and K. F. Pantzer, 2 vols. (London: The Bibliographical Society, 1986, 1976).

James Simpson, *The Oxford English Literary History, Volume Two, 1350–1547: Reform and Cultural Revolution* (Oxford: Oxford University Press, 2002).

Richard M. Smith, 'The English Peasantry 1250–1650', in Tom Scott (ed.), *The Peasantries of Europe* (London: Longman, 1998), 339–71.

Fiona Somerset, *Clerical Discourse and Lay Audience in Late Medieval England* (Cambridge: Cambridge University Press, 1998).

I. H. Stein, 'The Latin Text of Wyclif's *Complaint*', *Speculum*, 7 (1932), 87–94.

Emily Steiner, 'Commonalty and Literary Form in the 1370s and 1380s', in David Lawton, Wendy Scase, and Rita Copeland (eds.), *New Medieval Literatures*, Vol. 6 (Oxford: Oxford University Press, 2003), 198–221.

E. L. G. Stones, 'The Folvilles of Ashby-Folville, Leicestershire, and their Associates in Crime, 1326–1347', *Transactions of the Royal Historical Society*, 5th ser., 7 (1957), 117–36.

R. L. Storey, 'Ecclesiastical Causes in Chancery', in D. A. Bullough and R. L. Storey (eds.), *The Study of Medieval Records: Essays in honour of Kathleen Major* (Oxford: Clarendon Press, 1971), 236–59.

Paul Strohm, *Hochon's Arrow: The Social Imagination of Fourteenth-century Texts* (Princeton, NJ: Princeton University Press, 1992).

_____ 'The Trouble with Richard: The Reburial of Richard II and Lancastrian Symbolic Strategy', *Speculum* 71 (1996), 87–111.

Joanna Summers, *Late-Medieval Prison Writing and the Politics of Autobiography* (Oxford: Clarendon Press, 2004).

Walter Sinclair Thomson, 'A Lincolnshire Assize Roll for 1298', *The Lincolnshire Record Society*, 36 (1944).

Thorlac Turville-Petre, 'Politics and Poetry in the Early Fourteenth-Century: The Case of Robert Manning's *Chronicle*', *Review of English Studies,* n. s., 39 (1988), 1–28.

—— *England the Nation: Language, Literature, and National Identity, 1290–1340* (Oxford: Clarendon Press, 1996).

—— 'English Quaint and Strange in "Ne mai no lewed lued"', in O. S. Pickering (ed.), *Individuality and Achievement in Middle English Poetry* (Cambridge: D. S. Brewer, 1997), 73–83.

Claire Valente, *The Theory and Practice of Revolt in Medieval England* (Aldershot: Ashgate, 2003).

Roger Virgoe, 'Some Ancient Indictments in the King's Bench referring to Kent, 1450–1452', *Kent Records: Documents Illustrative of Medieval Kentish Society*, 18 (Kent Archaeological Society Records Publication Committee, 1964).

—— 'The Death of William de la Pole, Duke of Suffolk', *Bulletin of the John Rylands Library*, 47 (1964–5), 489–502.

John Watts, 'Pole, William de la, first duke of Suffolk (1396–1450)', *Oxford Dictionary of National Biography* (Oxford: Oxford University Press, 2004), http://www.oxforddnb.com/view/article/22461 (accessed 2 Oct 2005).

—— 'The Pressure of the Public on Later Medieval Politics', in Linda Clark and Christine Carpenter (eds.), *The Fifteenth Century IV: Political Culture in Later Medieval Britain* (Woodbridge: The Boydell Press, 2004), 159–80.

Helen C. White, *Social Criticism in Popular Religious Literature of the Sixteenth Century* (London: Macmillan, 1944, repr. New York: Octagon Books, 1965).

James I. Wimsatt, *Chaucer and his French Contemporaries: Natural Music in the Fourteenth Century* (Toronto: University of Toronto Press, 1991).

B. P. Wolffe, 'Acts of Resumption in the Lancastrian Parliaments 1399–1456', *The English Historical Review*, 73 (1958), 583–613.

Laura Wright, 'Bills, Accounts, Inventories: Everyday Trilingual Activities in the Business World of Later Medieval England', in D. A. Trotter (ed.), *Multilingualism in Later Medieval Britain* (Cambridge: D. S. Brewer, 2000), 149–56.

J. A. Yunck, *The Lineage of Lady Meed* (Notre Dame, IN: Notre Dame University Press, 1963).

Index

Page numbers in bold refer to illustrations.

A.B.C. ayenst the Clergye 156
Abingdon
  Abbey 19
  libels in 109
Adalbero of Laon
  Carmen ad Rotbertum regem 6
Adam 6, 7
  Adam and Eve 6
Ælfric
  Colloquy 6
Against the King's Taxes 10, 29–33, 176
Alansmore
  complaint of villagers of 13
almshouses 90, 98, 99, 100, 152
ancient demesne 9, 29, 100 n. 74
Annales Ricardi Secundi 94, 97, 144
Anonimalle Chronicle 63, 64, 83–4, 85, 144
Antwerp 151, 154, 156
appeals 44, 51, 56, 72, 179
  appeal of treason 65, 66
Appellants (of 1388) 63, 65–82, 179
  articles of appeal 66, 76, 80
Armourers' Guild (of London)
  petition concerning Brembre 67 n. 93
Arnold, Thomas 94
ars dictaminis 4, 171–3, 182–6
  see also formularies
Arthur, king 152
Arundel, Earl of
  appeal of 66
Arundel, Thomas, Archbishop of Canterbury
  Constitutions 156
Aspin, Isabel 19, 20, 21, 31, 42 n. 2, 48
Assize of Clarendon (1166) 45
Aston, Margaret 94
Ayscough, William, Bishop of Salisbury 129, 134

Babthorpe, Ralph 130
  petition and libels concerning 130
Babylon 97
bailiffs 46
Bale, John 95, 159
Bale, Robert 134, 135
  chronicle copied by 134–5
Ball, John 84
  sermon 5–6

Ballad set on the Gates of Canterbury 139–40, 186
ballades 1, 183, 184, 185
ballads 2, 140
Bannockburn 11
Barbour, Roger
  receipt of lollard bill by 101
Barlowe, Jerome (printer) 156
Barnak, Walter 97, 98
  libel concerning 97, 98
Barr, Helen 104
Battle of Northampton 140–1
Beatitudes 43
Beler, Roger 53
  plays on name of 53
  Versus compositi de Roger Beler 47, 52–4, 173
Belgrave, John 97, 98
  libel attributed to 97
  petition concerning 97
Benedict XII, pope 58
Benet, John 130–1, 135
  book copied by 145–6, 147
  chronicle copied by 134, 145, 148
Bernard (of Clairvaux)
  De consideratione 25
Bernewelle
  petition concerning tenants of 100 n. 74
Beverley 82
bill (meanings of) 1, 61, 165, 184
  true bill 45, 56
'Bille et supplicationes secundum novum modum' 183
Bishop, Nicholas
  historical notes by 109
Bisson, Thomas 10 n. 25
Blackfriars Council (1382) 95
Blackheath 110, 111, 112
Blakeney, John
  petitions and libel concerning 130
Blow Northerne Wynd 170–1, 173
Boke of Brut, see *Castleford's Chronicle*
Bolland, William Craddock 40, 41 n. 143
Boniface VIII, pope 21
Booth, William, Bishop of Coventry and Lichfield (Chester) 129, 130, 131

Booth, William, Bishop of Coventry and
    Lichfield (Chester) (*cont.*)
  petitions and libels concerning 130, 131,
    133, 183
  plays on name of 131
Boulers, Reginald, Abbot of Gloucester 130,
    131, 133
  petition and libel concerning 130, 131
Bracton 6 n. 9, 7, 18
Braybrooke 101
Brembre, Nicholas 66, 67–71
  appeals and petitions concerning 67–72,
    73, **74**, **75**, 76–7, 179
  plays on name of 76–7
Bridlington 27
Brigden, Susan 162
Brinklow, Henry 159, 160
  *Complaint of Roderyck Mors somtyme a gray
    fryre* 159–60
  *Lame<n>tacyon of a Christen agaynst the
    cytye of London* 159
  see also 'Mors, Roderyck'
Britons 27, 152
Brooks, Nicholas 84
Broughton, John 131, 145
Brut 145
burgesses (in parliament), *see* parliament
Bury, Adam 63
Bury St Edmunds
  libels in 134
But, John 175 n. 22

Cade, Jack 110, 112, 144
  see also Cade's rebellion
Cade's rebellion 87, 110–21, 125, 130, 134,
    136, 147, 158
  petitions of Cade's rebels 110–15, **116**,
    117, **119**, **120**, 128, 131, 139, 148, 157
Calais 89
Camargo, Martin 185 n. 62, 186 n. 63
Cambridgeshire 13, 14, 92
Canterbury 58, 108, 121, 129
  libels in 60, 107, 140
  province of 88
  see also *Ballad set on the Gates of Canterbury*
Carley, James 95
Cartlidge, Neil 43 n. 3
Castleford's Chronicle 28
Catalonia 10 n. 25
Catesby, William 142
  libel concerning 142
Cecil, Robert, Earl of Salisbury
  libels concerning 128 n. 151, 138
Chambers, R. W. and Marjorie Daunt 67
chancery 85
  bills and petitions 92 n. 40, 97, 174

clerks 92, 173
  see also scripts
Charles d'Orléans 1 n. 2, 121 n. 135
  lyric sequence associated with 185, 186–7
  manuscripts of works by 184, 185–6
Charter of the Forest 18
Chaucer, Geoffrey 2
  manuscripts of works by 77, 177, 184–6
  Anelida and Arcite 183, 184, 186
  'Bukton' 185 n. 61, 186
  Canterbury Tales, General Prologue
    (Prioress) 77; Merchant's Tale
    183–4
  'Chaucers wordes unto Adam, his owne
    scriveyn' 177
  dream visions 184, 185
  'Fortune' 184, 185, 185 n. 61
  'Lak of Stedfastnesse' 186
  'Mars' 184, 185
  'Pity' 181–2, 184, 186
  'Purse' 184, 185 n. 61, 186
  'Scogan' 185 n. 61, 186
  Troilus and Criseyde 177–8, 179
  'Venus' 184, 185
cherl (meanings of) 37 n. 124
Cheshire 46
Chester 133
Cheyne, Thomas 115
Christine de Pisan
  L'epistre au Dieu d'Amours 179–80, 184
chronicles 65, 100–1, 158
  London 146, 147, 148, 152
  Middle English 10
  of Norman conquest 6
  see also titles and authors of individual
    chronicles
Chronicon Angliae 64
Chroniques de London 57–8
Cicatrix cordium superbia 61
clamour (meanings of) 1, 3–4, 43, 64 n. 84
  clamour of the people (meanings of) 55–7
Claypole
  complaint concerning villagers of 13
Clehonger
  complaint of villagers of 13
'Clericos laicos' 58
Collyngbourne, William 141
  libel attributed to 141, 148–9
Colyns, John
  libels in commonplace book of 150
comaund (meaning of) 90 n. 27
commendere (meaning of) 90 n. 27
complaint (meanings of) 1, 183–4, 185, 185
    n. 62
  complaynyng wyse 1
  compleinen 1

Complaint of Roderyck Mors somtyme a gray fryre, *see* Brinklow, Henry
Confirmatio Cartarum 19
conspiracy 46, 47
‘De Conspiratoribus’ 46
Constantine, John
petitions concerning 68
Cook family 114, 118, 144, 146
Elizabeth, wife of Sir Thomas 146
Sir Thomas (son of Thomas Cook) 114, 146, 147, 149
Thomas 114, 146
coram regem (meaning of) 37
in English 37
Cordwainers’ Guild (of London)
petition concerning Brembre 67 n. 93, 68, 71
coroners 44, 51
counts (statements of legal cases) 49
‘Course of the Revolt’ 83–4, 186
courts
archdeacon’s 97
consistory 38
county 16, 44, 62 n. 77, 133
criminal 40, 42–82
ecclesiastical 89, 172
eyre 9, 44
king’s bench 54
oyer and terminer 44–5, 46, 55, 121, 129
royal 5, 7–9, 22–3, 37–8, 39, 40, 171
royal household 64 n. 83
seignurial 8 n. 14
trailbaston 43 n. 3, 46, 47
see also parliament
Coventry 94, 98, 102, 104, 105, 139
Leet Book 142
libels in 109, 142
coveren (meaning of) 37
Croft, Pauline 138
Cromer, William
petitions concerning 113
Cromwell, Thomas 157
Crowley, Robert
as printer 161
use of name of 161
Informacion and peticion agaynst the oppressours of the pore commons 160, 165, 183
Cumberworth, Sir Thomas 145
Cutlers’ Guild (of London)
petition concerning Brembre 67 n. 93, 72

Danes 152
Danyell, Thomas 125
petitions and libels concerning 125, 129, 130, 131

Dartford 115, 121, 129
Davenport, W. A. 2
Davis, Norman 177, 178
Day, John (printer) 160
De modo dictandi 170, 172, 182–3
Decaye of England, *see* ploughman petitions
‘Defend us all from Lollardy’ 102
Derby, Earl of
appeal of 66
Derbyshire 54
Despenser family 53
disendowment 94, 95, 98, 102, 105, 109, 152
Disputatio inter Clericum et Militem 21
Domesday Book 9
Dorset 12
Doyle, A. I. 146
Drapers’ Guild (of London) 146, 149
petition concerning Brembre 67 nn. 93, 94; 68, 71
Drayton, John
petition of 92
Duby, Georges 10
Dunstable
Priory 146
Durham 27, 46
Dyer, Christopher 10 n. 25
Dymmok, Roger 91, 144

Easingwold, Robert
will of, mentioning formulary 172
Edinburgh 108
Edward, Earl of March 139, 141
Edward I, king of England 1, 3, 9, 10, 12, 27, 28 n. 97, 85, 143
Edward II, king of England 45, 53 n. 42, 56, 62
Edward III, king of England 12, 13, 14, 22, 24, 45, 58, 86, 88, 91, 93
works addressed to, *see* William of Pagula
Edward IV, king of England 140 n. 16, 147
Edward VI, king of England 161, 168 n. 119
Edward, son of Henry VI 134
libel concerning 134
Edwards, J. G. 18
Egyptians, slaves of 6, 25
Elliott, Thomas J. 2
Ellis, Roger 184
Elvet, John, Archdeacon of Leicester
petition concerning John Belgrave 97, 98
Epistola ad Regem Edwardum III, *see* William of Pagula
Essex 84
Est, Robert
petitions concerning 113
Eugenius, pope 25

Eustace de Folville, *see* Folville family
exchequer 53, 85

Fabyan family
    John 149
    Robert (son of John) 149
    New Chronicles of England and France
        (attributed to Robert) 147–50
Fasciculi Zizaniorum 144
Fastolf, Sir John 114, 144
Favent, Thomas
    account of Merciless Parliament 69–71
felony 24, 45, 51
    felony (meanings of) 44, 50
'Ffor feer or for favour of any fals mane' 128
Fiennes, James, *see* Say, Lord (James Fiennes)
fifteenth (tax) 31
first person (writing in) 31–2
Fish, Simon
    Supplicacyon for the Beggers 137, 151–4,
        155, 156, 158, 159, 165, 167–8
Fisher, John 92, 173
Five dogs of London 135, 145
Folville family 55
    Eustace de Folville 53
    Robert de Folville 53
    Walter de Folville 53
formes fixes 1
formularies 172, 177 n. 26, 178, 179, 179 n.
        36, 184
    see also authors and titles of formularies
Fortescue, Sir John
    Governance of England 146
Founderers' Guild (of London)
    petition concerning Brembre 67 n. 93
Fourth Lateran Council (1215) 21
Fovent, Thomas, *see* Favent, Thomas
Fox, Adam 137
Foxe, John 102, 153
    Acts and Monuments 137
France 11, 12, 13, 14, 134
Francis, Viscount Lovell 142
    libel concerning 142
Freedman, Paul 6, 29
Friar Daw's Reply 97
friars 95, 168, 175
    libels and petitions falsely attributed to 97,
        159–60
    petitions and libels concerning 94, 95, 97,
        98

Gamelyngeye
    complaint of villagers of 13
Gascoigne, Thomas 112, 150
Gascony 11
George, Duke of Clarence 139

associated with 'Robin of Redesdale's'
        petition 139
    bills attributed to 139
Gerald of Wales 29
Gervase le Volore
    petition and libel concerning 130
Gilbertines 28
Gillingham, John 29
Gloucester 100
Gloucester, Duke of
    appeal of 66
Godfrey, Thomas (printer) 154
Goldeneye, John
    petition concerning 15
Goodman, Anthony 95
Gower, John
    manuscripts of works by 77, 177
    Cinquante Ballades 183
    Confessio Amantis 183
gravamina 38 n.129
Great Chronicle of London 148, 149
Greeks 152
Gregory, William
    chronicle of 118, 119
Green, Richard Firth 5 n. 2, 48
Gyles de Beauchamp
    petition concerning 34

Halley, Bartholomew
    petition and libel concerning 130
Halliday, Robert 14
Ham (son of Noah) 6
Hampton, John
    petitions and libel concerning 130
Hanley, Bartholomew, *see* Halley,
        Bartholomew
Hanna, Ralph 95
Harlington 145
Harriss, G. L. 29
Harvey, I. M. W. 111, 114, 115
Haskett, Timothy 173, 174, 178
Helton, John, *see* Holton, John
Henry II, king of England 8, 44
Henry III, king of England 10
Henry IV, king of England 102, 105, 106,
        108, 178
    libels concerning 102–5, 106
Henry V, king of England 101 n. 77, 105,
        106, 108, 173, 184
    libel concerning 101
Henry VI, king of England 140, 147, 184
    petitions and libels concerning 139–41
Henry VII, king of England 148, 169
Henry VIII, king of England 150, 160
'Henry A.'
    libel signed by 162, **163**, **164**

Hereford, Earl of
  petition of 17, 18
Herefordshire 13, 14
heresy 94, 95, 101 n. 77, 153, 155, 156
Hertfordshire 13, 14, 34, 50
Hilton, Rodney 5, 6 n. 9
hobelarii 50
hobeler, see *hobelarii*
Hoccleve, Thomas 179
  'Balade to Henry V' 184, 186
  Formulary 179
  'L'epistre de Cupide' 180, 184
  Regiment of Princes 181
  The Series 184
Holderness
  petition of men of 15–16
Holton, John 145
  libels attributed to 134
home counties 46
Hoo, Thomas
  petitions and libel concerning 130
Hudson, Anne 100, 154–5 n. 73, 156
Hugo de Wygthorpe 13
Humphrey, Duke of Gloucester 109, 111
Hungerford, Edmund
  petitions and libel concerning 130
Hurt, Roger
  complaint concerning 14
husbandmen 50, 168
  see also *Proper dyaloge, betwene a Gentillman
    and an Husbandman*; *Song of the
    Husbandman*

Ile, Thomas 101
  bills attributed to 101
impeachment 66
'In the moneth of May whan gres growes
    grene' 128–31, 145, 186
indictments 45, 51–2, 56, 131
Inquisition of the Ninth 12, 14
Isle, William
  petitions concerning 113

Jerusalem 19
Jews 6, 88
John, Viscount Beaumont
  libel concerning 141
John d'Arcy 61
John de Briggis
  ars dictaminis by 172
John de Kele
  complaint concerning 13
John of Gaunt, Duke of Lancaster 64–5, 84,
    94, 95
  petitions addressed to; forms of address
    to 94–5, 175, 175 n. 22

petitions and libels concerning 64–5, 84,
    144
judges 46, 47, 53, 97
  questions of Richard II to 66
  trailbaston 43 n. 3
  trial of (1290–3) 41
  see also justices; *Song on the Venality of the
    Judges*
judicial combat 65
juries 44–5, 46, 47, 49, 52, 53, 54
Jurkowski, Maureen 93
Justice, Steven 86 n. 10
justices 58
  Justice of the Peace 45
  see also judges
Juvenal
  Satire 6 26 n. 92

Kane, George 36
Kempe, Margery 101
Kent 84, 110, 112, 113, 114, 115, 129
Kent, Thomas
  petitions and libel concerning 130
Kerrigan, John 2
Kett's rebellion
  petitions attributed to rebels 158
Kilsby, William 58, 60, 61
  libels attributed to 61–2
King, Marjorie
  petition of 92
King, William
  complaint concerning 14
Knighton, Henry
  Chronicle 76, 80–1, 91, 92, 99
knights of the shire, see parliament
Köpfel, William (printer) 159

lament 2, 98, 140
*Lame<n>tacyon of a Christen agaynst the cytye
    of London*, see Brinklow, Henry
Lamentations of Jeremiah 19–20, 22, 97, 186
Lancastrians 105, 135, 141, 147
Lanfranc, *Surgery* 52
Langland, William, see *Piers Plowman*
Langlandian texts 152
  see also ploughman petitions
Langtoft, Peter
  Chronicle 26–7
Latimer, William 63–4
  petition concerning 63
law reports
  language of 39
law-writers 134
  see also notaries; scriveners
lawyers 85, 104
  associated with lollards 90, 93

lawyers (*cont.*)
  'country' 92
  professional 39, 40
  provincial 16, 92 n. 40
Leathersellers' Guild (of London)
  petition concerning Brembre 67 n. 93, 72
Leicester 101, 111
  Abbey 5, 19
  libels in 97, 101
  St Martin's Church 97
Leicestershire 53, 54, 55
libellus
  forms of 172
  libellus (meanings of) 61
  libellus famosus (meanings of) 61
Lincoln, John 150
Lincolnshire 12, 16, 27, 146
  rebellion in 139, 141
lollards 98, 101, 109, 152, 175
  bills, libels, and petitions of 4, 97, 101, 160, 175, 186
  complaint writings of, edited during Reformation 137, 154, 154 n. 71, 156
  views on eucharist 76
  views on law 93
  Clergy may not hold Property 156
  Epistola Sathanae ad Cleros 175 n. 22
  'Heu! Quanta desolatio' **96**, 97
  Lollard Disendowment Bill 87, 98–100, 105, 109–10, 148, 152, 167, 175, 176
  Petition to the King and Parliament 94–5, 98, 99, 152, 175
  'Plangant Anglorum gentes' 97
  Twelve Conclusions of the Lollards 87–94, 95, 97, 98, 99, 100, 108, 144, 152, 176
  see also Belgrave, John; Lucas, Thomas; Pateshull, Peter; Thorpe, William; Wyclif, John
London 64 n. 83, 90, 110, 114, 118, 131, 133, 138, 145, 162
  aldermen 61, 63, 134, 142, 151, 162
  Barking, All Hallows Church 150
  Bermondsey 105
  Bridge 146, 150
  chronicles 146, 147, 148, 152
  Common Council 114, 146, 147
  Gray's Inn 134, 151
  Guildhall 58, 70, 72
  guilds 67
  libels in 61, 64, 102, 105, 108–9, 125, 128 n. 149, 135, 139, 141–2, 150–1, 160
  mayor 61, 64 n. 83, 66, 139, 142, 146, 179
  prediction of Merlin concerning 162
  printing and circulation of petitionary pamphlets in 151, 153, 160
  St Mary Spital 150

St Paul's 64, 94, 97, 125, 141, 150
Southwark 114
stationers 146
Tower of 114, 125
see also Westminster; names of individual guilds
Long Stowe
  complaint of villagers of 13
Lord's Prayer 38
Lucas, Thomas 93, 108
Lucy, Sir Thomas 138
  libels concerning 138
  plays on name of 138 n. 6
Ludwig, emperor 24
Lydgate, John
  manuscripts of works by 146, 184–5
  Complaint of the Black Knight 184, 185, 186
  Serpent of Division 146
  Temple of Glass 184, 185
Lym cum Halghestok
  complaint of villagers of 12
Lyons, Richard 63–4
  petition concerning 63

Maddicott, J. R. 14, 29
Magna Carta 8, 18, 24, 58, 93
Maidstone 121, 129
maintenance 46, 90, 133, 182
Malpas, Philip 147
Man in the Moon 38 n. 129, 143 n. 24
mandare (meaning of) 90 n. 27
Manning, Robert
  Chronicle 28, 32
Manual of the Writings in Middle English 1
manuscripts
  early modern 4
  see also manuscripts (referenced); Charles d'Orléans; Chaucer; Gower; Lydgate; *Piers Plowman*
manuscripts (referenced)
  Cambridge, Cambridge University Library Ee.4.20 170, 182
  Cambridge, Trinity College R.3.20 184
  Dublin, Trinity College 516 130, 141, 145
  London, British Library
    Additional 10374 33
    Additional 24062 179
    Additional 34888 122, **123**, **124**
    Additional 48031A 111, 111 n. 109, 146–7
    Cotton Faustina B. i 90–1, 145
    Cotton Julius B. ii 148
    Cotton Julius D. vii 19
    Cotton Nero C. xi 149

Cotton Roll II. 23 111, 112, 113, 122, 128, 129, 131, **132**, 135, 146, 157
Cotton Roll IV.50 111, 111 n. 109, 112, 113, 114, 115, **116**, **117**, 118
Cotton Vespasian B. xvi 131
Cotton Vitellius E. xii 95 n. 58
Harley 543 111 n. 109
Harley 670 172
Harley 913 42, 43 n. 3, 47, 49
Harley 2252 150
Harley 2253 10, 33, 38 n. 129, 43 n. 3, 143, 176
Harley 3775 109, 148
Harley 3988 183
Harley 4971 183
Royal 12. C. xii 42, 43 n. 3
Royal 12. C. xiv 52
London, Guildhall
    3133 149
London, Lambeth Palace
    306 110, 112, 128, 131
Longleat
    53 148
Oxford, Bodleian Library
    Digby 86 176 n. 24
    Digby 98 **96**, 97
    Douce 137 19
    Eng. hist. b. 119 122, 125, 125 n. 144, **126**, **127**
    Fairfax 16 184, 185–6
Oxford, Magdalen College
    Magdalen Misc. 306 110, 111, 112, 113, 114, 118, **119**, **120**, 121, 139, 146
Margaret of Anjou 131, 135, 147
Marlborough
    libels in 109
Martinus de Keyser (printer) 154
Martyn, William
    libel concerning 48 n. 28
Matthew Paris 25–6
Maurice Fitz Thomas, Earl of Desmond 43 n. 3
mede 50
'Medieval Petitions' project 93 n. 48
mendicants, *see* friars
Mercers' Guild (of London) 67
    petition concerning Brembre 67 n. 93, 68, 69, 71, 72, **73**, **74**, 76–7, 91, 100, 173–4, 176, 177–9
Merke, Thomas
    ars dictaminis by 172
Merlin, *see* London
Michael de la Pole 65–6
    appeal concerning 66
Middle English, *see* vernacular
Middlesex 133
Modus Tenendi Parliamentum 66 n. 88, 91

Moffat, Douglas 29
monasteries 26
Monstraunces 17–18, 19, 24
Mooney, Linne 77
More, Sir Thomas 154
    Supplycacyon of soulys made by syr Thomas More 154, 155
'Mors, Roderyck' 160, 165
    see also Brinklow, Henry
Multon, John 146
Mum and the Sothsegger 91, 103, 104–5
Murimuth
    Chronicle 46, 58
Myners, William
    petitions and libel concerning 130

narracio (meanings of) 49
narrator (meanings of) 49
Neville, Alexander, Archbishop of York 66, 67
    libels concerning 67, 77, **78**, 79–82
    plays on name of 79
Neville, Richard, Earl of Warwick 139
    associated with 'Robin of Redesdale's' petition 139
    bills attributed to 139
New Chronicles of England and France, see Fabyan family
Noah 6
Nonarum Inquisitiones, see Inquisition of the Ninth
Norfolk 84
Norman conquest 6, 25–7, 148
Normandy 122
Northampton
    libels in 101, 109
Northampton, John 179
    appeal concerning 179
    see also *Battle of Northampton*
Northamptonshire
    petition concerning men of 140
notaries 115
notoriety 45–6, 51–2, 56–7, 65, 66–7, 113, 133
Nottingham, Earl of
    appeal of 66
Nottinghamshire 54
'Now is the Fox drevin to hole' 128

Oldcastle, Sir John 102, 108
    libels concerning 102
    rising associated with 101, 102
Oldhall, William
    libels attributed to 134
Oxford 93, 109
    dictamen in 183
    letter to university 175

Oxford (*cont.*)
  libels in 97, 102
Oxfordshire 169
  petition concerning men of 169

Painters' Guild (of London)
  petition concerning Brembre 67 n. 93, 75,
    88
papacy 24–5
parlement 112 n. 116
parliament 9–10, 15, 35, 58–9, 62, 64, 65,
    66, 113, 153, 159
  Act for the Advancement of True
    Religion 159
  Act of Suppression of the monasteries 157
  bills and libels circulated during 61–2, 78,
    94, 95, 111–12, 153–4
  burgesses 62, 108
  clerks of 15 n. 56, 16, 38 n. 129, 93, 130
  continental 15
  forms of petitions to 68, 86, 87–8, 92, 93,
    98, 99, 108, 110, 113–14, 153, 159,
    165–7, 175
  having status of a court 90, 112
  knights of the shire 62, 102, 108, 113, 157
  language of petitions to 67, 77, 91–2
  of birds 48
  printed petitionary pamphlets circulated
    during 153–4
  rolls of 67, 67 n. 93, 93, 94, 112
  Speaker 134, 142
  of 1334 (at York) 16
  of 1376 (Good Parliament) 63
  of 1382 (in May) 94
  of 1385 98
  of 1386 (Wonderful Parliament) 65–6
  of 1388 (Merciless Parliament) 67, 69
  of 1398 (at Shrewsbury) 104
  of 1404 (at Coventry) 98, 102, 104,
    105
  of 1407 (at Gloucester) 100
  of 1410 100
  of 1450 (January) 121
  of 1450 (April–June) 111, 118
  of 1450 (November) 118, 134
  of 1459 (at Coventry) 139
  of 1470 (November) 147
  of 1523 153
  of 1529 (October) 153
  of 1547 161
  see also *parlement; Parliament Rolls of
    Medieval England*; petitions; statutes
Parliament Rolls of Medieval England
    (*PROME*) 88
Paston family 122, 125, 144
  John Paston 114

Pateshull, Peter 160
  libels attributed to 97, 98
Paunfield, Thomas
  petition of 92, 100
Payn, John 114, 118, 144
peasants' revolt (1381), *see* rebellions
Penycoke, John
  petitions and libel concerning 130
Peter, John 1–2
petitions
  commons' 15, 38 n. 129, 93, 129–30,
    131
  petition (meanings of) 165
  private 15, 88, 93, 169, 183
  text preserved by Knighton 80–1, 91, 92,
    99
Petur, William 115
Philip, bailiff
  complaint concerning 14
Piers Plowman 2, 37 n. 124, 50, 91, 102–3,
    105, 131, 175 n. 22
  manuscripts 77, 177
  Reformation reception of 161
  see also ploughman petitions
Piggott, John 125, 129, 136, 186
Pilgrimage of Grace 157
  petitions associated with 157, 158, 159
Pinkhurst, Adam 77, 106, n. 91, 177, 177
    n. 25
planctus (words derived from) 1
plangere (relation with *pleinte*) 1 n. 3
pleinen (meanings of) 1
  pleinte 1
  pleinte wise 1
ploughman petitions 3, 154, 154 n. 73, 156,
    167, 167 n. 114, 168–9
  name Piers Plowman 3, 165, 167
  Decaye of England 168–9, 186
  *Praier and complaynte of the ploweman unto
    Christe* 137, 154–6, 167, 186
  *Pyers plowmans exhortation vnto the lordes
    knightes and burgoysses* 165, **166**,
    167–9, 183
  see also *Piers Plowman*
Plucknett, T. F. T. 63
Poem on Disputed Villein Services 5–8, 10, 41,
    173, 186
Polychronicon 145, 146
Pontefract 34
  petition drafted at 157
*Praier and complaynte of the ploweman unto
    Christe, see* ploughman petitions
presentments 45, 179
prise (meaning of) 12
  see also purveyance
privy seal, office of 179
  formularies associated with 179, 183

proclamations 40, 62 n. 77, 76, 133, 143, 155, 161
procurator (meanings of) 89–90
Proper dyaloge, betwene a Gentillman and an Husbandman 156
Protestants 155
Pulford, Thomas
  petitions and libel concerning 130
purgatory 154
purveyance 11–13, 15, 23–4, 27, 28 n. 97, 34–5, 50, 104, 111, 112, 157
Pyers plowmans exhortation vnto the lordes knightes and burgoysses, see ploughman petitions
Pynson, Richard (printer) 148

querela (meanings of) 1, 49, 61
'Quis dabit meo capiti' 97

Radcliffe, Stephen
  complaint concerning 13
ragman roll 133, 183
Rastell, William (printer) 148, 154
Ratcliffe, Sir Richard 142
  libel concerning 142
Reading
  libels in 101
rebellions
  after Norman conquest 27
  of 1381 4, 53 n. 41, 83–7, 99, 112, 118, 136
  of 1414, *see* Oldcastle, Sir John
  of 1431 109
  of 1450, *see* Cade's rebellion
  of 1469, *see* Lincolnshire
  of 1536, *see* Pilgrimage of Grace
  of 1549, *see* Kett's rebellion
Rede Me and Be Nott Wrothe 150
Remesbury 12
resumption 98, 99, 100 n. 74, 102, 105, 110, 112, 146
Revard, Carter 33, 176
Richard, Duke of York 139, 146, 147
  bills attributed to 146
  libels concerning 135
Richard II, king of England 44, 65, 85, 86, 88, 90, 94, 104, 105, 106, 108, 156
  forms of address to 175, 175 n. 22
  libel concerning 79–82
Richard III, king of England 141
  libel concerning 141
Richard the Redeless 103, 104, 105
Richardson, H. G. 9, 172
Richardson, Malcolm 173
robbery 24
Robert de Folville, *see* Folville family

Robert de Syward
  complaint concerning 14
Robert de Vere 66
  appeal concerning 66
'Robin of Redesdale' 139
  petitions and libels attributed to 139, 141, 145, 146
Rochelle 64
Rochester 121, 129
  indictment 129, 130, 130 n. 160, 131
Roger de Belafago
  libel concerning 48 n. 28
Roger le Draper
  complaint concerning 13
Rogers, Alan 63
rolls 41
  of court proceedings 39
Romans 152
Romeyn, Roger
  complaint concerning 15
Roye, William (printer) 156
Russhok, Thomas
  petition concerning 88, 89
Ryder, Robert
  appeal of 72

Saddlers' Guild (of London)
  petition concerning Brembre 67 n. 93, 68
St Albans 19, 25, 26, 63, 94,
  libels in 101
Salisbury
  libels in 109
'Salutaciones sive modo dictandi' 182–3
Sampson, Thomas
  ars dictaminis by 172, 183
Sandwich 140
Satire on the Consistorie Courts 38, 143 n. 24
Satire on the Retinues of the Great 33–5, 38–9, 41, 84
Saul, Nigel 67–8
Saunders, Laurence 142
  libels concerning 142–3
Saxons 152
Say, John 129 n. 155
  petitions and libels concerning 130
Say, Lord (James Fiennes)
  petitions and libels concerning 125, 129, 131, 134
Sayles, G. O. 9
Scattergood, John 29
Schepished, William
  complaint of 6–7
Scoloker, A. and W. Seres (printers) 159
Scotland 11, 12, 78, 105–6
scripts
  anglicana 72, 106, 145, 176 n. 24

scripts (*cont.*)
  chancery 72
  court 106, 176 n. 24
  secretary 125, 128
scriveners 92, 115, 134
Scrope, Richard, Archbishop of York 102–3,
     104, 105, 145
  Articles against Henry IV 102, 105, 130, 145
'Sedens super flumina' 97, 160
Seymour, Edward, Duke of Somerset 161–2,
     165
  libels concerning 161, **163**, **164**
  petitions of, in parliament 163
  proclamations concerning 161
Shakespeare, William
  A Louers Complaint 2
  libel attributed to 138
Sharp, Jack
  petition attributed to 109, 175
sheriffs 11, 46, 49, 133
Shirley, John 184
Shrewsbury 104
signet office
  formulary possibly associated with 183
'Simon O'
  ars dictaminis by 172
Singleton, Hugh (printer) 168 n. 119
Skegness 13
Slegge, Stephen
  petition and libel concerning 113, 129, 130
Smith, William 101
sokemen, legal status of 9
Somerset, Duke of, Lord Protector, *see*
     Seymour, Edward
Somerset, John
  petitions and libels concerning 130, 131
Somnium viridarii 21 n. 75
song 41, 140
Song of the Church 19, 21, 22, 24, 31–2, 186
Song of the Husbandman 10, 33, 35–8, 41, 84,
     173, 186
Song on the Times 47, 49–52, 54
Song on the Venality of the Judges 42–3, 44, 46,
     48–9, 173
Speculum Regis Edwardi III, *see* William of
     Pagula
Spigurnel, Henry
  libel concerning 48 n. 28
Stacy, Thomas
  petition and libel concerning 130
Stafford, Edmund, Duke of Buckingham 150
  lament for death of 150 n. 50
Stanley, John 184
Stanley, Thomas
  petitions and libel concerning 129, 130
statutes
  language of 39, 41

on treason, of 1547 161
Second Statute of Westminster 46
Statute of Pleading (1362) 40 n. 134
Statute of Treason (1352) 66
Statute of Winchester 103
Stein, I. H. 94
Steiner, Emily 64 n. 84
Stonor family
  letters 178
Stoughton 5, 6, 9, 18
  complaint of villagers of 8, 9, 11, 18
  libel concerning villagers of, see *Poem on
     Disputed Villein Services*
Stow, John 110, 111, 129, 131, 158
Strasbourg 159
Stratford, John, Archbishop of Canterbury
  complaints, libels, and petitions
     concerning 58–62
  excusaciones 60
Straw, Jack 135, 136
Strohm, Paul 179
Strood 115
Sudbury, Simon, Archbishop of Canterbury
  libel concerning 84
Suffolk 14, 84
Supplication of the Poore Commons 158–9,
     160, 167
Susanna 97
Sutton, John
  petition of 34
Swallow, Ralph
  petition concerning 13

Tailors' Guild (of London)
  petition concerning Brembre 67 nn. 93, 94;
     68, 71
Talbot, John
  libel concerning 141
tallage 18
  tallage (meanings of) 18, 19, 21, 28
tally sticks 12, 35
terms and processes (legal) 40
Thames, river 110
Thomas de Cressingham
  complaint concerning 14
Thorp, Thomas
  petition concerning 130 n. 160
Thorpe, William 106 n. 98
tithes 94
Trailbaston 42–3, 44, 46, 47–8, 53, 173
translation 40, 53, 91, 95, 100, 110, 175, 178,
     179, 179 n. 36, 180, 181
treason 45, 56, 65, 68, 111, 112, 113, 121,
     122, 128, 142 n. 20, 146, 147, 149,
     162, 182
Tresilian, Robert 66, 70
  appeal concerning 66

trespass 46
  trespas (meanings of) 50
Trevelyan, John
  petitions and libel concerning 129, 130
Tudors 137
Turks 152
Turville-Petre, Thorlac 28, 29, 34, 38, 38 n.
  129
Tyler, Wat 84–6
  petition of 84, 86
Tyndale, William
  translation of New Testament 151

Usk, Thomas 179
  appeal concerning John Northampton 179
  knowledge of *Troilus* 178 n. 31
  Testament of Love 178 n. 31, 179

Vale, John 111, 114, 149, 150
  book of 111 nn. 108, 109; 114, 115, 139,
  146–7
vernacular 3, 8, 38, 40, 41, 53–4, 60, 72, 76,
  91, 108, 173, 176, 177, 179
  letters 178
Versus compositi de Roger Beler, see Beler,
  Roger
villeins 3, 38 n. 129, 171 n. 3
  legal status of 6 n. 9, 7–8, 17–33, 36–7,
  171
  villein (meanings of) 8–9
  villenage (meanings of) 25
virelay 1

Wallis, Stephen
  complaint concerning 14
Walsingham, Thomas 5–6, 94, 97, 98, 101,
  102
Walter de Folville, *see* Folville family
Warwick, Earl of
  appeal of 66
Warwickshire 54, 138
Waynfleet
  complaint concerning villagers of 13
Westminster 108, 118
  Abbey 26, 61, 64, 106
  Hall 72, 94
  libels in 61, 64, 80, 94, 105, 121
Westminster Chronicle 70–1

Whitelock, John 105–6
  petition of 105–6, **107**, 177 n. 25
Wilkhous, Henry
  complaint concerning 115
William I, king of England 25–6
William de Knovill
  libel concerning 48 n. 28
William de la Pole, Duke of Suffolk 113,
  121, 128 n. 152, 129–30, 131, 134,
  135
  petitions and libels concerning 121–2, **123**,
  124, 125–9, **126**, **127**, 133, 144, 183
  plays on name of 133
William of Ockham 24
  An princeps 24–5
William of Pagula 22, 31
  Epistola ad Regem Edwardum III 22–4, 34,
  186
  Oculus Sacerdotis 22 n. 76
  Speculum Regis Edwardi III 22, 23–4, 31,
  34
William of Wallingford
  complaint concerning 13
Willoughby, Sir Richard
  complaints concerning 54–8, 60, 63
Wiltshire 12, 15 n. 52
Windsor 88
Wolde, John and John Reche
  petition of 174
Wolsey, Sir Thomas, Cardinal 150, 151, 153
  libels and satire concerning 150–1
Wright, Thomas 34, 37, 49
Wyclif, John 93, 94
  Complaint 94
Wycliffites, *see* lollards
Wykeham, William
  complaints concerning 63

'Ye that have the kyng to demene' 125, 128,
  183, 186
York 16, 27, 102, 142, 172
  aldermen 142
  libels in 102, 142
  mayor 142
Yorkists 134, 138–43
Yorkshire 27

Zouche, la, family 53

Printed and bound by CPI Group (UK) Ltd, Croydon, CR0 4YY